THE Involuntary American

THE Involuntary American

A SCOTTISH PRISONER'S

JOURNEY

TO THE

NEW WORLD

CAROL GARDNER

WESTHOLME
Yardley

Westholme Publishing, LLC
904 Edgewood Road
Yardley, Pennsylvania 19067
Visit our Web site at www.westholmepublishing.com

ISBN: 978-1-59416-312-8
Also available as an eBook

Printed in the United States of America.

He thocht weill he suld be worthy, For all his
eldris war douchty
　　　　　　—John Barbour, *The Brus* (ii. 166)

For my family: past, present, and future.

Contents

Introduction

S EVERAL YEARS AGO, while reading about early Maine, I stumbled upon the story of a group of Scottish prisoners of war who had been transported to New England in 1650. Numbering about 150, these prisoners had been captured at the Battle of Dunbar during the Wars of the Three Kingdoms (also known as the English Civil War), shipped to New England, and sold to farmers and industrial enterprises for £20 to £30 each. The more I investigated their circumstances, the more intrigued I became. The Dunbar prisoners had overcome tremendous odds to make it to New England alive: surviving a bloody battle; a forced march over a hundred miles; several months' imprisonment with scant food, warm clothes, or medical care; and a six- to eight-week journey across the Atlantic in the hold of a ship. A year later, 272 additional Scottish soldiers captured at the Battle of Worcester—the final battle of the war—arrived at the docks in Boston. They, too, were sold about New England for £20 to £30 per head. The communities these Scottish prisoners formed, as servants and later as free men, revealed a side of colonial life I never knew existed.

Twenty-one years of education had introduced me to New England's elite: pious, educated, and literate individuals like William Bradford, Anne Bradstreet, the Winthrops, Cotton Mather, Roger Williams, and Mary Rowlandson. But that education had neglected to turn up anything about those who couldn't express their thoughts on paper; who came to New England, not seeking freedom but bonded to others; who cut timber, cleared and cultivated fields, herded animals, built dams and mills and meetinghouses; and who, in the process of surviving, had little time to imagine more godly or peaceful societies. I wanted to find out more about this overlooked group: those who came to New England by force in the 1600s.

"We know only in the vaguest way who the hundreds of thousands of individuals who settled in British North America were, where precisely they came from, why they came, and how they lived out their lives," wrote historian Bernard Bailyn.[1] That knowledge gap is particularly wide when it comes to the working and servant classes, for whom few records have survived. Several histories, including Lawrence W. Towner's *A Good Master Well Served: Masters and Servants in Colonial Massachusetts, 1620-1750* (1998) and Wendy Warren's *New England Bound: Slavery and Colonization in Early America* (2016) have helped to fill the gap, arguing that servitude in New England was much more prevalent than previously acknowledged. But although I found those works fascinating, I was anxious to understand the practice in a narrower sense; what was life like for those who had had to surmount imprisonment, exile, servitude, and starting over in an unfamiliar land? I wanted to understand how challenging it was to navigate seventeenth-century society without money, education, or influence. Only an individual's experience could reveal the full extent of those challenges.

Thomas Doughty's long life recommended him. He survived to the age of seventy-five at a time when as many as one-third of children born in the British Isles never made it to age fifteen.[2] He endured some of the most compelling challenges and conflicts of his era: the severe weather of the Little Ice Age, famine and plague in Scotland, the Wars of the Three Kingdoms, the colonization of New England, the burgeoning transatlantic trade in servants and slaves, the First and Second Indian Wars, and the Salem witch crisis. His life offered a vehicle for understanding how these events affected individuals of modest circumstances, particularly those who arrived by force.

The broad arc of Doughty's life is traceable, but there are plenty of gaps in that record, too. We know he was a Scot through evidence of his servitude in New Hampshire, his appearance on an unofficial list of Dunbar prisoners, and his close association with other Scottish prisoners of war. No records detail his childhood, upbringing, parents, or where he was born. To flesh out that part of the narrative, I've drawn likely conclusions from Scotland's Old Parish Records, demographics, and cultural and historical sources on life in the Lowlands during the sixteenth and seventeenth centuries.

Doughty's adult life, from age twenty onward, is more certain. A fair amount of information survives on the Scots taken prisoner at Dunbar, particularly on those who died while imprisoned at Durham Cathedral, and on the comparatively small number who made it to New England alive. A few records also survive on Doughty's master at Oyster River, New Hampshire: the Puritan merchant Valentine Hill. And once Doughty emerged from servitude, he left behind his own paper trail in the vital, court, land, and probate records of Maine, New Hampshire, and Massachusetts.

What's missing is a record of Doughty's thoughts. Because he was illiterate, or at least unable to write, he left behind no account of himself. The literacy barrier provides a daunting obstacle for anyone seeking to uncover the past. And that barrier has in large part constrained our understanding of New England history. The Puritan educated class passed down a written legacy that places them squarely at the center of the region's historical narrative. Native Americans, women, and individuals like Thomas Doughty rarely appear, even as footnotes. I felt compelled to try and overcome that obstacle.

Only a single document written in Thomas Doughty's own voice later in his life survives: a letter to Sir Edmund Andros, governor of the Dominion of New England from 1686 to 1689. The Andros government had declared land titles throughout New England void; in response, Doughty wrote asking that he be allowed to retain land in Saco, in the Province of Maine, on which he had built a home and mill. Since Doughty signed all court documents and deeds with an "X," someone undoubtedly transcribed the letter for him. But it is, no doubt, in his voice; other letters written to Andros at the same time—of which dozens survive—show a range of personalities and styles, including those written by or for Doughty's immediate neighbors.

Apart from that letter, two depositions given by Doughty concerning his former master, Valentine Hill, also survive. Those are straightforward and pertain mostly to Hill. A dozen or so court, land, probate, and vital records allow us to trace Doughty's movements and his response to certain events. But his most closely held feelings, beliefs, and opinions died with him.

Nevertheless, I determined to see what his experiences could reveal. In some ways, detailing an individual's experiences—even without his thoughts or opinions—provides a platform for experiencing those events ourselves. Of course, there are risks; without a record of Doughty's thoughts, I felt acutely the danger that I would allow my own thoughts, emotions, and twenty-first-century prejudices to fill the gaps. To some degree, that's unavoidable. Literature and history, after all, are instruments for making other cultures pertinent to our own lives.

To keep my own biases in check, I employed Doughty's contemporaries as guides, allowing them to interpret seventeenth-century events in their own words. His peers, whether poor, well-to-do, influential, or not, offer us the most accurate portrayal of the culture and thinking of the times. In that regard, I've made liberal use of contemporary letters, reports, records, and narratives from those who experienced the same events as Thomas Doughty. Some of those are from the very people who've dictated the historical narrative: educated and influential English, Scottish, and Puritan writers. But many other voices moderate their influence: Scottish, English, and Irish servants and working-class individuals, African slaves, and Native Americans whose statements, letters, and court cases have largely lingered in obscurity. A different narrative emerges in examining history from their perspectives.

Where possible, I've quoted historical documents verbatim. To me, the originals provide authenticity and enhance our sense of the times. Some statements—especially those in the Scots language—require translation, which I've provided. And while English rules of punctuation, capitalization, and grammar were anything but consistent in the 1600s, I've tried to remain true to the originals, allowing writers and speakers to retain their own emphases.

Just as Puritan writers have directed the historical narrative of New England, descriptions of life in Massachusetts have long dominated our perceptions of what the region was like. Thomas Doughty lived largely in the frontier provinces of Maine and New Hampshire, a more diverse, less Puritan, and unrulier New England than Boston, Salem, Plymouth, Providence, or New Haven. Throughout the seventeenth century, Maine had an uneasy relationship with Massachusetts Bay. It began as an independent province, and later—despite significant protests from residents—fell under the authority of its more populated, and more Puritan, neighbor to the south. But it remained socially distinct. Life on the eastern frontier adds an additional layer in understanding the New England of the 1600s.

The narrative spends a fair amount of time outside New England, too, describing the social and political environment in Scotland where Doughty and the Dunbar and Worcester prisoners began. The powerful influence of that society didn't vanish once those men were shipped abroad. To this day, a section of York, Maine, is known as "Scotland," in deference to those who formed a tight-knit community there four centuries ago. While the Scots didn't separate themselves from their neighbors, they did consciously choose to live in and among their countrymen. And although they blended in physically among white New Englanders, their names, languages (many undoubtedly spoke either Scots or Gaelic), accents, and cultural behaviors readily identified them as Scots.

Events in England and Europe also continually reverberated throughout New England, as they do in this narrative. Regime changes, wars, and political decisions made abroad influenced the everyday lives of colonists. Just as Maine had an uneasy relationship with Massachusetts Bay, residents of New England had an uneasy relationship with English authority. Religion was at the heart of many disagreements, as England alternated between Puritan, Anglican, and Catholic rulers. Religion and politics formed a complex, tightly knotted web into which British subjects were swept.

In the pages that follow, readers won't find the religious interpretations for every action and event that are so prevalent among Puritan writers and diarists. But religion does show its powerful influence in politics and society. Doughty was, after all, conscripted to fight for the predominance of Presbyterianism throughout Scotland and England. Because English Puritans won that struggle, he was captured and transported to New England. Once there, he was expected to conform to Puritan worship and to attend weekly Sabbath meetings. Still, without a record of his thoughts, it's hard to say exactly what role religion played in his everyday life.

Doughty's journey offers us a sense of what life was like for the underclass. He lived much longer than the vast majority of his Dunbar comrades and eventually managed to build a livelihood and a family. Yet his experiences offer glimpses of what it meant to be powerless; to be subject to the whims of the ruling class; to rebuild one's life several times over out of necessity; to survive in a rapidly changing society. By rights, the central character should have lived out his life within a dozen miles of the spot where he was born. Instead, he was swept into the maelstrom of the First Global Age and transported to a different world altogether. Once in New England, he moved at least seven more times. That journey forms the backbone of this narrative.

The book's title, *Involuntary American: A Scottish Prisoner's Journey*, is not meant to describe Thomas Doughty's own sense of identity. After spending more than fifty years in America, he remained a Scot, just as the majority of his white neighbors remained "English." During the seventeenth century, the term "American" was used to describe this continent's native peoples. Only in the next century did it come to describe those of European ancestry who were born in, or had immigrated to, America. That shift mirrored what was happening in society: European colonists appropriated the term "American" just as they had appropriated American lands.

The title *Involuntary American* is intended to speak to modern readers, asking them to conjure an alternative image of the American colonist. Understanding that immigrants of many ethnicities came to this continent against their wills and displaced others in the process is essential to dispelling long-held myths and to understanding our true identities as Americans and as American nations.

Admittedly, I've taken some risks in my approach. This narrative doesn't pretend to comprehensively cover the seventeenth century, life in early colonial New England, or even the Dunbar prisoners of war. Numerous scholarly books examine those times, trends, and people. It's not my intention to challenge them, nor to offer a survey of the best and most original. Naturally, I consulted a wide array of modern scholars in my research, and many of their insights are presented here. They've been particularly helpful in making sense of seventeenth-century customs, laws, and social mores, and in considering voices and perspectives outside the powerful few who so successfully dictated the historical narrative for generations. Still, I've relied heavily on seventeenth-century sources, with all their contradictions, prejudices, and inaccuracies. That is intentional. I wanted those voices to be heard and heard loudly; I wanted the reader to experience the times as they did, not merely from the intellectual distance that four hundred years of history, scholarship, and cultural change affords.

Nor is this work intended as a biography of Thomas Doughty. As I've mentioned, we know little about his origins, and even less about what he thought or felt. But we do know what he experienced, and given those experiences, his life was extraordinary. Doughty may or may not have been a man of remarkable thoughts or actions; existing records simply don't offer that information. But what he endured was remarkable. This volume, then, is not so much the story of Thomas Doughty as it is the story of his *journey*. While it does not offer an exhaustive portrayal of Doughty or the times he lived in, it serves as a series of snapshots of Doughty and his working-class contemporaries during key moments of challenge and upheaval throughout the century.

What follows is a journey through the seventeenth century; a tale of an uneducated laborer who traveled much and witnessed firsthand many of the seminal events of a turbulent time—a man who did not choose to live in New England, but determined, once there, to make the best of it. For me, that journey was a lot more compelling than I had imagined it could be.

Chapter One

PASSAGE

Now would I give a thousand furlongs of sea for an acre of barren ground. —Shakespeare, *The Tempest*

IN NOVEMBER 1650, twenty-year-old Thomas Doughty lay between decks on a ship bound for New England. He was restrained, scantily clothed, half-starved, and packed in tightly with 150 other hungry, ragged, and seasick Scots. It had been many weeks since he had lain in a bed or eaten a decent meal. Now he and his fellow passengers lay practically on top of one another inside the dark, rank hold among livestock and other cargo as their ship lurched and bolted.

Yet Doughty and his co-passengers were among the lucky few. They had survived a bloody battle and a one-hundred-mile march without food or water, during which hundreds of Scots died by the roadside. They had spent two miserable months locked inside damp, cavernous Durham Cathedral, watching as Scottish soldiers continued to perish from malnutrition, dysentery, and other diseases.

Even if Doughty managed to take his mind off his miserable situation during the voyage, thoughts of the future gave him no quarter.

He and his co-passengers were on their way to "a hideous and desolate wilderness, full of wild beasts and wild men":[1] a land with a few thinly populated coastal settlements, an interior blanketed in dense forests and swamps, and natives who seemed peaceful, treacherous, and inscrutable by turns. If their ship managed to cross the North Atlantic without incident, and if they managed to survive the trip, the Scots would be sold or bonded to unknown masters. In all probability, they would never again see their families, loved ones, or homeland.

Thomas Doughty had been captured at the Battle of Dunbar on September 3, 1650, during the Wars of the Three Kingdoms.[2] He and other Scots taken prisoner there were being sent where they couldn't offer further resistance to Oliver Cromwell's New Model Army. On September 19, the English Council of State[3] ordered that 2,300 of the Dunbar prisoners be sent to Ireland to help suppress the Irish; 900 were to be shipped to Virginia and 150 to New England to serve as forced labor in the colonies. Sir Arthur Hesilrige, the governor of Newcastle, had been put in charge of the prisoners, who were marched to Durham from Dunbar and held in Durham Cathedral and castle. In a lengthy letter defending how well he'd fed and cared for the prisoners, Hesilrige replied that he couldn't fulfill those orders. Although he'd started with 3,900 Scots, Hesilrige no longer had enough men "because they still dye daily, and doubtless so they will, so long as any remain in Prison."[4]

For six weeks the prisoners had been languishing in Durham Cathedral under the oversight of Hesilrige and Major Samuel Clarke with scant food, heat, or medical care. Deaths were so numerous that English soldiers had taken to throwing the prisoners' bodies naked into large mass graves. The appalling truth behind Hesilrige's letter was that, of the 3,000 Scottish prisoners who marched into Durham in September, only 1,400 remained alive by the end of October, and only about 600 of those were healthy enough to travel. Perhaps as many as 700 had perished on the gruelling trek to Durham, and 1,600 had perished thereafter, in the cathedral and castle.[5]

On November 11 the Council of State determined to send Hesilrige a request they thought he could fulfill: "To write Sir Arthur Hesilrig to deliver 150 Scotch prisoners to Augustine Walker, master of the Unity, to be transported to New England."[6] The letter was a mere formality. Other documents suggest that the *Unity* already had her prisoners and lay in the Thames, awaiting permission to sail. On November 7 and 8, the Council of State called Major Clarke to task "concerning the ill-usage of the Scotch prisoners now on board a ship."[7] Most likely, the *Unity* departed on, or shortly after, November 11.[8]

Unknowingly, Doughty and his fellow prisoners aboard the *Unity* had become the property of the so-called "Company of Undertakers"—investors in two iron smelting factories in Massachusetts Bay. The Scots were consigned to company shareholders Joshua Foote, an ironmonger, and John Becx, a well-connected businessman. Becx also owned land in the Province of Maine and had interests in sawmills being built along the Piscataqua River and its tributaries. There is no indication that either man paid for the prisoners; instead, by shipping the captives to New England to serve as free labor, Becx and Foote were doing Cromwell and the English Parliament—and themselves—a favor. With an eye to business and profit, Becx stipulated that his prisoners be "well and sound and free from wounds."[9]

Very little information survives about the ship *Unity* in which the Scottish prisoners were transported to New England.[10] No ship's logs or diaries have been found. Some incomplete passenger lists have been compiled using a variety of evidence, but we don't know exactly how many prisoners died en route—though some surely did—or the conditions they were forced to endure.

Yet we can be sure that the Atlantic crossing was harsh. Passengers on seventeenth- and eighteenth-century voyages suffered deprivation beyond what most modern travelers can imagine. "Being in a ship is being in a jail, with the chance of being drowned," wrote lexicographer Samuel Johnson. And he was referring to paying passengers, not prisoners of war.

Voyages between London and New England could take from four to thirteen weeks,[11] and November and December were challenging months for travel. During the late fall, cold fronts begin to form on the American land mass, tracking their way across the Atlantic from west to east, bringing gales and storms. Cold weather not only made for tough sailing, it caused great discomfort for passengers and sailors. Rough weather tossed ships, throwing cargo, livestock, and passengers against each other; heavy seas swamped the decks, drenching those below.

In 1650, most immigrants—prisoners, slaves, servants, or paying passengers—came to America in merchant ships intended for freight. These individuals were relegated to the hold, or the area "between decks," along with the cargo, animals used to feed crew and passengers, and heavy guns used to defend the ship from pirates. Doughty and his fellow prisoners were likely kept in very close quarters for the entire voyage, fettered to prevent violence against their captors, and fed the absolute minimum necessary. If any among them had once had warm clothing or shoes, they had been stripped of those when captured.

Victorian historian Thomas Macaulay says of the 841 prisoners of the Monmouth Rebellion, shipped to Jamaica in 1685:

> The human cargoes were stowed close in the holds of small vessels. So little space was allowed that the wretches, many of whom were still tormented by unhealed wounds, could not lie down at once without lying on one another. They were never suffered to go on deck. The hatchway was constantly watched by sentinels armed with hangers and blunderbusses. In the dungeon below all was darkness, stench, lamentation, disease and death.[12]

The Dunbar Scots may not have even known where their ship was headed. Prisoners captured in an uprising against Cromwell in Salisbury four years after Dunbar were transported to Barbados "being all the way locked up under decks, . . . and they never till they came to the island knew whither they were going."[13]

Transportation beyond the sea for political prisoners wasn't unusual. But regardless of what awaited the Dunbar Scots in New England, for the time being, their lives wholly depended upon Augustine Walker, the ship's master. A merchant sea captain who traveled frequently between England and America, Walker hailed from near Berwick-on-Tweed, the northernmost town in England, just south of the Scottish border. He had moved to Charlestown in Massachusetts about 1640 and joined the local church there, which suggests his sympathies with the Puritan cause.[14] Still, since the *Unity* left no records in her wake, it's impossible to know whether, for Walker, the Scottish prisoners were countrymen, individuals, or commodities. From the Scots' perspective, Walker was merely one in a series of masters who would dictate the directions their lives would take: lairds and clan chiefs; military commanders; capitalists Becx and Foote; and masters who would purchase seven years of their lives upon arrival in New England.

Regardless of how Walker managed his human cargo, transatlantic crossings in the seventeenth century were almost always gruelling, even for well-to-do passengers. Firsthand accounts of seventeenth- and eighteenth-century voyages agree on the deprivations and the inevitable, violent seasickness that would overtake passengers, even among those who traveled in style. Francis Daniel Pastorius sailed from England to Pennsylvania in 1683 with six personal servants. On Pastorius's ship, "Almost all the passengers were seasick for some days."[15] Lutheran minister Henry Melchior Muhlenberg sailed from Rotterdam to Philadelphia in 1742 and wrote that "My stomach could retain neither food, drink, nor medicine; everything was expelled *per vomitum.*"[16]

Storms exacerbated seasickness and brought chaos to the spaces between decks. A Scot, John Harrower, traveled as a willing indenture from London to Virginia a century after Dunbar and detailed conditions between decks during a storm:

> The wind blowing excessive hard and a verry high sea running still from westward, at 8 pm was obliged to batten down both fore and main hatches, and a little after, I really think there was the odest shene [scene] betwixt decks that ever I heard or seed. There was some sleeping, some spewing . . . some damning, some Blasting their leggs and thighs, some their liver, lungs, lights and eyes, And for to make the shene the odder, some curs'd Father, Mother, Sister, and Brother.[17]

Methods to ventilate the air between decks weren't invented until the eighteenth century. When the weather grew stormy and the hatches had to be closed, fresh air was in short supply. Tightly packed with people, cargo, and livestock, and offering rudimentary sanitary facilities if any, the area below decks was unbearably oppressive, and the stench, overwhelming.

Extremely tight quarters, lack of hygiene, and the lack of fresh water made ships the perfect environment for spreading contagious disease. Harrower's diary relates how rapidly disease could sweep through a ship. He boarded the *Snow Planter*, which set sail on February 6, 1774, with about seventy-five indentures plus crew. By March 27, half of those were ill: "The sick, likways they being now in number about 37." So Harrower and his healthy co-travelers tried to stop the spread of disease by washing the entire area between decks with vinegar. But it was to little avail. By the thirty-first, more than two-thirds had succumbed: "The sick are now increased to the number of fifty betwixt decks besides three in the steerage."[18]

Travelers were also forced to weigh their hunger against unsavory rations. For paying passengers, provisions would consist of salt beef, pork or fish, cheese, dried peas, ale, and ship's biscuit. But passengers found themselves sickened by eating the over-salted meat and fish day after day. "The rations upon the ship were very bad," Pastorius complained. "Both the meat and the fish were salted to such an extent and had become so rancid that we could hardly eat half of them."[19]

For nonpaying passengers—servants or prisoners—the rations were simpler: ship's biscuit and water. And complaining about the food would often bring worse consequences still. On John Harrower's voyage, "There was two servants put in Irons for wanting other than what was served."[20]

The most complete description of the misery of transatlantic voyages comes from a German who made his voyage one hundred years after Thomas Doughty and the Dunbar prisoners. In 1750, Gottlieb Mittleberger, a paying passenger, traveled to Philadelphia from Rotterdam with four hundred others, many of whom intended to indenture themselves upon arriving in America for the cost of their passages. According to Mittleberger:

> There is on board these ships terrible misery, stench, fumes, horror, vomiting, many kinds of sea-sickness, fever, dysentery, headache, heat, constipation, boils, scurvy, cancer, mouth-rot, and the like, all of which come from old and sharply salted food and meat, also from very bad and foul water, so that many die miserably.
>
> Add to this the want of provisions, hunger, thirst, frost, heat, dampness, anxiety, want, afflictions and lamentations, together with other trouble, as c.v., the lice abound so frightfully, especially on sick people, that they can be scraped off the body.[21]

Mittleberger was convinced that food and water were largely to blame for the rampant illness aboard ships. Paying passengers had hot meals three times a week at most, so ship's biscuit comprised the bulk of their diet, too. And "in a whole biscuit there was scarcely a piece the size of a dollar that had not been full of red worms and spiders' nests." The water he described as "very black, thick, and full of worms."[22] Children suffered the worst. Mittleberger witnessed the death and burial at sea of some thirty-two children on his voyage.[23]

The lice that Mittleberger describes were an inescapable hindrance, regardless of shipboard accomodations. "My greatest annoyance during the whole voyage were the lice, from which none aboard were free, not even the captain," wrote Muhlenberg of his 1748 voyage.[24]

Kept in tight quarters and forbidden to go on deck, the Scots suffered unimaginable tedium during their weeks at sea. Even among the healthy, "impatience sometimes grows so great and cruel that one curses the other, or himself and the day of his birth, and sometimes come near killing each other,"[25] Mittleberger recounted.

Fortunately, the *Unity* made good progress across the Atlantic. The Dunbar Scots likely arrived in Boston in late December. Contemporaneous accounts suggest that losing 10 percent of a ship's passengers during transatlantic voyages wasn't uncommon.[26] So it's likely that the Scots saw some ten to fifteen of their countrymen buried at sea between London and Boston. Financial records of the Lynn and Braintree iron works show that a "windeing sheet" was purchased for "Davison the Scott" just after the *Unity* landed. They also show significant and recurring charges for "phisicke," or medicine, on behalf of the Scots, suggesting that the prisoners suffered ongoing health problems from their ordeal.[27]

Upon reaching Boston, sixty-two Dunbar prisoners immediately became property of the iron works under manager John Gifford and the Company of Undertakers. Augustine Walker sold the rest of the prisoners for £20 to £30 each on behalf of Becx and Foote. Several Scots were sold to merchants and farmers in the Boston area. Another fifteen to twenty-five were sent to Newichawannock (present-day South Berwick, Maine) to work with industrialist Richard Leader in building and running the Great Works Mill: a twenty-saw operation, outfitted to turn the northern forest into boards, ships' masts, and pipe staves. Still more went to other mills in Maine and New Hampshire. Perhaps as many as eighteen, including Thomas Doughty, were sold to Valentine Hill, a merchant and close friend of Massachusetts Bay Colony's first family, the Winthrops. Hill planned to build a mill complex at Oyster River: present-day Durham, New Hampshire.[28]

Cromwell and the Council of State had their reasons for transporting and selling these Scots as servants abroad: to prevent them from causing further problems for the English government and to provide desperately needed labor for New England. Their industrialist associates saw an additional benefit: to turn a profit. In 1650, a transatlantic passage cost some £5 per person, so Becx and Foote must have paid around £750 to ship 150 Scots to New England. If fifteen died on the voyage and sixty-two continued as their property at the iron works, Becx and Foote still made at least £1,000 (a handsome six-figure profit in today's market) from the remaining seventy-three Scots sold at Boston.[29]

In late December 1650, Thomas Doughty arrived on the frozen shores of Massachusetts Bay. We can only speculate on what he must have been thinking. From their writings, we know that passengers arriving on the *Mayflower* and the *Arabella* anxiously anticipated escaping tyranny, worshipping freely, and establishing a "citty upon a hill" dedicated to godliness.[30] But such motives were undoubtedly far from the minds of those on the *Unity*. Thomas Doughty's dearest hopes for the future likely involved a hot meal, a warm fire, clothing to protect him from the New England winter, and a bed in which to sleep. Yet even those things remained beyond his control; they depended entirely upon the Puritan merchant who had just purchased him.

Thousands of laborers, servants, and slaves were shipped to New England in the seventeenth century against their wills, but they have remained in the shadow of those who came of their own volition, seeking land, religious freedom, and opportunity. This narrative recounts the journey of one of the many who arrived not by choice, but by force.[31]

Chapter Two

RELIGIOUS WARS

*The King . . . looking upon the block, said to the Executioner, You
must set it fast.
Executioner: It is fast Sir.
King: It might have been a little higher.
Executioner: It can be no higher Sir.
. . . And after a very little pawse, the King stretching forth his hands,
The Executioner at one blow, severed his head from his Body.*
———King Charles I upon the scaffold at Whitehall Gate,
January 13, 1649[1]

B Y EARLY SEPTEMBER 1650, the Scottish army had Oliver
Cromwell's invading Parliamentary Army pinned down on a
coastal plain along the North Sea. For six weeks the Scots had
refused to engage openly with the invaders. They had removed livestock and destroyed all crops in their own towns east and southeast
of Edinburgh, where the English army was now quartering; they had
blocked transportation of goods from England, except by sea; they
had harassed the English troops without direct confrontation; and
they now occupied Doon Hill, the high ground above Dunbar, af-
fording them a sweeping view of the coastal plain. Their field leader,
David Leslie, seemed intent on waiting out Cromwell's New Model
Army, a professional and battle-tried force also known as "Ironsides,"
which was suffering from the extremely wet and cold weather, lack
of provisions, and disease.

"The Enemy hath blocked up our way at the Pass at Copperspath, through which we cannot get without almost a miracle," wrote a despondent Cromwell to the governor of Newcastle, Sir Arthur Hesilrige, on September 2, 1650. "He lieth so upon the Hills that we know not how to come that way without great difficulty; and our lying here daily consumeth our men, who fall sick beyond imagination."[2] Cromwell's army was trapped: they couldn't ascend Doon Hill to attack the enemy without terrific loss of life; they couldn't escape south to England, because the more numerous Scots had blocked the road to the border. They could wait for the Scots to change their positions, but waiting in the rain and cold had already cost them many soldiers. Or they could abandon the invasion altogether, returning to England by ship. For more than six weeks, Leslie and the Scots had engaged Cromwell and his troops in a cat-and-mouse game, and the lord general's patience, as well as his army's endurance and strength, was running thin.

But why had Cromwell invaded in the first place? Like so many wars, the Wars of the Three Kingdoms resulted from a confusing, often contradictory, mix of religious and political motives. In 1649, a powerful faction of the English Parliament ordered King Charles I executed. Charles, the son of King James VI of Scotland, was king of England, Scotland, and Ireland, so the Scots had a significant stake in the matter. They were incensed that the English Parliament had taken matters into its own hands without consulting them.

Ironically, Charles I had been unpopular in England, Scotland, and Ireland alike. He had engaged in a long power struggle with the English Parliament and managed to dissolve the body three times during his reign. He alienated many subjects by trying to enforce the supremacy of the Anglican Church and by persecuting Puritans, Presbyterians, and Catholics. He incited riots among Presbyterian Scots when he ordered them to adopt an Anglican prayer book. The Scots weren't sorry to see Charles removed from power; they were enraged that they had been given no say in the matter.

Earlier, in 1645 and 1646, the Scots Covenanter[3] army had allied with the English Parliament against Charles I's army. Charles fought himself into a corner, surrendered to the Covenanters, and tried to cut a deal to turn them against Parliament. It didn't work; the Scots turned him over to parliamentary forces.[4]

Eventually, the king was put on trial for treason. The ringleader of this effort was Oliver Cromwell, a member of Parliament and a devoutly religious Puritan. Charles I was found guilty and beheaded on January 30, 1649. Cromwell signed the king's death warrant and reputedly pressured others to do so, too.

As a result, English Puritans were no longer a persecuted minority, and England was no longer a monarchy. It was a republican commonwealth; Parliament and the Council of State, chaired by Cromwell, were responsible for governing all of Britain. But the Scots thought otherwise, and they weren't going to take this seizure of power sitting down.

The king's son, Charles II, who had fled to the Continent, tried to take advantage of the Scots' anger and rally them against Cromwell and regain the crown. He arrived in Scotland, where church and military leaders agreed to help him regain power if he would establish Presbyterianism as the official religion of England and Scotland. Charles reluctantly agreed, he was declared king, and the Scots' former allies—the Parliamentarians—became their new foes.

Hearing what was happening north of the border, the English decided to invade; Cromwell's New Model Army crossed the border in July, prepared to fight. Cromwell faced his former colleague and the leader of the Scottish Covenanters, David Leslie. Another Leslie, the seventy-year-old Alexander, Earl of Leven, was serving as strategic commander. Both were overseen by a Kirk Party commission. Although they were clerics rather than military men, the zealous Kirk Party commissioners meddled more than a little bit in military decisions.

At a distance, this war seems baffling. And it's fair to speculate that, for common Scots soldiers like Thomas Doughty, it may not have been an especially passionate cause. No doubt the patriotism of everyday Scottish foot soldiers was stirred by the English invasion. Yet Scotland had been divided in previous battles between royalist and anti-royalists, and it must have been hard for the laboring classes and men like Doughty to follow these allegiances, let alone fight with conviction. Many foot soldiers had fought with Leslie on the side of the Parliamentarians just a few years before. Some had fought with James Graham, Earl of Montrose, who led a Scottish force on behalf of Charles I. More confusing still, Montrose had earlier sided with the Covenanters: the Scottish forces who vowed to defend Presbyterianism against the likes of Charles I.

Because of these conflicts, Scotland had endured more than a decade of continuous conscription,[5] and so the 1650 levies, undertaken to raise a force of more than twenty thousand, were scraping the bottom of the barrel. Further, the Kirk Party ordered purges to remove officers whom they thought weren't truly committed to the cause, shrinking the number of experienced soldiers and potential leaders. The army had no choice but to fill those gaps with raw recruits. Charles II referred to the Scottish Army as his "Green Hornes."[6] At twenty years old, Thomas Doughty was not the youngest recruit, but he may well have been one of the greenest.

How were soldiers like Doughty recruited? The central government at Edinburgh would issue a call for men, and local committees would in turn call out all "fencible persons," or those between sixteen and sixty able to bear "arms defencible." Landowners had the power to order their tenants and servants to join. In exchange, the "lairds" were rewarded with the rank of captain or colonel. In the Highlands, clan chiefs compelled their tenants and clansmen to participate.

As often as not, the levies employed force to persuade the reluctant working class of their duty. In 1640, Major General Robert Munro had taken men "out of their naked beds" to bring his regiment up to strength.[7] That same year, "Seven score burgesses, craftsmen, and prentices, [were] prest and perforce taken, to help fill up Marischall's regiment to goe to general Lesslie. The honest men of the town wondering at this manifold oppression, fled, took fisher boats and went to the sea, lurking about the craigs of Downy whyle this storme past."[8] By 1650, it had become increasingly difficult to hide from the press gangs.

English eyewitness accounts[9] of the 1650 conflict suggest that nearly all able-bodied men between Edinburgh and the border had been recruited. "In the march between Mordington and Copperspith," wrote Captain John Hodgson, who served under Cromwell, "we saw not any Scotchman, in Eyton and other places that we passed thorow; but the streets were full of Scotch women, pitifull, sorry creatures, clothed in white flannell, in a very homely manner; very many of them much bemoaned their husbands, who, they said, were enforced by the lairds of the towns to gange to the muster."[10] When the

English arrived at Dunbar, Hodgson recalled, they found that "All the men in this town, as in other places of this daies march, were fled; and not any to be seen above seven or under 70 yeeres old, but onely some few decrepid ones."[11]

In seeking to muster a force of 20,000 from a standing army of only 5,500, the Scots had engaged in desperate measures. Virtually any male who could walk and carry a weapon was considered "fencible,"[12] regardless of age. In fact, archeological evidence has revealed that there were soldiers at Dunbar as young as thirteen and fourteen.[13] Small wonder that Hodgson noticed no men in the border towns between the ages of seven and seventy, except for the odd "decrepid" one. Clearly, laboring class Scots like Thomas Doughty had had little say in whether they would fight or not. Some may have willingly joined the effort, particularly at the prospect of having steady rations. But many were compelled to fight by political and social forces beyond their control.

By all accounts, August and September 1650 were especially wet and cold in Scotland.[14] It was, after all, the height of the Little Ice Age: a long period of cold and extremely unpredictable weather. Many English soldiers had gone without tents, sleeping outside in the worst weather, and this—combined with a severe shortage of provisions—had caused dysentery to flourish among them. After moving as far inland as Gogar, seven miles west of Edinburgh, to look for weaknesses in the Scottish defenses, Cromwell's army had to withdraw to the port town of Musselburgh, where English ships waited to carry the sickest troops off to Berwick. An English newspaper, *Mercurius Politicus*, offered Cromwell's point of view:

> Our bodies [were] enfeebled with fluxes, our strength wasted with watchings; want of drink, wet, and cold, being our continual companions, much impaired our strength and courage and made altogether useless above 2,000 men, which at severall times we were forced to send to Berwick.[15]

Hodgson concurred, describing himself and his comrades as "a poor shattered, hungry, discouraged army."[16]

The Scots were on home ground, and it's easy to assume that they were better off. But although the officers found refuge from the weather in nearby homes, the regular soldiers like Thomas Doughty sheltered themselves with newly cut stalks of hay, oats, and barley during the "exceeding foull" weather, "full of wind and weit."[17] As the weather worsened, they were even more exposed than the English, thanks to their position atop Doon Hill.

Nor were provisions a distinct advantage for the Scots. Many Scots soldiers fasted several days before the Battle of Dunbar.[18] Some historians have concluded that the practice was traditional and voluntary, intended to sharpen the soldiers' appetite for battle. But the Scots Army and the capital of Edinburgh were suffering food shortages just as the English were, making the need for fasting more than just a religious or pre-battle ritual.

Sadly, going without food was routine for some. Archeological evidence shows that many of the Dunbar soldiers suffered poor nutrition not just over the days and weeks before the battle, but for months and years at a time.[19] The worst and most frequent famines in all of Scottish history occurred between the middle of the sixteenth and the middle of the seventeenth centuries, just as Doughty and his fellow soldiers were being born and coming of age.[20] Between 1637 and 1649, Scotland suffered the longest drought in its history.[21] During the famine of 1649, the year before the battle, Scottish historian Sir James Balfour wrote: "The pryces of wictuall and cornes of all sortes wer heigher then ever heirtofor aney living could remember," and "The lyke had never beine seine in this kindome heretofor, since it was a natione."[22]

From Musselburgh, the English continued to move eastward to Haddington and finally to Dunbar, where they began shipping out the sickest of their soldiers. From the Scots' perspective on Doon Hill, it looked as though the English were giving up on the invasion entirely. On September 2, David Leslie told his troops that, by seven the next morning, he would have the English Army dead or alive.[23] So, after spending a miserable night atop the hill, the Scots soldiers began moving down into the valley to level the final blow to the demoralized Ironsides.

Cromwell and his generals were, of course, watching the Scots' every move. And as they saw Leslie and his men descend to new positions, they noted two opportunities: the Scots' right flank didn't extend all the way to the shore, and their left flank was wedged into

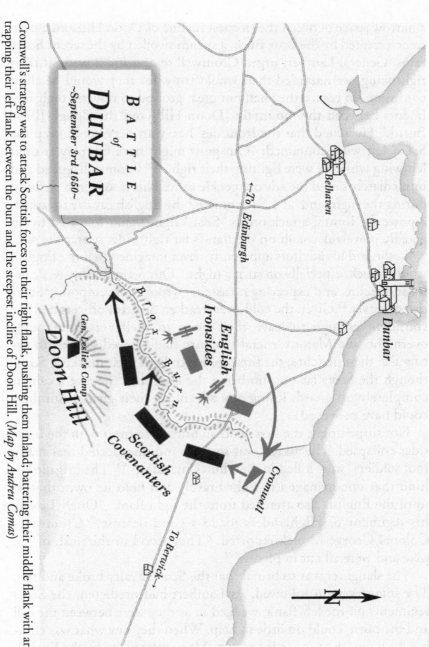

B A T T L E
of
DUNBAR
~September 3rd 1650~

To Edinburgh →

Belhaven

Dunbar

Gen. Leslie's Camp

Doon Hill

English
Ironsides

B r o x   B u r n

Scottish
Covenanters

Cromwell

To Berwick →

N

Cromwell's strategy was to attack Scottish forces on their right flank, pushing them inland; battering their middle flank with artillery; and trapping their left flank between the burn and the steepest incline of Doon Hill. (*Map by Andrew Comas*) a narrow space between the steepest incline of Doon Hill and a deep trench created by the Brox Burn, a stream swollen by the recent heavy rains. General Lambert urged Cromwell to attack: "If we beat their right wing, we hazarded their whole army, for they would be all in confusion, in regard they had not great ground to traverse their regiments between the mountain [Doon Hill] and the clough [Brox Burn]." He added that the Ironsides' heavy artillery could keep the Scots' left wing contained: "Our guns might have fair play at their left wing while we were fighting their right." [24] Cromwell agreed and immediately seized the advantage. He moved his troops into position during the night and, at 4 A.M., ordered the English cavalry to launch a powerful frontal attack on the Scots' right flank, followed by an equally powerful assault on the flank's far right side, nearer the sea.

Leslie and his advisors apparently never imagined that the English would attack, especially on such a night. "Our Scottis airmy wer cairles and secure, and expecting no assalt," wrote a contemporary Scottish observer.[25] Given the cold, wet weather, Scottish officers had felt confident enough to leave their posts to shelter at farmhouses overnight, and Major General Holburn had allowed soldiers to extinguish their matches: the fires needed to light their muskets. So although the Scots far outnumbered the English,[26] they were caught completely off guard, losing any advantage their greater numbers could have conveyed.

Not surprisingly, the first Scottish brigade to meet with the Ironsides collapsed. The assault was so early and unexpected that many foot soldiers "were killed in their hutts fast asleep."[27] The brigade behind that one managed to fight bravely and hold its own: that is, until the English also attacked from the right flank. "Onely Lawers his regiment of Highlanders made a good defense," Cromwell's Colonel George Monck reported. "They stood to the push of the pike and were all cut in pieces."[28]

The slaughter was so brutal that the Scots cavalry broke and ran. The infantry soon followed. As Lambert had predicted, the Scots regiments on the left flank, wedged in as they were between the hill and the burn, could do little to help. When they saw what was coming for them, they, too, tried to run. Many were taken by the English trying to cross the burn. Still others were captured on their way south toward Berwick. Those who did make it past the English lines were chased by the English cavalry a dozen miles to Haddington. "They run," said a giddy and disbelieving Cromwell, "I profess they run." But some Scots didn't run; they simply threw down their weapons and surrendered. Most likely Thomas Doughty was among them.

It was a thorough rout that neither Cromwell nor Leslie expected. The battle lasted no more than two hours. And because of the Scots' humiliatingly rapid capitulation and retreat, it became known as "the Race of Dunbar."

At a distance, the Scots' rapid demise isn't so surprising. The most influential Scots—lairds, clan chiefs, and the Kirk Party clerics—had shifted loyalties and alliances multiple times over the preceding months and years, even fighting among themselves. Each time, common men like Thomas Doughty were expected to fall into line. For the 1650 levies, the government seemed more interested in mustering a large force rather than a well-trained one. And pressured by clerics, the army removed many of its most experienced and effective leaders. Perhaps most important, those commanders who remained failed to persuade foot soldiers of the justness and urgency of the cause. Lacking experience and morale, Scottish foot soldiers simply didn't have the resolve to stand up against a professional fighting force that shrewdly exploited the Scottish commanders' errors of judgment.

Cromwell claimed his army lost "not twenty men" in the battle. But some three thousand Scots were killed and nine thousand more threw down their weapons and surrendered. Cromwell eventually saw fit to release 5,100 of those: the ill and severely wounded.

Though we can't confirm what regiment he was attached to, Thomas Doughty survived the battle and was taken prisoner. It must have been harrowing to witness the chaos and slaughter around him, and a relief to know that he'd survived, largely unscathed. But that relief was short-lived. Doughty and the other 3,900 Scots prisoners considered fit enough to be a threat to the Commonwealth were about to face an ordeal that was, in many ways, far more horrific than the battle itself.[29]

Chapter Three

DEATH MARCH

They throw in Drummer Hodge to rest,
Uncoffined—just as found.

—Thomas Hardy

IN SEPTEMBER 2015, Durham University archeologists confirmed
that up to twenty-nine skeletons found in a corner of the church-
yard near Durham Cathedral in England were the remains of
Scottish soldiers from the Battle of Dunbar. An archeological inves-
tigation—launched when excavations for a new café hit a mass
grave—showed that the naked bodies had been tossed into the grave
without coffins and, presumably, without ceremony. Isotope analyses
determined that almost all the individuals hailed from Scotland. Car-
bon dating, the presence of clay pipes—widely popular in the mid-
1600s—the fact that the dead were all male and almost exclusively
between the ages of thirteen and twenty-five helped to confirm that
these were indeed Dunbar soldiers.

A magnificent stone structure dating from the 1100s, Durham
Cathedral is today part of a UNESCO World Heritage Site. But it
was once a grisly prison and the site of an appalling human disaster.

The skeletons found at Durham tell a troubling story about deprivation and hardship. The age range of the remains was much lower than for those recovered from other battles of the English Civil Wars, suggesting that Scotland had indeed had trouble raising troops for battle and resorted to recruiting very young and inexperienced men. And the skeletons showed little trauma, except for widespread evidence of malnutrition. This, too, suggests that they weren't battle-hardened. "These were young men compared to other civil war casualties. That reflects the difficulties for the Scots in drawing together people from villages and clans at that particular moment during the campaign. These were young, green, raw recruits," professor of archeology at Durham University, Chris Gerrard, told the Scottish newspaper, *The National*.[1] Said Gerrard's colleague, Pam Graves, "These were lads recruited fresh from the fields."[2]

"It was obvious right away that the bodies had been slung into the pit and become entangled with each other," wrote Janet Beveridge, one of the archeologists who helped recover the human remains found at Durham. "It seemed to me at the time that little care had been taken over their burial."[3]

The dead bodies had been thrown naked into two pits; no bits of clothing, no shoes, nor any possessions were found with them. These pits were located at the far end of the Durham Castle grounds, as far as possible from the castle itself: "out of site, out of mind," said Durham University senior archeologist Richard Annis.[4]

Annis speculated that there could be more mass graves near the site: under the Library's Learning Centre, and part of the music studios, the café, and as far as the Exchequer Building and the Fellows' Garden. "All of these areas could have been open ground in the early to mid-seventeenth century."[5] But since Durham Cathedral is a World Heritage Site, there are no plans to excavate further.

The Durham University archeologists' findings reveal poignant details about the Scots Army, the war, and life for the vast majority of those who lived during the seventeenth century:

One thirteen- to fifteen-year-old boy suffering from scurvy had infections in his leg and foot bones.

A fourteen- to fifteen-year-old appears to have suffered from malnutrition for several years and had had severe tooth decay and a leg infection.

A twelve- to sixteen-year-old had leg and foot infections and probably also suffered from rickets—a weakening of bones due to severe vitamin D deficiency.[6]

Approximately one-third of individuals studied suffered from rickets.[7]

Several individuals had dental enamel hypoplasia (characterized by thin, mottled, or pitted enamel) suggesting that they suffered from malnutrition, illness, and stress.

Two had gnawing marks on their skeletons, indicating that they had been left unburied for a time, or that the mass grave was open or shallow enough that rodents were able to molest the dead.[8]

But how did the bodies of Scottish soldiers from the Battle of Dunbar reach Durham, over one hundred miles to the south? After the battle, Cromwell wrote that he had taken some ten thousand Scots prisoner and released five thousand sick and wounded. Sir Arthur Hesilrige, governor of Newcastle, was put in charge of the prisoners and gave a more detailed account. According to Hesilrige, 9,000 were captured, 5,100 wounded were set free, and 3,900 Scottish prisoners, including Thomas Doughty, were force-marched roughly 107 miles from Dunbar, across the Scottish-English border to Durham.

The Scots were hungry before the march began, "they having fasted, as they themselves said, near eight days," Hesilrige wrote in his "Letter to the Council of State for Irish and Scottish Affairs Concerning the Scots Prisoners." By the time they had marched the first thirty miles to Berwick, many were exhausted and refused to continue unless they were given something to eat. English soldiers shot thirty Scots on the spot, persuading the rest to continue. At Morpeth, some fifty miles from Berwick, the prisoners were enclosed in a walled garden. By this time, they were so desperately hungry that they found and devoured raw cabbages, stem, seeds, roots, and all, which "poysoned their Bodies." Scores of soldiers died the next day on the march to Newcastle, another fifteen miles away.

"The next morning, when I sent them down to Durham," wrote Hesilrige, "about Sevenscore were sick, and not able to march, and three dyed that night, and some fell down in their march from Newcastle to Durham, and dyed." By the time the prisoners arrived in

After being taken prisoner at the Battle of Dunbar, 3,900 Scots were marched south to Durham, England, without food or water. Some 700 likely died along the way, with about 3,000 entering Durham. Deprivation and disease continued to ravage the prisoners. Fifty-five days after the battle, a mere 1,400 remained alive. Despite the nearly 3-to-1 odds of dying, Thomas Doughty managed to survive the ordeal. (*Map by Andrew Comas*)

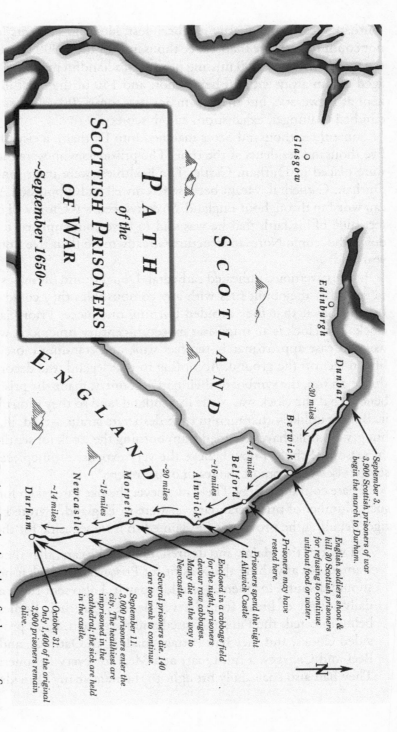

PATH
of the
SCOTTISH PRISONERS
OF WAR
~September 1650~

Glasgow

Edinburgh

SCOTLAND

ENGLAND

Dunbar

~30 miles

Berwick

~14 miles

Belford

~16 miles

Alnwick

~20 miles

Morpeth

~15 miles

Newcastle

~14 miles

Durham

September 3. 3,900 Scottish prisoners of war begin the march to Durham.

English soldiers shoot & kill 30 Scottish prisoners for refusing to continue without food or water.

Prisoners may have rested here.

Prisoners spend the night at Alnwick Castle.

Enclosed in a cabbage field for the night, prisoners devour raw cabbages. Many die on the way to Newcastle.

Several prisoners die. 140 are too weak to continue.

September 11. 3,000 prisoners enter the city. The healthiest are imprisoned in the cathedral; the sick are held in the castle.

October 31. Only 1,400 of the original 3,900 prisoners remain alive.

N

Durham, nearly one-quarter had been lost. Hesilrige's officers "could not count them more than Three thousand" of the 3,900 that began the march. Of those 900 missing prisoners, a handful may have managed to run away without being shot, and 140 of the most ill were kept at Newcastle, but the vast majority—some 700 soldiers—succumbed to hunger, exhaustion, and dysentery.

Some three thousand Scots marched into Durham, a city of only five thousand residents at the time. The prisoners who were most ill were placed in Durham Castle. The healthiest were imprisoned in Durham Cathedral, vacant because Cromwell had suppressed Anglican worship throughout England. So convinced was Cromwell of the rectitude of his faith that he was said to have contemplated tearing down the iconic Norman structure, already more than five hundred years old.

In the cavernous, unheated cathedral, Doughty and his mates were so cold that they built fires with any combustibles they could find. Legend has it that they avoided burning one piece: Prior Castel's clock. The clock is an imposing sixteenth-century timepiece, with a wooden case approximately ten feet wide and standing more than fifteen feet off the ground. According to that legend, the decorative thistle on top, the symbol of their native country, made the prisoners believe that the clock was made in Scotland, and so they didn't burn it. But it's unlikely that men in such desperate straits—cold, ill, and hungry—would have refrained from burning the clock for sentimental reasons. Scholars now believe the very expensive timepiece was stored elsewhere, out of the reach of prisoners.[9]

"I dare confidently say, There was never the like care taken for any such Number of prisoners that ever were in England," wrote Hesilrige, detailing the provisions he claimed to have set aside for them:

> I writ to the Major, and desired him to take care, that they wanted not any thing that was fit for Prisoners, and what he should disburse for them, I would repay it. I also sent them a daily supply of bread from Newcastle. . . . But their Bodies being infected, the Flux encreased amongst them. I . . . provided Cooks, and they had Pottage made with Oatmeal, and Beef and Cabages, a full Quart at a Meal for every Prisoner: They had also coals daily brought to them; as many as made

about a hundred Fires both day and night, and Straw to lie upon . . . and the Marshal was allowed Forty men to cleanse and sweep them every day.[10]

Whether Hesilrige was completely honest, or whether his charges carried out his orders at Durham, we cannot know. Rumors abounded that the guards intercepted food for the prisoners and sold it to townspeople and even to the prisoners themselves, who surely had little to offer in exchange. Or maybe, having been deprived of nutrition for so long, their bodies rejected the food they were given. What we know for sure is that the Scots continued to die at the rate of thirty per day while kept at Durham, and that Hesilrige's associates buried some 1,600 on or near the cathedral grounds.[11]

In his letter, Hesilrige did appear to feel some shame in reporting this disaster to the council: "Gentlemen, You cannot but think strange this long preamble, and to wonder what the matter will be." The "matter" was that the math revealed a horrible fact: of the 3,900 Scots taken prisoner at Dunbar, a mere 1,400 remained 58 days later. So, when the Council of State requested 2,300 be shipped to Ireland for service there, Hesilrige was forced to explain that he simply no longer had the men.

Hesilrige laid some of the blame on the prisoners themselves. They were, he says, "unruly, sluttish and nasty," and

some were killed by themselves, for they were exceeding cruel towards one another. If a man was perceived to have any Money,[12] it was two to one but he was killed before morning, and Robbed; and if any had good clothes, he that wanted, if he was able, would strangle him, and put on his clothes.

This would not be the first or last time that desperately hungry and cold prisoners would fight each other for food or warm clothing, or would become violent and unmanageable after suffering the trauma of battle, being imprisoned under horrible conditions, or watching their comrades die daily in front of them.

Yet there are indications that the prisoners crowded into the cathedral had in fact organized themselves in some ways. In the late 1960s, caretakers noticed that paving stones in a far end of the cathedral proved repeatedly slippery. When those stones were chemically analyzed, researchers found high levels of uric acid seeping out of the stones, suggesting that the prisoners had, perhaps, established that area of the cathedral as the designated latrine.[13]

Still, while there is undoubtedly some truth to Hesilrige's portrayal of the desperate prisoners, the massive loss of life in Durham Cathedral can't be laid to unruly behavior. Clearly, dysentery among the prisoners had gotten out of hand, and those in charge had little capacity to stop it. Moreover, the Parliamentarians were simply overwhelmed with so many prisoners and had trouble supplying their basic needs for food, warmth, and sanitation while waiting for boats to carry them away.

In the face of terrible carnage—and despite the nearly three-to-one odds of dying during the ordeal—some Scots, including Thomas Doughty, made it out alive. Some were to be sent to Ireland to help Cromwell suppress the Irish, engaged in their own political uprising against the Parliamentarians; others were to be shipped to Virginia as laborers. But there is no evidence that either directive was carried out. We do know that a significant number of prisoners were sent to fight in France; others were put to work at salt mines at Shields; a handful were engaged as weavers and laborers locally; and some remained in the cathedral and were finally pardoned and released in 1652.[14] One hundred and fifty Dunbar prisoners, including Thomas Doughty, were shipped to New England to labor at whatever enterprises Cromwell's associates there had in mind. Under these circumstances, Doughty became an unwilling immigrant to the New World.

Chapter Four

ORIGINS

Dowchty man he wes and stout.
— *The Orygynale Cronykil of Scotland,*
Andrew of Wyntoun *(before 1420)*

I N 1700, Thomas Doughty deposed to a New Hampshire court
that he was "Aged seventy Years or theraboughts."[1] That would
mean he was born in 1630. But he didn't say where, or to whom,
or how many siblings he had. And it appears no records survive to
fill in those details. An uncorroborated list of Dunbar prisoners, the
time and location of his servitude in New England, and his close association with other Scots prisoners there point to his Scottish heritage.[2] With such scant information, can we even pretend to know
where he was from?

There are at least a dozen variants of his last name: Doughty,
Doughtie, Dughtie, Duchti, Dochtie, Dowchty, Dufty, Dowty,
Doubty, Doutey, and Doty, among others. The fact that Thomas
couldn't write his own name complicates the puzzle, but even if he
could have, there is no guarantee that he would have used a consistent spelling. Spelling, at the time, was open to interpretation and
whim. Shakespeare famously signed his own name as "Shaksper,"
"Shakspere," and "Shakspeare."

The first-known occurrence of the name Doughty and its variants in Scotland was in 1365, when "Ricardus Duchti held land in the vill of Traqwayre."[3] Traquair is a small village on the Scottish Borders, home to Scotland's oldest continually inhabited house: Traquair House.

Old Parish records of baptisms, marriages, and deaths kept by the Church of Scotland during the seventeenth and eighteenth centuries show one or two Doughties in areas including Edinburgh, Glasgow, and Perth. But, by far, the vast majority of vital records involving Doughties in seventeenth-century Scotland is found in Lothian: the area from the Firth of Forth south to the Lammermuir Hills. With Edinburgh as its urban center, that region is today separated into East Lothian, West Lothian, and Midlothian.

These records show a high concentration of Doughties in the 1600s and early 1700s in the town of Prestonpans—some ten miles east of Edinburgh along the Firth of Forth—with a few more records scattered among the nearby towns of Musselburgh, Newbattle, and Tranent. When the spelling "Duchtie" is added to the mix, a large concentration occurs in Musselburgh and Tranent, with a few in Prestonpans. Almost all of these family records are found within ten kilometers of one another, south of the Firth of Forth and east of Edinburgh. This cluster may give us a clue as to Thomas's origins.[4]

Locating Thomas Doughty's likely origins in the Lowlands is important: as important to understanding his cultural background as knowing whether a modern American hails from New England, the West Coast, or the Deep South. Highland and Lowland Scotland have been historically distinct, separated not merely by geography but by culture, social structure, religion, and especially language. "Scotland is indefinable. It has no unity except upon the map," wrote Scottish novelist Robert Louis Stevenson in 1883. "Two languages, many dialects, innumerable forms of piety; and countless local patriotisms and prejudices part us among ourselves more widely than the extreme east and west of that great continent of America."[5]

Stevenson's portrayal of his homeland was equally true of Scotland two centuries earlier. Even in 1650, Lowlanders had more in common with their neighbors across the border in Northumberland than with the clan-organized society of the Highlands. It's not entirely surprising: during the sixth and seventh centuries, the Scottish Lowlands

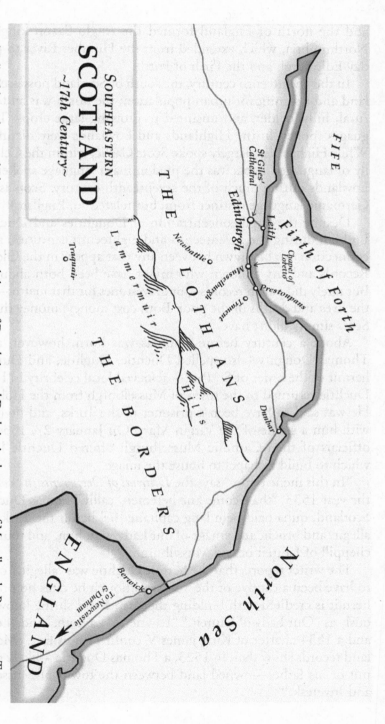

Scotland's Old Parish Records show a concentrated cluster of Doughties and Duchties in the towns of Musselburgh, Prestonpans, Tranent, and Newbattle during the seventeenth and early eighteenth centuries. (*Map by Andrew Comas*)

and the north of England formed the Anglo-Saxon kingdom of Northumbria, which extended from the Humber River to present-day Edinburgh and the Firth of Forth.

In the seventeenth century, the south of Scotland possessed arable land and a significant urban population; the north was and is more rural, hilly, colder, and unsuited to growing large crops. The languages spoken in the Highlands and Lowlands were distinct, too. While Highlanders largely spoke Scots Gaelic, within the Celtic family of languages, Scots was the predominant language spoken in the Lowlands during much of the seventeenth century. Scots is a West Germanic language distinct from, but related to, English.[6]

Despite the large concentration of Doughties and Duchties in Lothian during the seventeenth and eighteenth centuries, no clear connection can be drawn between any that appear in the Old Parish Records and any children who might have been born about 1630. But rarely did parish records—or gravestones for that matter—record the lives and deaths of the poor. Both cost money: money that most Scots simply didn't have.[7]

About a century before Thomas was born, however, another Thomas Doughty (also spelled Duchtie, Dughtie, and Duthy)—a hermit of the order of St. Paul—achieved local celebrity in Lothian. Duchtie returned to the town of Musselburgh from the Holy Land. He was said to have been a prisoner of the Turks, and he brought with him a statue of the Virgin Mary. On January 27, 1534, town officials of then-Catholic Musselburgh offered Duchtie land on which to build a chapel to house the image.

"In this mene tyme," says the *Diurnal of Occurrents in Scotland* of the year 1533, "thair come ane heremeit, callit Thomas Duchtie, in Scotland, quha haid bein lang capitane [*sic*] befoir the Turk, as was allegit, and brocht ane ymage of our Lady with him, and foundit the cheppill of Laureit besyid Mussilburgh."[8]

The writer reports that the hermit Duchtie was "allegit," or "said" to have been a captive of the Turks. Although he cites no proof, the hermit is credited with building the chapel and shrine known variously as "Our Lady of Laureit," "Lawriet," "Laureto," and "Loretto," and a 1534 charter of King James V confirms it as fact.[9] Moreover, land records show that, in 1523, a Thomas Dughtie—likely the hermit or his father—owned land between the towns of Musselburgh and Inveresk.[10]

Sites such as Our Lady of Loretto were the tourist traps of their day; they attracted pilgrims from all over who would pay tribute to the shrines and spend their money at local alehouses, inns, and taverns. For twenty to thirty years, Our Lady of Loretto was an extremely popular site, drawing religious pilgrims, including King James V himself, to Musselburgh.[11] The shrine was said to confer blessings upon those about to marry or bear children, and was believed to heal the sick and infirm.[12] That was its reputation at least.

But not everyone was a devout believer. In a 1555 poem, Sir David Lindsay, a poet and Scottish officer of state, portrayed Thomas Duchtie, the hermit of Loretto, as one of many professed holy men, a "Fained false hermite,/Abusing the people of this region,/Only for their particular profit." Lindsay singled out Duchtie for special attention:

> And 'specially that hermite Lawriet,
> He put the common people in believe
> That blind got sight, and crooked got their feet,
> The which the paillard by no means can prieve."[13]

Lindsay charged that Duchtie was a "paillard" (or "palliard"): a scoundrel who preyed upon the uneducated, convincing them that the shrine could make the blind see and the crippled walk. And the poet, it seems, was clairvoyant. Around 1560, the Reformation swept through Scotland, driving Catholicism and idolatry before it. Desperate to preserve the shrine from zealous reformers, the hermits of Loretto set out to prove that it could truly muster miracles. The hermits—no one knows whether Thomas was still among them—found a local man who was widely believed to be blind. His mother, a gypsy, had taught him as a young child to roll his eyes back in his head for hours at a time to appear sightless: a skill that greatly enhanced his success as a beggar. In collusion with the monks, the man agreed to act out a miracle upon a stage erected near the shrine: to have his sight restored. Crowds gathered to witness the event. The gypsy beggar came before them with the whites of his eyes showing. When he was told to open his eyes, he did so, to the great amazement of those gathered.

But it wasn't long before the truth came out. The beggar was persuaded by the sword of a skeptic to tell the truth. When he did, local residents rioted, destroying the chapel and shrine of Loretto. For this act, the townspeople of Musselburgh were afforded the honor of being excommunicated from the Catholic Church by the pope himself annually for the next 250 years.[14]

We do not know what ultimately became of Thomas the Hermit, and no obvious connection exists between him and our Thomas Doughty. Of course, hermits, or monks, took an oath of celibacy, so it's unlikely a direct connection exists, though Thomas the Hermit appears to have had questionable morals. But combining an actual event—Musselburgh's granting the land for a church to Thomas Duchtie, a man of some local renown—with the concentration of vital records for Doughties in the same region a century or so later, suggests that we may be on the right geographical track, at least.

Yet the story of Thomas the Hermit offers something equally important: a valuable glimpse of local history and culture in the decades just before our Thomas Doughty was born. Sixteenth-century Scotland was in flux, and people, like those of today, were naïve and skeptical, ignorant and learned, devout and doubtful. The upheaval caused by the Reformation, and the notion that Catholicism was growing increasingly corrupt, reverberated throughout Scottish culture for the next century. Events such as the destruction of Loretto Chapel laid the groundwork for a century of disputes among Catholics, Anglicans, Puritans, and Presbyterians, including the Wars of the Three Kingdoms and the Battle of Dunbar. In fact, from the time Thomas Doughty was nine years old until he was twenty-one, war—fought mostly on the grounds of religious ideology—was a constant in his life.

During the Reformation, John Knox, a Scot who studied with John Calvin in Geneva, became Scotland's most influential leader. Knox returned to Scotland in 1559 and was elected minister of Edinburgh's iconic St. Giles' Cathedral, where he espoused Calvinist principles: the importance of faith, the priesthood of all believers (and the superfluity of bishops), and the authority of scripture. This was the beginning of Presbyterianism; today the Presbyterian Kirk is the national church of Scotland.

By the 1630s, many Lowland Scots were Presbyterian; some were beginning to embrace the religion as fundamental to Scottish sovereignty. But the king, Charles I, wanted the Scots to worship as the

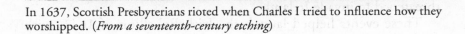

The Arch-Prelate of St Andrewes in Scotland reading the new Service-books in his pontificalibus assaulted by men & women, with Crickets stooles — Stickes and Stones.

In 1637, Scottish Presbyterians rioted when Charles I tried to influence how they worshipped. (*From a seventeenth-century etching*)

English did, with bishops governing local churches and worshippers following an Anglican liturgy. Religious conformity, he hoped, would help bring about political conformity. So in 1637, he ordered the Scots to adopt a new Anglican prayer book. They were outraged. For them, the Anglican faith was tantamount to popery, and the prayer book, an attempt to undermine their religious autonomy.

Street vendor Jenny Geddes attended church in St. Giles' Cathedral in Edinburgh on Sunday, July 23, 1637, the day Charles I's new prayer book was introduced. She was seated on a small stool, and when the dean began reading from the prayer book, she allegedly stood up and threw her stool at his head, shouting, "Deil colic the wame o' ye, fause thief; daur ye say Mass in my lug?" In other words: "The Devil give you colic, you false thief; do you dare say mass in my ear?" Jenny's passionate reaction inspired a riot, and the unrest spread from St. Giles to churches throughout Scotland.[15]

The popular unrest inspired a revival of the Scots Confession, or the National Covenant: the agreement among many influential Scots that they would defend Presbyterianism as the official religion of Scotland. But the king would have none of it. He mustered an army to try and force the Scots into submission. The first Bishops War, as it was called, comprised several minor skirmishes on the border before a tenuous agreement, the Pacification of Berwick, was signed. Charles I simply didn't have the money or soldiers to carry out his plans. Yet, sometime later, the king learned the Scots had been colluding with France, and he became even more determined. Parliament was unwilling to support Charles's plans for war, so he summarily dismissed the body, raised his own army, and marched his soldiers north. Once again, the Scots gained the upper hand; the second Bishops War resulted in the Scots seizing English territory as far south as Durham.

The Scottish Army's success against Charles inspired his opponents in Ireland and England to rebel, which caused a cascade of confusing and violent events. Desperate for troops, Charles proposed to abolish discrimination against Irish Catholics if they would fight for him. In response, the English dissenters and the Scottish Covenanters threatened to invade Ireland.

These events helped launch the Irish Rebellion of 1641, with Catholics trying to unseat the English-run government to force concessions. But the conflict soon turned ugly; some Catholics turned to killing their Protestant neighbors, many of whom were English and Scottish transplants. To protect the Ulster Scots, the Covenanters sent an army to Ireland.

Back in Scotland, the Royalists, who supported Charles I under James Graham, First Marquis of Montrose, clashed with the Covenanters from 1644 to 1645. The Covenanters ultimately won and, in 1644, signed an agreement to fight alongside the Parliamentarians in the English Civil War.

Amid this religious and political turmoil, Scots, like their counterparts all over the globe, were coping with an especially tough climatic period known as the Little Ice Age. Throughout the century, long, cold winters and very short, cool summers dominated, stunting crops, bringing drought, inundations, and famine, and enflaming political and social turmoil.[16]

Just before Thomas Doughty was born, the country endured two disastrous harvests in a row, and Scots suffered dearly from a lack of grains and other staples. In 1622, the *Chronicle of Perth* reported that "about the harvest and efter, their wes suche ane universall seiknes in all the countrie as the ellyke has net bene hard of. . . . Thair wes also grat mortalitie amongs the poore."[17]

In 1637, when Doughty was seven years old, Scotland endured one of the worst floods in its history. In October, it rained for ten days straight:

> Waters and burns flowing up over bank and brae; corn-mills and mill-houses washen down; houses, kilns, cots, faulds wherein beasts were keipit, all destroyed. The corns, weel stacked, began to moch and rot till they were casten over again. Lamentable to see, and whereof the like was never seen before.[18]

The Earl of Lothian wrote to his father in October 1637: "There have been such inundations and floods and winds, as no many living remembers the like. This has shaken and rotted and carried away the little corn came up."[19] The harvest of 1637 was ruined, and that was followed by a year of terrible drought.[20]

During the decade of the 1640s, summers in Scotland were extremely cold and wet, ruining crops and causing many farms, particularly in the Lammermuir Hills, to be abandoned. Between the years of 1600 and 1650, some one hundred thousand Scots voluntarily left the country seeking better opportunities abroad.[21]

Because the climate reduced yields and destroyed crops, hunger and malnutrition, particularly among the lower classes, took their toll on Scottish children during the 1600s. The worst famines in Scottish recorded history occurred between 1550 and 1650.[22] And, as we've seen, malnutrition left its mark on the skeletons of Dunbar soldiers.

Diseases also had a powerful impact on families and child survival. In seventeenth-century Western Europe and the North American colonies, 12 to 13 percent of infants would die before reaching their first birthday.[23] Once a child survived birth, any number of diseases could threaten: measles, mumps, rubella, whooping cough, scarlet fever, smallpox, diphtheria, tetanus, not to mention diarrheal diseases, tuberculosis, and streptococcal infections. Many of these diseases have since been prevented by vaccination and inoculation, as well as improved hygiene, medical care, and better nutrition. But in seventeenth-century Scotland, they were frequently deadly. Scot John

Maxwell wrote in August 1629 of the physical and emotional consequences of smallpox in his household:

> My whole and greatest part of my household has taken the pox, and my second son Patrick is departed this life and my eldest daughter at the point of death also, and if she dies I will be utterly wrecked. Beseeching God of His great mercy to send me a part of Job's patience, because I am not able to reach to the whole, in regard my heart is half rent out of me.[24]

In the summer of 1655, the Countess of Lothian wrote to her husband about how their three children were enduring a bout with the measles:

> We are as you left us. Lilias has had the measles and is recovering, John has; this is the fourth day of a hot fever and is not got a cool as yet. He has taken it with a great cold, going too soon out after the measles. Margaret is not fully well as yet. I know not what the will of God is, but I submit to His will. I trust they will be well.[25]

Epitaphs tell an equally poignant story of the tremendous toll that childhood mortality had upon Scottish families. The monument of the Laird of Enterkin's wife, who died in 1676, reads, "Twice five times suffered she the childbed pains, yet of her children only five remains." George Foulis of Ravelston "left six sons surviving and as many daughters; he had five sons dead before himself and one daughter." In the Howff Cemetery in Dundee, Grisel Scott was buried "with children six, sprung from her fruitful womb, as many live."[26]

Some diseases didn't discriminate between children and adults. Scotland endured its second major outbreak of the bubonic plague between 1644 and 1648, when Doughty was between fourteen and eighteen years old. The disease may have been introduced by Scottish soldiers returning from the Bishops Wars in northern England.

This was the last bout of the plague to affect Edinburgh but also the most severe. The Scottish capital is thought to have lost as many as half of its thirty-five thousand residents,[27] though exact numbers are hard to come by, since many, including city officials, left Edinburgh for rural areas.[28] In the nearby port of Leith, fully half of the town's six thousand inhabitants perished. The South Leith Kirk Session Register of 1645 reported that:

Leith . . . doe lye for the present, being visit with the plague
of pestilence in such sort that the nomber of the dead exceeds
the nomber of the leiving, and amongst them it cannot be de-
cernit quha are clean and quha are foulle; and make the
calamitie greater, the are visit with ane lamentibill famine,
both for penurie and also for laicke of means.[29]

Despite the challenges of armed conflict, climate, and disease,
however, Scotland was making strides to improve life for its children.
The School Establishment Act of 1616, adopted fourteen years before Doughty's birth, ordered that schools be set up in every parish
to teach reading and writing. These schools were to be publicly
funded, supervised by the church, and were to teach not just the sons
of wealthy families but those of ordinary means, as well.

Scottish schools had political and religious aims, reflecting a rapidly changing society and cultural biases. The School Establishment
Act sought to homogenize Scottish culture, to remove what it saw as
the "barbarite and incivilitie" of the Highlands and islands, and to
establish Protestantism and the English language as cultural bench-
marks. Schools would help ensure that "the trew religioun be advancit and establisheit in all the pairtis of this kingdome"; that the
"Inglishe toung be universallie plantit"; and that "the Irische language,"—or Scots Gaelic—"whilk is one of the cheif and principall
causes of the continewance of barbarite and incivilitie amongis the
inhabitantis of the Ilis and Heylandis, may be abolishit and removeit."[30]

Literacy in Scotland was not widespread when the seventeenth
century dawned. But as a result of educational reform, by the end of
the century, the majority of Scottish men could at least sign their
names.[31] Thomas Doughty could not: a detail that strongly indicates
very modest origins.

We don't know for sure what Doughty's family did for work, but
the odds suggest that they were agricultural workers. In the 1630s,
nine out of ten Scots worked the land,[32] and in Lowland parishes,
the vast majority of the population consisted of cottar families who
worked small plots of land leased from a handful of great
proprietors.[33]

Boys from ordinary circumstances might attend school for a few
years and then apprentice to tradesmen or begin to work with their

fathers at a trade or in agriculture at about age fourteen. Boys from poorer families typically went to work at age seven, either at home or for a local farmer or tradesman. Although work began for boys and girls alike at a young age, life was not all drudgery. Hiring fairs or feeing markets, for example, were held in late fall, and they were a chance for farmers to find servants, and laborers to find work and potential mates, for both men and women attended. Workers would deck themselves out to look strong, capable, and attractive; peddlers were there to sell trinkets and treats to the crowds; and children tagged along, too, giving these hiring events the atmosphere of a festival. Drinking was pervasive; once the employer and servant agreed on a wage, the employer would often stand the new employee a drink at the local inn or tavern as part of the deal.

The harvest, too, was another opportunity for celebration, with music, dancing, and drinking. In seventeenth-century Scotland, "hijinks" was not "boisterous or rambunctious activity," but a drinking game. Players rolled a die, and the one scoring the lowest had to perform a humiliating forfeit or take a drink. Weddings, funerals, and wakes also provided time for socializing, storytelling, eating, and imbibing. At working-class penny weddings, attendees would pay a shilling, and the money went to the young couple or to purchase food and drink.

Town commons served not only for grazing animals but also as sports fields. Scots enjoyed ball games including shinty and football; at Fisherrow, near Musselburgh, such games pitted single fishwives against married fishwives.[34] Bowls, ninepins, golf, and archery contests were popular, as were horse races. Cockfights were a common occurrence in Scottish schoolyards, and occasionally, children would see exotic animals, including bears and elephants, paraded from town to town.[35]

Archaeological evidence shows that children, like their parents, did have time for fun, and that toys were as popular in early modern times as they are now. When workers unblocked a long-unused stairwell at Market Harborough Church in England, they found over two hundred children's toys from the sixteenth and seventeenth centuries, likely placed there by children attending the nearby grammar school. The toys included tipcats—long sticks used to play an early ancestor of rounders or baseball; spinning tops; whistles; knucklebones, or dice; balls; whip handles; and teetotums—a form of spinning top used in gambling or games of chance.[36]

Yet children and young adults—particularly those from poor families—faced an additional peril during the seventeenth and eighteenth centuries that is only infrequently acknowledged. The colonization of America and the great demand for labor to help settle new lands inspired a surge in human trafficking. Convicts, persons considered to be beggars or idlers, as well as young adults, youths, and children were taken, legally and illegally, from the streets of port cities such as London, Bristol, Edinburgh, Leith, and Aberdeen and shipped to the New World as laborers.[37]

The practice was officially sanctioned early in the century. In 1620, the English Privy Council, an advisory body to the king, noted,

> Wee are informed that the Citty of London hath, by an act of comon councell, appointed one hundred children, out of the multitudes that swarme in that place, to be sent to Virginia there to be bound apprentices for certaine yeares with very benificall condicions for them afterwardes.

According to the Council, "the citty deserveth thankes and comendacions for redeemeing so many poore soules from mysery and ruyne and putting them in a condicion of use and service to the State."[38] Given the short-term hazards (the heightened chances of dying during the Atlantic crossing; children's vulnerability to malnutrition and contagious diseases; and their lack of endurance for hard labor), any beneficial conditions for the children over the long term were unlikely. The potential gains for the traffickers, masters, and the government, however, were palpable and abundant, and included profit from selling the children, a relatively cheap source of labor, and a means of shifting social problems caused by poverty and unemployment to the colonies.

We can track at least one shipment of children from London to New England. In June 1642, John Winthrop, in his third term as governor of Massachusetts, wrote that "One of our ships, the Seabridge, arrived with 20 children and some other passengers out of England." "Those children," wrote Winthrop, "with many more to come after, were sent by money given on fast day in London, and allowed by the parliament and the city for that purpose."[39]

What happened to one of those children may or may not have been typical, but it is troubling. According to Winthrop, a farmer named Franklin engaged one boy on that shipment, young Nathaniel Sewall, as an apprentice. Nathaniel was hard to handle, so Franklin, according to Winthrop, "used him with continual rigor and unmerciful correction, and exposed him many times to much cold and wet in the winter season." Franklin also employed unusual punishments, such as "hanging him in the chimney" until Nathaniel was "very poor and weak." Exasperated with the boy's behavior, Franklin determined to bring him before the court. So he "tied him upon an horse and so brought him (sometimes sitting and sometimes hanging down) to Boston." Along the way, Nathaniel called out for water, but Franklin "would give him none, though he came close by it, so as the boy was near dead when he came to Boston, and died within a few hours after."

In May 1644, a court of assistants found Franklin guilty of murder. But doubts among some magistrates caused his sentencing to be put off until the next court session in August. At that time, some assistants argued that Franklin shouldn't be put to death, because "it did not appear that the master's intention was to hurt [Nathaniel], but to reform him." By bringing the boy before the magistrates, they argued, Franklin showed that he was innocent of evil intent. But Winthrop cited Exodus 21:20, which indicates that "if a master strike his servant with a rod, which is a lawful action, and he die under his hand, (as this servant did,) he was to die for it." In the end, Franklin was executed, though he "continued even to his execution, professing assurance of salvation, and that God would never lay the boy his death to his charge, but the guilt of his blood would lie upon the country."[40] Franklin may well have been guilty, but he was also correct in suggesting that "the country" was complicit in the crime. Massachusetts Bay had willingly accepted the boatloads of children so generously sent to them from London.

By mid-century, child-stealing had become so rampant that the government had to step in. "Divers lewd Persons do go up and down the City of London, and elsewhere [and] in a barbarous and wicked Manner steal away many little Children," reported the English Parliament in 1645. In response, they passed an ordinance to search all vessels and to imprison anyone caught stealing children "until they may be brought to severe and exemplary Punishment."[41]

Scotland faced similar challenges. In 1668, a Captain Guthrie, master of *The Ewe and Lamb*, announced to the Scottish Privy Council that his vessel was "ready to transport vagabonds, idle beggars, and other criminals to Virginia, Barbadoes and other remote islands," and he "crave[d] delivery of such according to the intention and custom of the Council."[42] Yet Guthrie wasn't above scaring up passengers on his own. That same year, the Privy Council, "being informed that some persons are by compulsion and violence caryed aboord the ship called . . . *The Ewe and Lamb* at present in the roads of Leeth . . . to be caryed to Virginia, do . . . command the magistratts of Edinburgh or Leeth to send some fitt person or persons aboord . . . and to report ane accompt of their diligence to the Councill."[43] While there's no indication that Guthrie was carrying children, Scottish officials, like their London counterparts, found it necessary to search his vessel and others headed to America to ensure that their cargo didn't include kidnapped individuals.

Because they proved highly profitable, kidnapping schemes continued into the next century, as illustrated by the story of the most famous kidnapped Scot, Peter Williamson. In 1743, Williamson was seized from the docks in Aberdeen at a young age, shipped to America as a servant, and ultimately returned to tell his story. It was quite a tale, and was published in his book, *French and Indian Cruelty: Exemplified in the life and Various Vicissitudes of Fortune, of Peter Williamson.*

According to Williamson's account, several Aberdeen merchants and magistrates colluded on a scheme to kidnap children from the streets of the town, ship them abroad, and sell them at a profit. The conspirators held the children in barns, in the Tollbooth Prison, aboard ships in the harbor, and at other locations until they were ready to sail and were said to have hired pipers to play near these locations so that passersby couldn't hear the noise of the children inside.[44]

Williamson was brought on board a ship that lay at anchor in Aberdeen Harbor and kept below deck for "about a Month's Time," until the perpetrators of the scheme had enough children to set sail. The ship crossed the Atlantic safely but ran aground in a storm near Cape May in present-day New Jersey. He and his fellow travelers survived and were eventually sold in Philadelphia for sixteen pounds a

PETER WILLIAMSON.

Remarkable for his Captivity & Sufferings

Peter Williamson was undoubtedly a showman, as this image of him impersonating a Native American demonstrates. But records show that he was kidnapped as a child or young man from Aberdeen and shipped to America where he was a servant. (*Wellcome Collection*)

head. "It was my Lot to be sold to one of my Countrymen, a *North-Briton*, for the Term of seven Years, who had in his Youth undergone the same Fate as myself; having been kidnapped from St. *Johnstown* in Scotland," wrote Williamson.[45]

According to his account, Williamson became a free man in Philadelphia upon the death of his master. Soon after, however, he was captured by Cherokees and forced to live among them as a slave for several months, or so the story goes. He eventually escaped and, after serving as an Indian fighter with the British army in Pennsylvania, returned to Scotland to publish his memoir and seek revenge against the Aberdeen merchants.

Scholars have long doubted the veracity of Williamson's story. One called Peter "One of the greatest liars who ever lived."[46] Scholar Timothy J. Shannon referred to *French and Indian Cruelty* as "factual fiction": a heavily embellished narrative based on fact. It is "reasonable to conclude," writes Shannon, "that Williamson came to America as a youth bound into servitude, that he was shipwrecked off Cape May, and that he was sold to a master in northeastern Pennsylvania. It is equally likely that he lied about the age at which he was indentured, his marriage, and his Indian captivity."[47]

What we know for sure about Peter comes from a series of court proceedings. In 1762 and 1765, Williamson successfully sued the conspirators who had run the child-kidnapping scheme. A "kidnapping book" containing Peter's name—and the names of others—turned up as incriminating evidence. And Williamson went so far as to print some of the more damning depositions from the trial in the 1762 edition of his book, *French and Indian Cruelty*. During the trials, evidence emerged that the scheme was active between 1740 and 1746, and likely consigned scores of Scottish children to involuntary servitude.[48]

Human trafficking schemes during the seventeenth and eighteenth centuries demonstrate the powerful influence that the colonies exerted on English and Scottish society. America's labor needs made poor and laboring class Britons and Scots marketable commodities, vulnerable to legal and illegal transportation abroad. For the merchant class, trafficking in servants and slaves proved a profitable business. And for the ruling class, transportation to the colonies served as a satisfactory solution for social problems such as crime, unemployment, and poverty.

Though likely quite poor, Thomas Doughty managed to survive the mortal hazards around him throughout his childhood. And for a time, he managed to avoid the strong gravitational pull that the American colonies had for people of his station. By the time he was a young adult, however, his luck changed, and he found himself among those undesirables who were to be disposed of across the sea.

The seventeenth century was a turbulent time in Scotland. The upheaval from the Reformation had not yet sorted itself out, the climate was unstable and unpredictable, and diseases ran rampant. Most Scots were sucked into this maelstrom in one way or another, as Thomas Doughty was when he was conscripted to fight for the Covenant. As it has for countless young men over the centuries, war and its aftermath changed his life forever, exposing him to a much larger and even more chaotic world, and making it impossible, figuratively and literally, for him to return to his rural Scottish roots.

Chapter Five

PRISONERS, SERVANTS, OR SLAVES?

God Almithie in his most holy and wise providence hath soe disposed
of the Condicion of mankind, as in all times some must be rich some
poore, some highe and eminent in power and dignities; others meane
and in subjeccion."

—John Winthrop, *A Modell of Christian Charity*

ONE HUNDRED AND FIFTY SOULS who survived the Durham ordeal set sail for New England aboard the *Unity* on or about November 11, 1650. The trip was another prolonged trial for the Dunbar Scots. And it's hard to imagine that they felt much relief arriving in New England in late December, not knowing what lay in store for them, or perhaps, even where they were.

Still, the site of Boston Harbor may have helped to allay their fears of being shipped to a desolate wilderness. Just two decades earlier, the very year that Thomas Doughty was born, John Winthrop and company had founded the Massachusetts Bay Colony. Winthrop and his Puritans settled at Charlestown first, but many moved across the Charles River to the narrow Boston Peninsula, where fresh water was more abundant. The two towns formed a snug port. Houses and wharves hugged the coastline, and a ferry carried passengers back and forth.

The harbor saw plenty of traffic, even in the 1630s. William Wood, one of the first long-term visitors to write a description of New England, noted in 1634 that "Here may ride 40 ships at a time."[1] But according to another English visitor, John Josselyn, Boston itself was still something of a backwater. As he observed in 1638, "Boston . . . was rather a Village, than a Town, there being not above Twenty or thirty houses."[2]

Sixteen years later, not long after the Dunbar Scots arrived, Captain Edward Johnson described a different Boston altogether:

> The Chiefe Edifice of this City-like Towne is crowded on the Sea-bankes, and wharfed out with great industry and cost, the buildings beautifull and large, some fairly set forth with Brick, Tile, Stone and Slate and orderly placed with comly streets, whose continuall inlargement presages some sumptuous City.[3]

Johnson's description was meant to render the town in its best light and to praise its potential. He had come to New England with Winthrop in 1630, and the colony actively sought to attract newcomers, particularly pious Puritans and reliable, hard-working servants. He described the harbor as a busy international port:

> Good store of Shipping is here yearly built, and some very faire ones: both Tar and Mastes the Countrey affords from its own soile; also store of Victuall both for their owne and Forreiners-ships, who resort hither for that end; this Towne is the very Mart of the Land, *French*, *Portugalls* and *Dutch* come hither for Traffique.[4]

Ten years beyond the Great Migration (1629–1640), during which twenty thousand people left England to settle in New England, Boston was home to some four thousand inhabitants. What the Scots prisoners must have glimpsed, then, was the waterfront of a bustling town—nothing compared with London (four hundred thousand inhabitants) or Edinburgh (thirty-five thousand)—but still, a small, thriving seaport with a cosmopolitan character.

A map of the city based on land records from 1648 shows a good deal more houses than the twenty or thirty Josselyn saw a decade earlier.[5] Showing the names of property holders, it reads like a list of

New England's elite, including two powerful men who would hold a number of the prisoners' futures in their hands: Richard Leader and Valentine Hill.

The prisoners' relief at arriving on land was short-lived. Soon after disembarking, some thirty-five Scots were transported by boat to the Lynn iron works (at present-day Saugus); perhaps twenty to thirty more were sent to the iron works at Braintree; and the rest were sold at Boston to a variety of masters, including Richard Leader and Valentine Hill, and scattered across Massachusetts, New Hampshire, and Maine.

Captured, transported, and sold, Doughty and the other Dunbar Scots have been called both "slaves" and "indentured servants." In common parlance, if you weren't a slave, then you were an indentured servant. While the Scots were taken prisoner and sold, much like chattel slaves, their terms of servitude were finite—at least for those whom we know ended up in New England. And there was no thought that their offspring would be born into perpetual slavery, as was the case for millions of kidnapped Africans, particularly those arriving after 1700.

The myth persists that, in New England, the vast majority of servants came willingly by an indenture or contract. Immigrants arrived in New England, contracted to a local employer who paid the immigrant's passage or fare over, and in exchange, the passenger agreed to serve the master for up to seven years. During that time, the master was to feed, clothe, and house the servant, and to teach him or her a trade. And local laws dictated that servants were not to be "sent away empty" when their contracts ran out. Most benefited from grants of land or money.

But, like Doughty and the Dunbar Scots, not all servants came willingly; many were forced into ships under a variety of pretenses and had no say in the contracts that bound them to others. So the common understanding of "indenture" is deceptive. In using the term "indentured servant" so loosely, says scholar John Donoghue, some historians have followed the lead of slave masters themselves, who sought to hide their transgressions "under the rhetorical cloak of the tradition of English service."[6]

Even in the seventeenth century, there was considerable discussion about what constituted a slave versus a servant. Puritan clergyman Samuel Willard, pastor of Boston's Third Church, wrote:

> The word *Servant* . . . is applied to all such in a Family as are under the command of a *Master*, and owe to him Subjection: And we know by Experience, that these are not all of a sort, or come under the same degree of Servitude; some are more Free, and others more in Bondage; hence the word Servant is sometimes used in common language, distributive with that of a *Slave*.[7]

Were the Dunbar Scots, then, prisoners, servants, or slaves? They were, without doubt, involuntary immigrants who found themselves in a variety of situations after arriving in America. They had been torn from their families, homes, and homeland against their wills and transported across the ocean to be sold as laborers for a price. They didn't spend their entire lives in servitude, yet they enjoyed little freedom for those first seven or eight years in New England. Except for the occasional runaway or disobedient individual, the Scots prisoners rarely show up in the court records of New England towns before 1657 or 1658, when their terms began to expire. That suggests that they were kept under close rein and had little time for much beyond work.

Forced labor was vitally important to early New England's economy and culture. A good deal of it has lain hidden behind the word "indenture," and the arguable notion that most workers arrived in New England voluntarily. Yet it has also been overlooked because the sheer numbers of slaves and servants shipped to Virginia, Maryland, and the West Indies were much greater. Those regions' larger plantations and longer growing seasons benefited from wholesale chattel slavery. New England presented a smaller, but still thriving, market for prisoners, slaves, and kidnapped individuals.

Social context is vitally important for understanding the importance of forced labor and the Scottish prisoners' place in the world. African slaves could be found in Massachusetts even before the Scots arrived. John Josselyn witnessed as much in October 1639. Josselyn was lodging on Noddles Island in Boston Harbor with a man named Samuel Maverick when, he wrote, "Mr. Mavericks Negro woman came to my chamber window." The woman was very upset, and "willingly would have expressed her grief in English; but I apprehended it by her countenance and deportment." Concerned, Josselyn went to his host to find out what was behind the woman's anguish. Maverick explained to his guest that he

> Was desirous to have a breed of Negros, and therefore seeing she would not yield by perswasions to company with a Negro young man he had in his house; he commanded him will'd she nill'd she to go to bed to her, which was no sooner done but she kickt him out again, this she took in high disdain beyond her slavery, and this was the cause of her grief.[8]

Maverick had ordered a young black man, presumably also his slave, to rape the woman so that he could have "a breed of Negros." Not surprisingly, the woman took this injustice "in high disdain beyond her slavery." Although the enslavement of Africans had not yet risen to the entrenched institution it would achieve in later centuries, the incident speaks to the uniquely dehumanizing treatment that servants and slaves of color faced from the start. Though they were often treated cruelly, no white or Native American slaves that we know of were subjected to any such "breeding" schemes.

Samuel Maverick's scheme was just the beginning. Letters and court and probate records prove that African slaves and servants were more numerous in New England than Puritan writers and diarists and even many modern historians have acknowledged. In *New England Bound: Slavery and Colonization in Early America*, scholar Wendy Warren found documentary evidence of nineteen trading voyages that "followed the telltale slaving route of New England to Africa to the West Indies and back." And that was in the seventeenth century alone. "Even more trading voyages carrying slaves went back and forth between the Caribbean and New England, a slow but steady influx," wrote Warren.[9]

Keeping Africans as servants and slaves seems to have picked up steam toward mid-century, and not just in Boston. The eastern frontier also had its share. Captain Brian Pendleton, a landowner in Saco, Maine, and sometime magistrate, owned at least two black servants. Their "untimely death" by fire became the subject of a court inquiry in 1663.[10] In 1676, Robert Cutt, a prominent citizen of Kittery,

Maine, died, leaving "Three Negro men," "Two Wimine Negros," "Two Negro Wimine Children," and "one Negro Lad" as part of his estate.[11] That same year, his neighbor Nicholas Shapleigh purchased a "Certaine Negro man Called Coffe" to "Have and to hold . . . during the terme of the naturall life of him the s^d. Coffe."[12]

Even the most prominent New Englanders became slaveholders. In 1689, former Massachusetts Bay governor Simon Bradstreet wrote a will leaving two slaves, Hannah and Bilhah, to his second wife.[13] And at the turn of the century, Cotton Mather's own congregation procured an African slave for him named "Onesimus," demonstrating the broad acceptance of chattel slavery in the eyes of both law and religion in Massachusetts.[14] "A pretty intelligent fellow," Mather wrote of his man, Onesimus had been inoculated against smallpox in Africa and helped the minister, who had a lifelong interest in medicine, to understand how important inoculation could be in ridding Massachusetts of the scourge of smallpox.[15] Onesimus may well have been the Reverend Mather's intellectual companion, but he remained the white man's property, a gift from his appreciative congregants.

In the 1600s, it was equally common practice for prisoners of war to be sold into bondage, as Doughty and the other Dunbar Scots were. In 1602, John Smith, the famed explorer and admiral of New England, was wounded in a battle in Transylvania. There, he and his comrades were "sold in the market place as if we were beasts":

> None but those who have undergone this degradation, can have any conception of the feeling. Stripped naked in order to show the soundness of our limbs, with muscles being handled and felt, as a butcher does an ox; a kick, a blow, or a lash from a whip, and a curse, were you not quick enough in obeying such orders as "Turn round," "Put out your arm," &c.; whilst now and then we were set a-wrestling, one with another, in order to show our strength.[16]

In New England, too, enslaving conquered warriors after battle was practiced throughout the century. The English and their native allies in the Pequot War of 1636–1637 killed some 700 Pequot men; 250 captives were ordered "to be disposed aboute in the townes" of

Connecticut and Massachusetts as household servants; and 17 Pequot boys were shipped to the Caribbean.[17] The ship captain who sold them, William Pierce, exchanged the boys for salt, cotton, tobacco, and Africans.[18] Presumably, the Africans were in turn sold about Boston. Later in the century, in the aftermath of King Philip's War, some one thousand Native Americans were sold into captivity in Bermuda, Cadiz, and elsewhere.[19]

Nor were the Dunbar prisoners the only Scots sold in New England. One year to the day after Dunbar, Cromwell fought the final battle of the civil war at Worcester, England. Once again, he faced David Leslie and the Royalists. And once again, Cromwell's New Model Army defeated the Scots, taking ten thousand prisoners. Many were transported to Ireland and Barbados, and 272 were shipped to New England on the *John and Sara*. When they arrived in late 1651, Thomas Kemble, a Boston resident and business associate of John Becx and Valentine Hill, sold the captured Scots to local tradesmen, industrialists, and farmers.

Like the Dunbar prisoners, many of the Worcester captives had been pressed into the Scots Army; after losing the battle, they faced either death or banishment and hard labor. This time, though, they weren't needed for the iron works at Lynn. Only one of the Worcester soldiers is known to have been employed there;[20] the rest went to farms, workshops, and mills scattered throughout New England.

Profit was a primary motivating factor behind their sale, as this communication from the businessmen in charge of the prisoners— Robert Rich, William Green, and John Becx—to Kemble makes clear:

> Wee . . . doe consigne the said Shipp & servants to be disposed of by you for our best Advantage & account & the whole proceed of these Servants & voyage Retourne in a Joinct stocke without any Division in such goods as you conceive will turne best to acco[nt] in the Barbadoes.[21]

As the letter indicates, a triangular trade had developed, whereby prisoners captured—not in Africa, but in Scotland and England— were sold in New England or Virginia for money or goods, which was in turn traded for sugar, tobacco, or cotton at Barbados to be returned to England.

Barbados, of course, welcomed even larger numbers of servants and slaves who had no say in the matter. Many prisoners from the Wars of the Three Kingdoms ended up there, including some 1,300 captives from the Battle of Worcester.[22] Hundreds who participated in the 1685 Monmouth Rebellion, an attempt to overthrow James II, were transported to the island. And combative Native Americans, too, were shipped to Barbados from New England. The influx of Native Americans immediately after King Philip's War caused great concern for Barbadians; in June 1676 they passed a law expressly forbidding the importation of Indians from New England. Barbadians were worried that the New England natives would serve as tinder to an already heated situation. In May 1675, African slaves had plotted against their Barbadian masters with the design of eliminating whites (who were the minority) from the island altogether. The plot had been discovered before it could be carried out. New England Indians were seen as "being of a Subtle and dangerous Nature and able more cunningly to contrive to carry on those dangerous designes which our Negroes of the[ir] Owne Nature are prone unto."[23]

In the seventeenth century, slavery and forced servitude weren't merely matters of ethnicity. During the Wars of the Three Kingdoms, voluntary migration from England to the American colonies dropped sharply: in part because young men were being conscripted, and in part because English Puritans wielded political power under Cromwell, and so prospects improved for them at home.[24] The sudden drop-off of voluntary migration created a serious labor shortage for Massachusetts Bay. In April 1645, Governor John Winthrop noted in his journal that "The warres in England kept servantes from comminge to us, so as those we had, could not be hired when their tymes were out, but upon unreasonable termes: & we fonde it very difficult to paye theire wages to their content."[25] That situation likely helped to inspire Cromwell's shipping the captive Scots abroad.

Yet defeated soldiers and combatants weren't the only ones to be forced into service abroad. Throughout the century, England's population continued to grow, even as farmland became scarce and the demand for labor ebbed. In contrast, the American colonies offered abundant land to claim and cultivate, coupled with a huge demand for labor. The demand for labor was so great that many schemes arose, legal and otherwise, whereby the poor and disenfranchised from England, Scotland, and Ireland were shipped and sold abroad.

Early in the century, English and Scottish governments encouraged the transportation of those without work or resources. In 1623 and 1632, the Council for New England urged letters be sent "from his Matie to the Lieuts of every Shire for the Setting forth of their poorer sort of people for New England." Such letters were sent and effectively ordered English officials to gather up the poor for shipping abroad.[26] One of the main arguments for this practice was that "Itt will thereby disburthen the Comonwealth of a multitude of poore that are likely dayly to increase, to the infinite trouble and preiudice of the publique state."[27] During the 1660s, Edinburgh magistrates petitioned for the right "to send all such men and women who shall be legallie found guiltie of whoredom or theift aff this kingdome with the first conveniency to Barbados."[28] According to scholar Simon P. Newman, ships' inventories recorded such individuals as "freight," or, in the case of children, "half-freight."[29]

The demand for servants and the profitability from their sale abroad were so great that, throughout the century, illicit trafficking rings developed. Records from the London courts suggest that ships bound for the West Indies regularly contained, not soldiers or prisoners of war, but individuals obtained by the work of "spirits," the common term for operatives of professional kidnapping rings. In 1645, 1646, and 1647, Parliament records demonstrate members' concerns about this growing trade.[30] In 1657, the *Conquer* was about to depart London for Barbados when officials found eleven persons "taken by the Spirits" aboard.[31] An East End shoemaker is said to have tricked some 840 unsuspecting persons into involuntary servitude abroad, and another ring in the Katherine's Stairs section of London managed to deceive more than 6,000 individuals into bondage in America. The Katherine's Stairs neighborhood contained waterfront buildings known as "cookshops," where stolen individuals—including children—were kept in secret until they could be loaded onto ships departing for America.[32]

Many British subjects were spirited away from their homelands without warning; these included convicts and "vagrants," though some of the latter group were taken, not from the streets, but from their own homes. In Ireland, kidnapping was carried out to fulfill the labor and capital needs of merchants and adventurers, and to satisfy Cromwell's desire to cleanse Ireland of Catholics, beggars, and criminals, and, some believe, the Irish themselves. Many Irish, as well as other nationalities, were stolen, transported, and sold as laborers on—where else—Barbados. Conditions there were harsh: the climate was hot, and the servant culture, brutal. Being "Barbadosed" was to the seventeenth century what being "sold down the river" was to the nineteenth: the step tantamount to signing another's death certificate.

Other Caribbean islands became destinations for servants and slaves, too. In August 1654, perhaps the very same *Unity* that carried the Dunbar Scots to Boston waited in Dublin Harbor for two hundred Irish servants to come aboard to be transported to America. When the captain of the voyage, Jacob Moulson arrived, however, the local prisons yielded only thirteen or fourteen potential servants. So as to not disappoint his investors and ruin his chances for profit, Moulson hired "a joiner" to scare up thirty-nine more. The other unfortunates came randomly from the streets of Dublin.[33] Once the ship reached Antigua, the captives were "sold at the best rates obtainable," according to the deposition of a mariner on the voyage.[34]

In New England, "man-stealing" was a capital offense.[35] But plenty of kidnapped individuals ended up there, and prominent New Englanders did more than look the other way. Richard Leader was the one-time manager of the Lynn iron works and part-owner of the Great Works saw mill at Piscataqua, for which he purchased some seventeen to twenty-five of the Dunbar prisoners. Three years later, in 1653, Leader engaged in another business deal with Boston merchant David Selleck to transport four hundred Irish children to New England and Virginia as servants. The Council of State in London approved a permit for the scheme. Leader and Selleck then employed agents to scare up 250 women between the ages of 12 and 45 and 300 men from 12 to 50 years of age. Clearly, they took some liberties interpreting the word "children." Some of these captives were transported to Virginia on the ship *Providence* out of London. Others came to New England on the ship *Goodfellow* from Boston, England, under the command of George Dell.[36]

John Ring was one of the passengers on that ship who was sold into servitude in Massachusetts. Here is what he had to say about his experience on that voyage to a Salem court in 1661:

That he, with divers others, were stolen in Ireland by some English soldiers out of their beds in the night and brought to Mr. Dell's ship when the boate lay ready to receive them; and in their way, as they went, some others they tooke with them against their consents and brought them aboard the said ship [the *Goodfellow*] where there were divers others of their countrymen, weeping and crying, because they were stolen away from theyr friends, they all declaring the same.[37]

It wasn't a particularly isolated instance. Nearly eighty years later, in 1730, Colonel Josiah Willard of Lunenburg went to the docks in Boston to view some arriving laborers. He spoke with one Irish boy who said that he had been kidnapped from his home and sold in the Irish Sea by pirates to a Boston-bound vessel.[38]

In 1650, slavery, servitude, and kidnapping were widely practiced almost without discrimination; they were not yet the contentious political issues that they would grow to be. Neither Cotton Mather nor Samuel Willard had delivered their well-known sermons on the subject. Nor had Samuel Sewall composed his equally well-known antislavery tract, "The Selling of Joseph: A Memorial."[39] Instead, the Massachusetts Body of Liberties of 1641 served as both a legal guide and an expression of individual rights for the colony. That document is infamous for sanctioning slavery in Massachusetts. It established that the normal term of servitude was seven years, though it left room for exceptions:

Servants that have served diligently and faithfully to the benefit of their masters seven years shall not be sent away empty. And if any have been unfaithful, negligent, or unprofitable in their service, notwithstanding the good usage of their masters, they shall not be dismissed till they have made satisfaction according to the judgment of authority.[40]

The document also seems to forbid slavery by kidnapping, except as a consequence of battle: "There shall never be any bond slavery, villeinage, or captivity amongst us unless it be lawful captives taken in just wars, and such strangers as willingly sell themselves or are sold to us."[41] The phrase "just wars" conveniently legitimized the influx of Scottish prisoners, as well as the outflux of Pequot men and boys. And the term "strangers" left open the door for purchasing those of African or other backgrounds who had been simply stolen and "willingly" sold.

New Englanders were not above flouting the prohibition of man-stealing, either, regardless of who the victims were. In 1661, two other servants from the *Goodfellow*, Philip Welch and William Downing, refused to work any longer for their master, Samuel Symonds of Ipswich, a prominent merchant. So Symonds brought them before the Essex County Court. In their own defense, Welch and Downing argued that, since they had already worked seven years under Symonds, by law they should be free. As the court transcript states:

> We were brought out of or owne Country, contrary to our owne wills & minds, & sold here unto Mr Symonds, by ye master of the Ship, Mr Dill, but what Agreement was made betweene Mr Symonds & ye Said master, was never Acted by our Consent or knowledge, yet notwithstanding we have indeavored to do him ye best service wee Could these seven Compleat yeeres, which is 3 yeeres more then ye use to sell ym for at Barbadoes, wn they are stollen in England. And for our service, we have noe Callings nor wages, but meat & Cloths. Now 7 yeares service being so much as ye practice of old England, & thought meet in this place, & wee being both above 21 years of age, We hope this honored Court & Jury will seriously Consider our Conditions.[42]

Symonds produced the bill of sale from Captain Dell, which promised that the two Irishmen would serve him until 1663. So, despite their never having agreed to servitude, nor having signed the contract, to say the least of being shipped across the Atlantic illegally—and despite their service's extending beyond the normal terms of indenture—the court ordered Welch and Downing to serve out a term of nine years without consideration for the original wrong done them. It likely didn't help their case that Symonds, their master, was wealthy and well-connected; he eventually served as deputy governor of Massachusetts Bay.

The stealing of individuals into servitude during the seventeenth and eighteenth centuries was a profitable business. Colonial merchants and adventurers needed laborers, and English authorities complied, signing permits allowing kidnapping throughout the British Isles, having their own political and economic motives for doing so. We've already seen how eight-year-old Peter Williamson was kidnapped from the Aberdeen waterfront, kept in the hold of a ship with other children for a month and transported to Philadelphia where he was sold, coincidentally, to a Scot who himself had been kidnapped as a child years before. Williamson was lucky; his master was "a humane, worthy, honest Man," who treated Peter with kindness, helped him learn to read and write, and, upon his death, left Williamson two hundred pounds, his best horse and saddle, and all his clothing.

Williamson knew he was fortunate. Regardless of whether they entered servitude via kidnapping or voluntarily, individuals, according to Williamson, "Often meet with very bad, and I may say, cruel Masters; through whose barbarous Treatment, they are often induced to elope, to avoid Servitude, or (more properly) *Slavery* under such Tyrants."[43]

In the seventeenth and early eighteenth centuries, trafficking in people of all races was common. Almost any excuse was sufficient to consign individuals to servitude: crime, poverty, vagrancy, ethnicity, class status, political or religious nonconformity, poor luck. And as Williamson points out, neither the system of laws nor the contract was the ultimate authority; the master's disposition dictated the true terms for the servant.

In practice, seventeenth-century slavery was much murkier than it came to be in the eighteenth and nineteenth centuries. Twenty-first-century scholar John Donoghue has argued that "the drive to maximize profits in the early plantation complex gave rise to different 'slaveries.'"[44] Margaret Ellen Newell has demonstrated that consigning Native Americans to servitude was common in New England, and that they endured different degrees of bondage: "Chattel slavery and freedom were at opposite ends of a broad spectrum, and many Indians occupied points along that spectrum in varying degrees of unfreedom."[45] Captured and kidnapped Scots, Irish, and English also occupied varying points along that spectrum. It's fair to say, however, that almost none were enslaved for life (though many died before being freed) or had offspring who became the property of their masters. Despite the indiscriminate nature of servitude, true chattel slavery remained the exclusive domain of people of color.

In the seventeenth century's more random culture of servitude, the roots of institutionalized slavery based on race are evident, even in the minds of prominent New Englanders, including the most illustrious family of New England at the time: the Winthrops. Governor John Winthrop, who had a hand in shaping the Massachusetts Body of Liberties in 1641, was known to have kept a Narragansett and his wife as servants. His son, Samuel, who built a sugar plantation on Antigua, owned at least sixty-four slaves.[46] And Emmanuel Downing, Winthrop's brother-in-law, famously wrote to his nephew, John Winthrop, Jr. in August 1645:

> I doe not see how wee can thrive untill wee get into a stock of slaves suffitient to doe all our buisines, for our Childrens Children will hardly see this great Continent filled with people, soe that our servants will still desire freedome to plant for them selves, and not stay but for verie great wages. And I suppose you know verie well how wee shall maynteyne 20 Moores cheaper than one Englishe servant.[47]

Downing's comment reflects wealthy New Englanders' belief that servants and slaves would be essential to the colony's economic future. The American continent's vast spaces offered an incentive for fixed-term servants to leave their masters and build their own independent livelihoods, rather than stay on as employees. Downing's message eerily presages the notion that trading exclusively in African slaves, consigned to perpetual servitude, would offer a more permanent and economical solution for America's labor needs. What he couldn't imagine was the extent to which future generations would act on, implement, defend, and struggle to overturn that sinister notion.

Once in New England, the Dunbar prisoners met with various fates. Sixty-two became property of the iron works at Braintree and at Lynn, where John Gifford oversaw production and William Awbrey ran the business side of the operation. An impersonal ledger entry offers a glimpse of the miserable condition of the Scots upon arrival.

Gifford's first expenses on their behalf included payments for "the cure of two Scotts," "a windeing sheet for Dauison the Scott." Numerous outlays for "phisicke," or medicine, on behalf of the Scots continued throughout the duration of operations at Hammersmith.[48]

More information survives on the Scots employed at Hammersmith and Braintree than on those sold elsewhere, perhaps because of the financial troubles and lawsuits that the company ultimately faced. Gifford employed the Scots in mining the ore, cutting wood and making charcoal for the iron furnaces, keeping cattle for the company farm, and cultivating gardens. Most likely, the prisoners also built their own living quarters: the "Scotch-men's House," a dormitory about a mile from the Lynn iron works. That building is believed to have had two rooms with a central fireplace and chimney. We know from Gifford's financial records for the Braintree Furnace that he also purchased eleven beds and bolsters, and twice as many blankets and coverlets, suggesting the Scots slept two to a bed at both sites.[49] A deposition by William Emery, a Scot and "servant at the company," suggests that others who were not iron works employees lived for a while at the Scotch-men's House.[50] Other Scots were lodged with farmers nearby, and seventeen appear to have been returned to Boston to work in a warehouse connected with the iron works.[51]

Gifford's ledgers also detail that he purchased hops, malt, bread, mackerel, wheat, peas, and pork—and "a Case of strong Waters for ye Scotts and other menn."[52] The Company of Undertakers in London—the iron works shareholders—kept a close rein on Gifford, complaining that he was spending too much on food for the Scots: "I have advised with some of the Company & thay tell me that 3s 6d p. weeke is a sufficient allowance for every man; Considering the cheapness of provision their," they wrote in a letter of April 1652, "you haveing ther plenty of fish, both fresh & salte & pidgions & venison & corne & pease at a very cheape Rate."[53]

All this sounds like very lavish fare for the seventeenth-century worker. And there is little doubt that the Scots ate better upon arriving in New England than they had in a long time. But the servants may not have consumed all the provisions charged to their account. Willliam Emery stated that "divers men"—that is, others not affiliated with the iron works—"were boarded at the Scotchmen's house on the company's provisions"; that barrels of beef for the Scots had eighteen or twenty pieces missing after Gifford had opened them first; that mackerel and soap meant for the Scots was given to Samuel Bennett, the Giffords' neighbor and good friend; and that "thousands of biscuit" purchased on the Scots' accounts went to Gifford's family and others.[54]

At some point, the English Parliament, or perhaps Cromwell himself, inquired what had become of the Dunbar prisoners. The Reverend John Cotton, a close associate of Governor John Winthrop, the grandfather of Cotton Mather, and a friend of Cromwell, wrote this 1651 letter to the lord protector on the treatment the Scots had received upon arriving in New England:

> The Scots, whom God delivered into your hand at Dunbarre, and whereof sundry were sent hither, we have been desirous (as we could) to make their yoke easy. Such as were sick of the scurvy or other diseases have not wanted physick and chyrurgery. They have not been sold for slaves to perpetuall servitude, but for 6 or 7 or 8 yeares, as we do our owne; and he that bought the most of them (I heare) buildeth houses for them, for every 4 an house, layeth some acres of ground thereto, which he giveth them as their owne, requiring 3 dayes in the weeke to worke for him (by turnes) and 4 dayes for themselves, and promiseth, as soone as they can repay him the money he layed out for them, he will set them at liberty.[55]

While many have taken this letter at face value, Cotton seems ill-informed about the true conditions of the Scots. His assertion that Scots lived four to a house wasn't accurate. And while they probably did have their own gardens to defray the cost of their "dietting," it is highly unlikely that the Scots had a four-day work week with three days off to tend their crops and earn money on the side.[56] Free time, after all, was anathema to Puritan doctrine. Individuals were regularly presented at court for being idlers, and Puritan ministers, including John Cotton himself, preached passionately against the sin of idleness. In his sermon "A Good Master Well-Served," Cotton Mather exhorted masters not to "countenance . . . *any Idleness*," in their servants, "whereof there comes *no Goodness*."[57]

Yet another impression of the iron works comes from the journal of Obadiah Turner, an English immigrant to America who "possessed a considerable estate, and carried on farming to some extent." Turner visited the foundry in August of 1651, some eight months after the Scots arrived. "At ye Iron Workes wee founde all ye men wth smutty faces and bare armes working lustilie," wrote Turner. He found the site to be "a delightfull place, beside ye river Saugust," with plenty of lumber nearby: "Manie tall pines grow neare by; also oakes and walnuts. And it is pleasant to see ye smoke of ye workes curling up among ye trees." But Turner seems to have had some doubts as to the moral character of the laborers, many of whom were Scottish prisoners: "Ye headmen be of substance and godlie lives. But some of ye workmen be young, and fond of frolicking, and sometimes doe frolicke to such purpose that they get before ye magistrates." Worse, still, "One or two hath done naughtie workes with ye maidens living thereabouts."[58]

It's equally doubtful that the Scots had much time to "frolicke" with the maidens living nearby. As servants, they were of course forbidden to marry until their tenures were expired, though contact with women was not entirely out of the question.

Despite these two very positive impressions of life at Hammersmith, there is no doubt that the Scots worked hard, had limited freedom, and sorely missed their families and native land. Still, no existing records hint at any especially cruel treatment or unrest among the Scots who lived and worked there.

In summer of 1652, Hammersmith began to have credit problems, and William Awbrey, hired to handle the business side of the effort, mortgaged the Iron Works. He may also have sold some of the Scottish servants to other masters at this time, including to sawmilling operations in the Piscataqua region of Maine and New Hampshire.[59] Then, in fall of 1653, just two years after the Scots' terms of service had begun, the Hammersmith Iron Works faced bankruptcy, and Manager John Gifford was jailed. At that point, the company's creditors took control of all assets, including the Scottish bond servants. Some likely remained on to continue the work under new managers, while some were sold. Two years after the bankruptcy, some Scots—very likely from Dunbar or Worcester—petitioned a Massachusetts court to set them free. "In answer to the petition of severall Scotsmen who desire to be freed from their masters, the Court, seeing no proofe nor pbabilitye appearing of what they affirme, se no reason to graunt theire requests."[60] This is virtually all we know of their circumstances; even their names are lost to history.

But what of the Scots who didn't end up at the ill-fated iron works? Some twenty-five of the prisoners were sold to Richard Leader upon arriving in New England. Leader had taken possession of an abandoned mill on the Asbenbedick River in York County, Maine, and was said to be outfitting the mill with up to twenty saws. It was one of the largest sawmills of its time and was commonly referred to as "the great mill works." Eventually, the Asbenbedick came to be known as the Great Works River.

Leader was an ambitious capitalist who traveled widely in search of personal wealth. He managed the Hammersmith Iron Works from 1645 to 1650 before John Gifford took over, replacing the project's founder and original manager, John Winthrop, Jr. "You know the man," wrote Emmanuel Downing, to his nephew, the younger Winthrop, just before Leader set out for New England. "He lived in Ireland, he is a perfect Accountant, hath skill in mynes, and tryall of metals."[61]

While managing the iron works, Leader lived, not at Lynn, but in style at Boston in a "Mansion house" with "Orchard gardens Tymber yeards wharfes wayes water courses Grounds" worth two hundred pounds.[62] But in August 1650, he resigned as manager of the iron works. The circumstances aren't fully clear, but more than five years on, the venture hadn't yet turned a profit. In a letter to the younger Winthrop two years earlier, Leader had admitted that he and the Company of Undertakers didn't see eye-to-eye:

> The Company are very much discontented; and use me not as I have deserved. They have sent one over to take account of things; and to give them sattisfaction how things stand with us. . . . For my part I am resolved they shall provide them an other Agent, except a more cleere understanding cann be mainetained betwext us.[63]

Soon after resigning, Leader found himself in a world of trouble with the local magistrates of Massachusetts Bay. The outspoken and bitter Leader was said to have "threatnd, & in high degree reproached

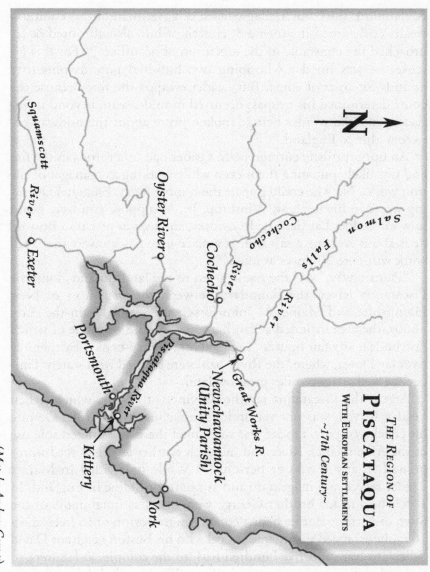

THE REGION OF
PISCATAQUA
WITH EUROPEAN SETTLEMENTS
~17th Century~

Squamscott River

Oyster River

Cochecho River

Salmon Falls River

Piscataqua River

Exeter

Cochecho

Portsmouth

Great Works R.

Newichawannock
(Unity Parish)

Kittery

York

(Map by Andrew Comas)

& slaundrd, the Courts, magistrates, & goverment of this common weale, & defamed the towne & church of Lin, also affronted & reproached the constable in the execution of his office."[64] For this offense, he was fined a whopping two hundred pounds plus fifty pounds for costs of court. But Leader escaped the fine because the court determined his trespass occurred in mid-ocean, beyond its jurisdiction: "the wordes beinge spoken neere about the midway betweene this & England."[65]

An opportunistic entrepreneur, Leader had other irons in the fire and was likely pursuing them even while working as manager of the iron works. Now he could pursue them more freely. Emanuel Downing wrote to his nephew, Winthrop, Jr., "I suppose you have heard how mr Ledder Late left the Ironworks, and lives at prsent in Boston, he is about erecting a saw mill at a place nere pascattaway that shall work wth nere 20 sawes at once."[66]

"Pascattaway," was the name given to the lands in and along the Piscataqua River, the boundary between the provinces of New Hampshire and Maine. As John Josselyn described it in the early 1660s, the area included a "fair harbour," on the west side of which "are built many fair houses . . . called Strawberry-bank." Farther upriver lay Dover, where "the River-banks are clothed with stately Timber" as well as "two miles meadow land."[67]

Across the Piscataqua lay the province of Maine, which, when Leader arrived, was not yet under Massachusetts Bay rule. Despite his checkered past, Leader was welcomed there and offered sole use of the Asbenbedick River and "all such tymber as is not yet Impropriated to any towne or persons."[68] While he resided in Maine, Leader served as a magistrate and as agent for Maine in England. In 1652, he and his brother George were listed as inhabitants of the town of Kittery. But he hadn't cut all ties to Boston or to Ireland. In 1653, he arranged the infamous deal with his Boston neighbor David Selleck to transport five hundred Irish to the colonies as laborers.

Leader's business venture at the Great Works mill didn't prove any more profitable than his stint at the Hammersmith Iron Works. So sometime around 1655, he sold his share of the mill to John Becx and Richard Hutchinson of London and moved to Barbados, where he engaged in yet another scheme: salt works. He died in 1661.

We know very little about the Scots in his employ: how they lived or what work they performed. But, given Leader's disposition, it is hard to imagine he was an indulgent master. His brother George, who stayed behind to manage the Great Works after Richard left for Barbados, had problems with at least one Dunbar Scot named Alexander Maxwell or Maxell. A court case from 1654 offers some details:

> It is ordered that Allexander Maxell for his grosse offence in his exorbitant & abusive carages towards his Maister Mr. George Leader & his Mistresse as by evidence doth appeare shall bee publiquely brought forth to the Whipping Post whereunto hee shall bee fastened till 30 lashes bee given him upon the bare skine. The sayd Maxell is here by injoyned to give full satisfaction to his aforesd Maister for the expence of tyme & dyett dureing the tyme of his imprisonment with other charges amounting to the valew of seaven pounds, 10s, And in case that Maxell do att any tyme for the future misbehave him selfe towards his Maister George Leader that then his sayd Maister hath full Lyberty to make sayle of the sayd Maxell to Virginia, Barbadoes, or any other of the English Plantations.[69]

Whatever Maxwell's offense was, it was serious enough to merit his being publicly whipped and imprisoned. And he was required to compensate Leader for his food and the time spent away from work while in jail. The incentive for mending his disobedient ways was the threat of being sold to Virginia or Barbados.

Maxwell survived the controversy and gained his freedom along with a grant of land around 1657. He is believed to have built a garrison house on Cider Hill Road in present-day York, Maine. Today, on the same site, stands one of the oldest-known houses in the state, known as the McIntire Garrison House. In 1707, Maxwell sold the property to his neighbor John McIntire, the son of Micum McIntire, another of the Dunbar Scots.[70] Also known as "Scotland Garrison," this house helped give this York County neighborhood its current name of "Scotland."[71]

At Exeter, New Hampshire, Nicholas Lissen purchased between four and seven Scots to help run his two mills,[72] and mill owner Henry Sayword of York may have purchased at least one Dunbar Scot, Thomas Holme, for thirty pounds.[73]

Thomas Doughty and seven or more[74] Dunbar and Worcester prisoners were purchased by another "adventurer," a merchant trader by the name of Valentine Hill. Hill was a devout Puritan. He arrived in Boston in 1635, when he was twenty-five, and became a neighbor and good friend of Massachusetts Bay governor John Winthrop. Hill served as a deacon in the First Church of Boston,[75] a selectman alongside Winthrop from 1641 to 1646, and at one time, owned more land than anyone else in the Boston area, including sixty acres at Pullen Point, now Point Shirley. He built wharves along the harbor, owned interests in several ships, and ran a lively trading business, shipping goods from Massachusetts and Maine to Virginia, Barbados, Newfoundland, and London.[76]

In 1643, Hill was granted land near the mouth of the Oyster River in New Hampshire. But he didn't move north until 1649, shortly after the death of John Winthrop, Sr. In September of that year, he was granted the rights to use the falls of that river—at the head of tide in present-day Durham—along with a local carpenter named Thomas Beard.[77] There, he built New Hampshire's first sawmill in 1651. Or, more likely, Hill provided the funds and the impetus for the project, while Scottish laborers built the mill under the direction of Beard. Hill eventually resigned as a member of the Church of Boston and became a member of the Church at Dover, New Hampshire. In 1653, with the help of Beard and the Scots, he built the town's first meetinghouse. He built another mill on the Lamprey River in 1657[78] and served as a selectman in Dover from 1651 through 1657.[79]

The town of Dover gave Hill some five hundred acres—nearly the entirety of present-day Durham—adjacent to his mill for a house and farm.[80] There is little doubt that Doughty and his fellow Scots also helped Hill to build his house there, a portion of which still stands today as part of an inn overlooking the Oyster River dam. In 1652, the town gave him additional acreage: "Given and granted unto Mr. Valentine Hill, his heires, Executors, administrators or assigns foure acres of land adjoining to Goodman Hudsons Lott for his Scots."[81] Most likely, the Scots built shared dwellings or bunkhouses and cultivated vegetable gardens on the site.

Apart from a few towns—Strawberry Bank, Kittery, Dover—Piscataqua was still largely wild and unsettled. But local authorities were

The McIntire Garrison, perhaps the oldest building in Maine. In 1707, Alexander Maxwell sold the property to his neighbor John McIntire, the son of Micum McIntire, another of the Dunbar Scots. Also known as "Scotland Garrison," this house helped give this York County neighborhood its current name of "Scotland." (*Author*)

doing their best to tame it. At a Dover town meeting in 1657, it was announced that "Homesoever Einglesh or Indian shall kill aney wolf or wolfes within this Township shall have for soe doeing fower pounds for every wolf soe kild."[82]

Lumbermen and mills, too, were making quick work of the stately forests. The towns' records are full of accounts of persons poaching: cutting down trees not their own. And, as currency, pipe staves and merchantable boards were more common than English pounds.[83]

How did they live, these Scottish prisoners sent to the frontier in New Hampshire and Maine? Chances are, the Scots' days from dawn to dusk were dedicated to physical labor: felling trees; preparing timbers and boards and pipe staves for use nearby and shipment out; cutting and curing firewood for heating and cooking; building a dam, mills, a large timber frame house for Valentine Hill, simple living quarters for themselves, and a meeting house for the community; cutting roads and paths; tending livestock; clearing land for cultivation; growing crops; and loading boats with timber products.

Most likely, Doughty and the other Scots were given provisions and prepared their own food. And their diets changed wholesale upon arriving in New England. In Scotland, oats had been staple and substance for the masses. Dr. Johnson's *Dictionary of the English Language* (1755) famously defined oatmeal as "A grain, which in England is generally given to horses, but in Scotland supports the people." Behind the bigoted comparison, Johnson's definition holds a kernel of truth; oats did form the bulk of Scots' diets. Soldiers in the seventeenth-century Scottish covenanting armies received two-thirds of their calories from oat bread, while oat bread comprised 82 percent of nutrition for orphans in Hutcheson's Hospital in Glasgow.[84]

Few Scots in the seventeenth century enjoyed meat in their diets. Game laws prevented all but the wealthiest landowners from hunting, and butchered meat wasn't readily available. Overwhelmingly, their food consisted of oatmeal porridge and bread, with peas, peas porridge, kale, and barley. The little meat that was eaten came in the form of haggis, blood pudding, or broth.[85]

Upon arriving in New England, the Scots would have had to adapt to eating corn meal porridge, or "samp," three meals a day. In his *A Key into the Language of America in 1643*, Roger Williams noted that the Narragansetts called their corn meal porridge "Nasàump."

> From this, the *English* call their *Samp*, which is the *Indian* corne, beaten and boild, and eaten hot or cold with milke or butter, which are mercies beyond the *Natives* plaine water, and which is a dish exceeding wholesome for the *English* bodies."[86]

Because corn was the most successful crop in New England throughout the colonial period, samp (later known as "mush" or "hasty pudding") made up a huge portion of the diet for wealthy and poor alike. Wild game was available, especially turkey and venison, but whether the Scots were provided with game isn't clear. Because the fishing industry was already well established in Maine and New Hampshire, dried fish, especially cod and mackerel, presumably formed a part of their diets, as did beans, peas, squash, and pumpkins, which tolerated New England's indifferent soils and cool climate. Even accounting for variations among their masters, the Scots likely ate a more varied diet in New England than they had at home. And although fresh, clean water was readily available, servants, like their masters, drank mostly beer, ale, and cider.

Regardless of their social status, everyone in New England was forced to attend the Sunday meeting and forbidden from performing work. In addition, masters and heads of families were required to instruct their servants and family members in religion at least once a week.[87] So, between working long days, cooking their own meals, and attending church and religious study, servants had little time left for leisure activities. As scholar Lawrence Towner has written: "The servant had to steal time to lead a personal life. Either he stole it from his master when he was supposed to be working, or he stole it from himself when he was supposed to be sleeping."[88]

It's hard to say exactly what kind of master Valentine Hill was, but the Scots he owned were relatively silent in the public record until 1658, when the town of Dover received several as tax-paying inhabitants: Thomas Doughty, Henry Brown, Richard Hubbard, James Oare, Patrick Jameson, Walter Jackson, Edward Erwin, James Merry, and James Middleton.[89] That they lived in Oyster River largely without controversy suggests that they were under tight rein while in Hill's service. Once freed, however, several of Hill's Scots received land parcels that had been granted to him. Henry Brown and James Oare, who lived together upon being freed, came into possession of some of Hill's property. Patrick Jameson, a captive from the Battle of Worcester, received land from Hill on the north side of the Oyster River in 1659. In a deposition some decades later, a neighbor testified "That he asked Mr. Valentine Hill why hee would sell that land to Patrick Jemison. Hee answered mee, because he was a usefull man to mee aboutte my mills. Hee was my servant and I would have him settled by mee."[90] Hill also stood up in court for one of his former servants, James Middleton, who was "Convicted of frequenting the Tavernes & quarrelling & fighting." Hill not only paid Middleton's fine, but served as security for the Scot's good behavior until the court convened its next session.[91] At the very least, such evidence suggests that Hill was a man of conscience and felt responsible for the men who had served him.

Many years later, Thomas Doughty briefly deposed about his years with Valentine Hill to a New Hampshire Court:

> Abought Forty years a goe or more I lived with Vallantin Hill when the said Hill was in possession of ffive hundred Accers of Land ajassent to his Mill. . . which land The said Hill

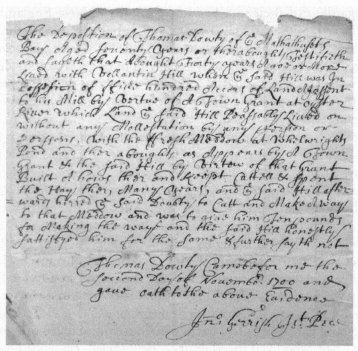

Thomas Doughty's deposition of November 2, 1700, recorded by Justice of the Peace Jonathan Gerrish. (*New Hampshire State Archives*)

Peassably Lived on without any Molestation by any Person or persons, with the ffresh Meddow at Wheelwrights Pond and there a boughts . . . the said Hill . . . built a house ther and keept Cattell & spent the Hay ther, Many years, and the said Hill afterwards hired the said Dowty to Cutt and Make a way to that Meddow and was to give him Ten pounds for Making the way and the said Hill honestly sattisffyd him for the same & further sayeth not.[92]

Doughty became Hill's servant, not by choice but by force. Yet even after Doughty's term of servitude expired, he contracted with Hill to cut a road to an outlying pasture in a deal that appears to have satisfied both. There is little to be envied in seven years of servitude. But Doughty and the other Scots at Oyster River were in many ways fortunate to have had Valentine Hill for a master.

Chapter Six

LAND, WOODS, AND WATER

Here every man may be master and owner of his owne labour and land; or the greatest part in a small time. If hee have nothing but his hands, he may set up this trade; and by industrie quickly grow rich; spending but halfe that time wel, wch in England we abuse in idleness. —John Smith, *A Description of New England*

W HAT DOES ONE DO after being freed from seven years' servitude? In 1657, most of the Dunbar prisoners who made it to America alive were released from bondage and scattered across New England without families, employment, homes, or any sort of safety net. Few if any had the resources to return home, even if Cromwell's government had allowed it.

So they banded together. On January 6, 1657, twenty-eight former prisoners living in the Boston area helped form the Scots' Charitable Society: the first, and longest-lived, private charitable organization in America. The members agreed to give small amounts of money to the society on a quarterly schedule. "Our benevolence," stated the founding document, "is for the releefe of our selves being Scottishmen or for any of the Scottish nation whome we may see cause to helpe."[1]

While the Scots had many advantages over the permanently enslaved, they did suffer from being forcibly separated from their native culture, friends, and family. So even those in remote and sparsely populated New Hampshire and Maine formed tight units once freed. They teamed up on work contracts, shared households, and stood up for one another when called before the provincial courts. Because so many Scots settled at present-day South Berwick, Maine, it began to be known as "the parish of Unity," after the ship that brought the Dunbar prisoners to New England. That name was also a metaphor for how the Scots intended to survive on New England's eastern frontier.

Like immigrants everywhere, the Scots gained security and comfort by living together. Many of their neighbors were Native Americans, whose culture and behaviors were entirely unfamiliar. Nor did the Scots feel fully a part of Puritan society: the languages they spoke[2] and their accents set them apart; they weren't sure they could trust English-run courts to deal fairly with them; and they knew they'd find kinship and familiarity among their countrymen. This was especially important since all had left their families behind. So the Scots created their own extended families: fellow prisoners from Dunbar and Worcester. Their solidarity helped them integrate into a society that was still largely foreign to them.

The first thing Thomas Doughty did upon being freed was to buy land. In 1657, Doughty purchased property from William Roberts on the south bank of the Oyster River, across from the land of his former master, Valentine Hill. His purchase included a spring, fresh and saltwater marshes, thirty acres of upland, and a house and other structures. Most likely, a parting sum of money from Hill allowed him to buy it.[3]

America in the 1600s wasn't the land of freedom for everyone. Yet in many ways it was the land of opportunity, even for some who had been transported against their wills. A large part of that had to do with the availability of land. The native population had declined precipitously as a result of diseases such as smallpox and hepatitis introduced through trade and exploration. And English colonizers were anxious to fill the void by helping as many British subjects as possible settle in New England. So many servants received land grants once their terms were finished, and many others used money they received at termination to purchase land.

For Doughty and the other Scots, this was opportunity indeed. Land in Scotland had become nearly impossible to obtain for members of the working class. The mid-seventeenth century saw the enclosure of most grazing and agricultural land, and common lands became privately owned, causing the rise of large landowners and the demise of small farms. All but the very wealthy found themselves without access to land except as renters and wage laborers, which made it extremely difficult to improve their circumstances.[4]

The plight of Scotland's landless laborers improved little over the centuries. In 1832, William Cobbett visited a farm in Dunfermline, just across the Firth of Forth from Edinburgh, and described how single male laborers lived:

> The custom here is for men to plough with a pair of horses; to go out at daylight . . . and plough till night . . . it was a great slavery both to the horses and the men.
>
> There is generally a BAILIFF upon these farms, . . . and he is a sort of sergeant or corporal over the common men, who are continually under his eye day and night; and who being firmly bound for the year, cannot quit their service till the year be out.
>
> The single men lived in a sort of shed . . . with a fire-place in it to burn coals in, with one doorway, and one little window. The floor was the ground. There were three wooden bedsteads, nailed together like the births in a barrack-room, with boards for the bottom of them. . . . There was no back door to the place and no privy.
>
> Each has allowed him two pecks of coarse oatmeal a week, and three "choppins" of milk a day, and a "choppin" is, I believe, equal to an English quart. They have to use this meal . . . either by mixing it with cold water or hot.
>
> Here are these men, who work for so many hours in a day, who are so laborious, so obedient, so civil, so honest, and amongst the best people in the world, receiving for a whole week less than what an American labourer receives for one day's work not half so hard as the work of these men.[5]

The Scots Cobbett describes were considered free men, but their living and working conditions suggest otherwise. Obviously, a variety of working conditions—good and bad—existed on either side of the Atlantic. But in early New England, at least, the greater availability of cheap land gave workers a clear advantage; once free, they at least had the possibility of owning property and using it according to their own designs.

Doughty, it seems, didn't intend to live on, or to farm, his land at Oyster River. Records indicate that William Roberts and his family continued to inhabit the dwelling on the property. Instead, Doughty likely purchased the parcel for its trees. We know he was skilled with an axe; after he left Valentine Hill's service, Doughty agreed to cut a road to one of Hill's outlying pastures for ten pounds. The thirty acres of upland that Doughty now possessed were most likely forested. They would supply plenty of lumber that he could cut, transport, and sell, while the grasses from his marshes would supply fodder for oxen, which were used to move logs from the woods to the river, where they could be transported to nearby sawmills.

Doughty's intent to become a lumberman isn't surprising. Along with fish and furs, lumber was New England's most prized commodity, in large part because the international demand for wood was enormous. While England was too far away to be much of a market for anything but ships' masts, its Caribbean possessions—especially Barbados—had used up most of their own forests by the mid-seventeenth century. Yet lumber remained a key element in Barbados' sugar industry: as a raw material for building mills, equipment, buildings, and storage containers, and as fuel. Farther afield, wine-producing regions including the Canary Islands, Madeira, and Málaga purchased boatloads of New England oak staves for manufacturing barrels.[6]

White pine, then commonly known as "board pine," was particularly valuable. The tallest trees in New England, white pines, impressed the English, who had depleted their own forests at least a century before.[7] John Josselyn described the pine as "a stately large Tree, very tall, and sometimes two or three fadom about"—or some eighteen feet in circumference.[8] The most massive white pines could reach 220 feet tall and eight feet in diameter. "There is reason to fear that this noblest of all vegetable productions will be unknown in its proper size and splendor to future inhabitants of New England," wrote Timothy Dwight in 1821 in his *Travels in New England and New York*. And he was right. Today white pines rarely reach two hundred years old; forests full of towering four-hundred-year-old pines, like those of the seventeenth century, have long since disappeared.

Early in the century, Piscataqua settlers had begun harvesting pine and other trees and exporting boards, pipe staves, clapboards, shingles, and later, more famously, masts for the king's navy. But wood had plenty of local uses, too. Nearly all buildings, except for a few in Boston, were made of wood cut from nearby forests. While Hammersmith was in operation, the iron furnaces at Lynn required a constant supply of charcoal, and Scots had been employed in cutting trees for that purpose. Wooden zigzag fences enclosed New England farms and pastures, keeping livestock confined and crops protected; the stone fences that are today so common didn't come into use until much later.[9] Farm tools—shovels, pitchforks, rakes, and mallets— were made of wood, as were many dishes and kitchen implements. Most important, wood was virtually the only fuel used for cooking and heating. A typical household could easily run through thirty to forty cords of wood annually, which required cutting more than an acre of forest.[10] It took an experienced lumberman about one month of steady work to cut an acre of forest by hand.[11]

Although New England's winters were very long and cold, even by Scottish standards, winter was the high season for logging. Cutting the wood in spring and summer, when the sap was running, made it rot faster.[12] But winter also made it much easier to drag large logs over the snow to the water's edge on sleds or sledges pulled by oxen. Equally important, as anyone who has lived in New England's woods knows, swarming, biting insects didn't bother the lumbermen or livestock in winter.

Loggers typically finished cutting by the end of January or beginning of February, and hauling could continue into April, as long as cold weather kept the ground frozen.[13] Once ice was gone from the rivers, logs were transported with boats or barges to sawmills or ships. The high season for milling, or sawing, was spring, when freshets provided plenty of power to drive the mill wheels.

In 1663, while still living at Oyster River, Doughty entered a joint contract with John Wingate to provide lumber to John Wincoll, a local magistrate and militia captain who owned two sawmills on the nearby Salmon Falls River. Wingate, like Doughty, was a former servant; born in England, he came to America in the service of settler Thomas Layton. And Wingate's case shows that the availability of land spelled opportunity for many former servants. At the end of his tenure, Wingate was granted twenty acres of land on Hilton Point in present-day Dover. The town then granted him another twenty acres adjoining his parcel. In succeeding years, he accumulated one hundred acres, so that by 1683, he was one of the area's principal landowners.[14]

The lumbering contract for Doughty and Wingate didn't go smoothly; that's why we know about it. The two were called into court for "breach of covenant for Logging."[15] But the case was immediately withdrawn without further explanation, suggesting that they were late on delivery but were able to settle their dispute with Wincoll. Surviving records point for the most part to business deals gone sour, not to those that went smoothly. So it's likely that Doughty and Wingate—and potentially other partners—were successful at fulfilling a number of lumber contracts.

Lumbering is among the most physically taxing occupations, even when mechanized; felling giant trees, stripping the branches with hand tools, hitching logs to ox teams, and guiding the teams over rocky and steep terrain was both exhausting and dangerous. In March 1654, Thomas Tuttle of Dover was found dead near the stump of a tree: "a tree which he had newly fallin upon another lime of the other tree Rebounding backe and fell upon hime which was the Caus of his Death."[16] In 1659, a jury at Oyster River found that James Morray (or Murray), another former Dunbar prisoner, was a victim of a "widowmaker"; he was "Acedently killd" by "A Lime of A Tree falling downe upon his head."[17] Morray survived only a year after earning his freedom. In 1660, Thomas Canyda was found with a tree "uppon him, [which] was forced to be cut before he could be gott from under it, & this . . . was ye cause of his death."[18]

So, after seven or eight years of logging, Doughty jumped at another opportunity; he opted to take over management of the vacant

Great Works sawmill, renting it from wealthy merchant Eliakim Hutchinson of Boston. It was an ambitious plan for a former servant, especially given Richard Leader's difficulties there, even with the free labor of some twenty-five Scots. Still, Doughty took it on, with James Grant of York, Peter Grant, and John Taylor (all former Scottish prisoners) as his bondsmen on the agreement of June 1, 1665. It's possible that they agreed to work together at the mill and chose Doughty as the primary on the contract.

Sawmills were the frontier colonies' most important engine of industry. Without them, no ships could be built or fitted out; nor houses, apart from the rudest log structures; and no exports could be sent to Salem and Boston, Barbados and Jamaica, or England in exchange for capital, sugar, or manufactured goods. So important were sawmills that towns made grants outright of forested acreage to those, like Richard Leader and Valentine Hill, willing to build and run them. Kittery granted Leader "property and liberty of all such timber as is not yet appropriated to any town or person."[19] Hill was granted the rights to "the fall of the Oyster River . . . for the Erickting and setting up of a sawe mill," along with the rights to forested lands nearby. He was also awarded five hundred acres for a farm, "foure acres of land . . . for his Scots," and mill privileges on the Lamprey River along with timber rights on land a mile wide on both sides of the river.[20] Small wonder that millers were among the most prosperous citizens in northern New England.[21] And small wonder that Doughty saw the chance to run a sawmill as an important opportunity.

Doughty's business venture at the Great Works didn't last long or may never have gotten off the ground at all. Four years after he took over the contract, an inventory was taken at the mill, which included: "a broaken dwelling house ready to fall, & a barne much out of re-

Overleaf: This map is a copy of the original "Pascatway River in New England" on file in the British Museum. The original was likely drawn between 1660 and 1685 and shows some fifteen mills in the Piscataqua region alone (see lettered key at upper left). At the time, mills were also in operation at Wells, Cape Porpoise, Saco, Black Point, and other locations along the Maine coast. The mapmaker, signed "J.S.," is believed to have been Captain John Scott of Long Island. (*Maine State Archives/digitalmaine.com*)

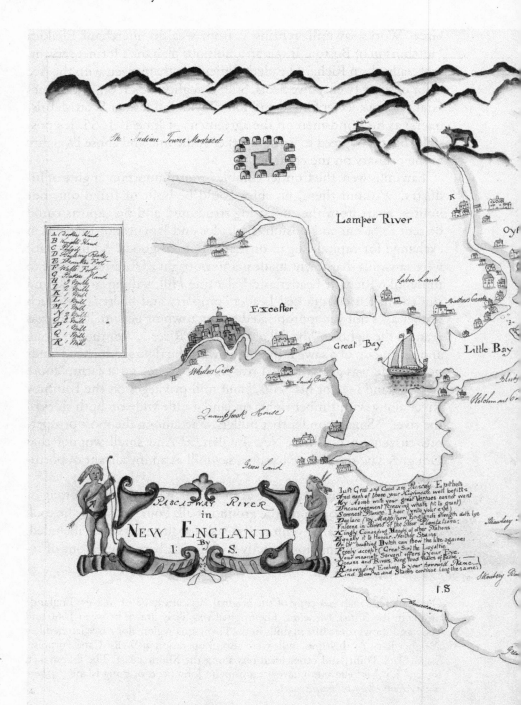

payre"; a "broaken Mill with the Irons & Vtensills," and several other items.[22] Two years after that, in 1671, Eliakim Hutchinson filed a case with the Suffolk County Court of Massachusetts[23] against "Thomas Doughty as prinsipall, & James Grant of Yorke, Peter Grant & John Taylor as seuerity or either of them Defend[ts] in an Action of the Case for forfeiture or breach of Bond or obligacion of twelve hundred [5] pounds . . . for non performance of a Covenant or Agreement."

The jury "found for the plaintiff the forfeiture of the bond & costs of Court," all of which amounted to 1,201 pounds and 16 shillings.[24] For Doughty, this had to have been a crushing defeat. Yet no records exist to explain how, or whether, this enormous debt was paid.

Still, the experience doesn't appear to have deterred Doughty from his ambition. In 1667, he had sold his property in New Hampshire: "Thomas Doutie now Resident at oister Riuer, sells to Jno Cutt of Portsmouth, land, marsh &c. dwelling house, &c, now in occupation of Wm. Roberts of O. R. and purchased of him; Oct. 1657."[25] By then, he had more than likely cut the best timber, making way for pastures and agricultural land, and prepared to move across the Piscataqua to Maine. The purchaser was John Cutt of Portsmouth, who became the first president of the New Hampshire Province in 1680. The property is today known as "Cutt's Hill," and lies along present-day Route 108 in Durham.

Why did Doughty move to Maine? First, he had friends there. While a dozen or so Scottish servants of Valentine Hill had settled near Oyster River, the Maine side of the Piscataqua was home to two dozen or more, some of whom had been bonded to Richard Leader and inhabited Unity Parish. Equally important, sawmills in the frontier provinces were going up fast, and the forests along the coast were disappearing at a rapid pace. A map of "Pascatway" made sometime between 1660 and 1685 shows some fifteen sawmills, not including the many that had been built beyond York in settlements such as Wells, Saco, Cape Porpoise, Black Point, and Casco. As the forests nearby were leveled, mills crept farther and farther inland. By century's end, sixty mills were operating between Hampton, New Hampshire, and Casco: present-day Portland, Maine.[26] At mid-century, those interested in the lumber business had either to move up the coast or upriver to find profitable stands of timber.

A sawmill under construction along the Machias River, Maine, in an eighteenth-century sketch. (*Norman B. Leventhal Map Center, Boston Public Library*)

Even before Doughty arrived in America, Piscataqua towns had tried to control wanton deforestation. In 1642, Dover town officials ordered that no man could fell more than ten trees for clapboards or pipe staves until he had "wrought them up." For every tree above ten that a lumberman had not processed, he had to forfeit ten shillings.[27] In December 1643, Dover ordered that no man should fell any timber for clapboards or pipe staves, plank, or board on public land without the approval of the town.[28] And by 1665, officials declared that "Many persons do fall timber and make staves without order, whereby the town and the settled inhabitants are much injured." Doughty's neighbors John Roberts, Thomas Nock, and Philip Chesley were ordered to search for poachers and seize their wood; half would be for the use of the town, and Roberts, Nock, and Chesley could retain the other half for themselves.[29] In 1656, the town of Kittery declared that if any person felled timber and let it lay unused for one month's time, another citizen could claim it as his. In 1660, Portsmouth exacted a fee of five shillings for citizens who cut wood from the town common except for use as domestic building, fencing, or firewood.[30]

By 1677, northern New England, from Hampton, New Hampshire, to present-day Portland, Maine, was booming with sawmills. According to seventeenth-century historian William Hubbard:

> All or most of the . . . Towns and Plantations are seated upon, and near some River greater or lesser, whose Streams are principally improved for the driving of Saw-mills. . . . There is scarce a River or Creek in those parts that hath not some of those Engines erected upon them.

But good quality lumber in the Piscataqua watershed was already becoming scarce: "[In] the upper Branches of the famous River Pascataqua," wrote Hubbard, "[the] principal Trade is in Deal-boards, cut by those Saw-mills, since their Rift Timber is near all consumed."[31]

After leaving the Great Works at present-day South Berwick, Doughty was clearly in search of optimal conditions for a sawmill. He moved eight or so miles upriver where he constructed his own dam and mill, at a spot today known as Doughty Falls in the center of North Berwick. We know little more, though, because he didn't stay long there, either. Sometime around 1667, after selling his property in New Hampshire, he moved north to Saco.

The Saco River's first sawmill had been built sometime around 1653 to 1654.[32] The town granted Roger Spencer rights to the falls and land for his mill, stipulating that he had to build it within a year and that local residents were to be charged cheaper rates for lumber than outsiders.[33] It's not clear, though, whether he built the mill, or whether John Davis, who received a similar grant about a year later, did so, either.[34] In 1660, the well-to-do William Phillips, a Boston neighbor of Valentine Hill and Richard Leader, moved to Maine and acquired timberlands throughout the area through purchase and negotiation with native sachems.[35] Phillips built a mill on the southwest bank of the river, in present-day Biddeford. Benjamin Blackman, a Harvard graduate and minister, later purchased significant property on the opposite side of the Saco and erected a sawmill. He owned yet another sawmill at Black Point, farther north.[36]

But the Saco is a large, long river; it flows 136 miles from its headwaters in New Hampshire's White Mountains to its mouth in the Gulf of Maine. Doughty likely recognized the river's capacity, not only to support multiple mills but as an important link to the dense interior forests of southern Maine and eastern New Hampshire. In fact, the Saco supported a vibrant logging industry well into the twentieth century.[37]

By his own account, Doughty settled near the confluence of the Saco and Swan Pond, or Swan Pond Creek, a few miles upstream of the falls. We know he built a grist mill and dwelling and lived there for most of the next twenty years.[38] It's unclear whether he purchased the land or received a grant from the town or from William Phillips. It's possible Doughty did neither, instead following the cultural lead of Puritan New Englanders, such as John Cotton, who preached "That in a vacant soyle, hee that taketh possession of it, and bestoweth culture and husbandry upon it, his Right it is," or John Winthrop, who argued similarly that land "taken and possessd as vacuum domicilium"—that is, unoccupied lands—"gives us a sufficient title against all men."[39] Doughty didn't hail from a culture where ownership was conveyed by hard work alone, but, once in America, he may well have benefited from that doctrine. His indigenous neighbors, however, had a radically different concept of ownership; to them, the notion of "vacant soyle" was entirely foreign. Those very distinct concepts of ownership were already causing tensions in southern New England.

Doughty wasn't the only Oyster River Scot to move to Saco. In October 1667, he, Henry Brown, and Patrick Denmark were present in Saco to witness William Phillips selling a portion of an island in the Saco River (most likely present-day Factory Island) to John Bonighton (or Bonython). And James Oare was with them: a New Hampshire deed states that "James Oare of Sacoe Falls" sold land on behalf of himself and Brown to "James Smith of Oyster River, tailor, October 9, 1669." So four Dunbar Scots—Doughty, Brown, Oare, and Denmark—came to Saco together, likely lured by Phillips to provide timber for, and help him run, his large sawmill operation there.[40]

Not long after, James Oare and Henry Brown moved south to a mill site on the Cape Porpoise River owned by Henry Sayword. The site was at the head of tide of the present-day Mousam River. Oare and Brown managed Sayword's sawmill with the help of a third Scot, Robert Stewart, from the Battle of Worcester. In 1675, Oare and Brown even purchased some two hundred acres from Sayword below the mill. A small tributary, Scotchmen's Brook, is said to be named after the three who lived along its banks.[41]

But this didn't spell the end of the Scots' joint business dealings, or their support for one another. At the time, the two settlements, Saco and Mousam, were connected by a winding overland trail called the "Saco Path." And court records indicate that Doughty, Oare, and Brown continued to have joint contracts. Another of the Oyster River Scots, Patrick Jameson, appears with Doughty, Oare, and Brown in court records, as well.

By 1674, Thomas Doughty must have had a thriving business on his own, because he willingly took on Richard Gibson as his servant. Like all male citizens, Gibson was required to participate in the local militia and to attend training days. But he was called to court for striking his superior officer, Captain Charles Frost. Gibson was ordered "to be layd & Tyd Necke & Heeles togeather at the head of his Company for the tyme of 2 houres or to ride the wooden horse[42] at the head of his Company," at the next training day at Kittery. He was also ordered to provide bond of £20 to the court to ensure his good behavior until the next session. Thomas Doughty not only paid the bond but agreed to take Gibson into service for one year, offering to pay him twenty-six pounds at year's end: "Gibson hereby stands Ingagd to performe honest service unto the sd Doughty or his order for one whoole years tyme . . . for which years service truly performed Tho: Doughty Ingageth to pay the sd Gibson Twenty six pounds."[43]

No records exist to demonstrate what sort of master Doughty, as a former servant, turned out to be. But his willingness to take on Gibson undoubtedly relieved York County of the inconvenience of incarcerating Gibson and saved Gibson jail time and the costs associated with it, which drove many individuals deeper into debt. The town was relieved of responsibility; Doughty received help at his milling operation; and Gibson had his large fine paid off, as well as the prospect of earning a modest sum for a year's work. As was the custom, Gibson likely also received room and board during the time of his service. All around, it was a much better solution than condemning Gibson to waste away in a frigid jail cell.

Doughty, in fact, would serve as a bondsman in several court cases during his lifetime. While the conditions aren't always spelled out in the court records, he often stood up for others in court and helped them pay their fines or reduce their charges.[44] Perhaps he was practical and compassionate; perhaps he was seeking ways to ingratiate himself to local magistrates; perhaps he needed to clear his conscience.

Eight years earlier, just after he'd moved to Maine, Doughty had served on a grand jury in the death of Nicholas Woodman. Woodman was the servant of Nicholas and Judith Weeks, and Judith admitted in court to chopping off Woodman's toes with an axe in a fit of anger. Woodman died soon afterward. So, in June 1666, Judith Weeks was called to court "upon suspition of some further matter which possibly might appeare concerneing the death of the said Nicho: Woodman."

Under the Massachusetts Body of Liberties, murder—resulting from premeditation or from a fit of anger or passion—was a capital offense. The likelihood that Woodman would die from his wounds was huge, especially since wound hygiene wasn't understood or widely practiced until the nineteenth century. But the very language of the court presentment ("upon suspition of some further matter which possibly might appeare concerning the death") shows the court's reluctance to find Judith responsible. The magistrates questioned Goodwife Weeks but did not pursue charges: "upon further Inquiry into the matter & nothing appeareing shee is hereby Accquitted from her bond of fivety pounds."[45]

Troubled by Woodman's death, yet reluctant to fully prosecute it, magistrates ordered a grand jury to convene at the next court session in September to investigate further. Thomas Doughty served on that grand jury along with Peter Cloyce, whose eventual wife, Sarah Towne, would be imprisoned in Salem as a suspected witch. Nicholas Weeks, Judith's husband, was called before the grand jury to "answere his Inditement by the Coroners quest for being suspitiously guilty of the death of the said Nicho: Woodman, his servant." But Doughty, Cloyce, and their peers on the grand jury cleared Weeks. Once again, no one was called to account for Woodman's death.[46]

The acquittal of Judith and Nicholas Weeks appears—at least from several centuries' distance—to have been a serious miscarriage of justice. Yet many important details are missing. We do not know whether the grand jury vote was unanimous or contentious; whether Judith Weeks felt threatened by Woodman; nor what went on in the Weeks household day to day. Nor do we know why Nicholas, and not Judith, Weeks was called before the grand jury. Yet even if unintended, Woodman's death should have prompted accountability or punishment.

Neither the magistrates nor the grand jury had had the nerve to find the Weeks guilty of murder. The Weeks were, after all, everyone's neighbors. The truth is, throughout Massachusetts Bay, hangings for capital crimes were uncommon; magistrates and grand juries alike found it difficult to condemn individuals whom they knew well.

In Woodman's case, the grand jury's decision wasn't the end of the saga. At the general court session the following summer, magistrates[47] declared the matter "a mischarage both in bench & Jury." They noted that the grand jury had failed both to "take notice of the Charge that had been occasioned by the Coroners Inquest," and "to lay it upon the right persons." The grand jury pled that they had been confused about their role and legal responsibilities. Unnamed jury members declared that "they were noe grand Jury, but a particular Jury of paress": they may have meant "peers." And they admitted that they "could not find the bill referred to their considerations."[48] Their reluctance to take responsibility for the difficult matter was clear.

Magistrates of the general court, who had tried to foist responsibility onto the grand jury's shoulders, were forced to take matters into their own hands. Though they found Nicholas Weeks guilty of neither murder nor manslaughter, he was found to be "defective in his duty to his servant, which occasioned the death." Magistrates also declared "the Townes men of Kittery" at fault, because "when Complaynt to them being made they had not caused [Woodman's] Master to provide for him," suggesting that selectmen, constables, and others had been negligent in ignoring previous complaints about Woodman's situation. In the end, Woodman's life was worth little: Weeks was fined some twelve pounds, fifteen shillings.[49]

Participating in the grand jury must have been a challenge for Doughty, who fully understood the humiliations, pressures, and daily injustices of living as another man's servant. But he had also proven that he aspired to a higher station. It's possible that he participated in the grand jury's majority decision and found it reasonable; it's equally possible that he didn't. It's unlikely that he was confused about what he was being asked to do and more likely that he and his peers were simply uncomfortable doing it. Because it was one of

Doughty's first experiences in fulfilling his civic duty as a free man and taxpayer, the Woodman affair must have chafed his conscience and made a lasting impression. That may be why he became useful in the community as a bondsman for others.

In fact, at the very court session where the grand jury proclaimed Nicholas Weeks innocent, Doughty engaged in a bond of ten pounds with Thomas Chicke. Chicke, it seems, had been charged with fighting with the wife of David Hamilton, a Scot and former prisoner from the Battle of Worcester. The joint bond was meant to ensure that Chicke would "bee of good behavior towards all persons, espetially towards the wife of Davie Hamilton."[50] Doughty's stepping in suggests a willingness to ease community tension where he could.

As a lumberman and miller, at least, Doughty seems to have found his niche in Saco: that is, until the Indian raid of September 18, 1675, when Native Americans burned nearly all the town's mills and dwellings. Saco wasn't the only town destroyed. Houses at Winter Harbor (present-day Biddeford Pool) and Black Point were burned, and five Englishmen in a canoe were killed.

Although King Philip's War had begun in Massachusetts in June 1675, violence didn't break out in Maine until early September, when natives sacked Thomas Purchase's trading post at Pejepscot (Brunswick). No one was injured during the raid, which may have had less to do with the war to the south and more to do with Purchas's unfair trading practices. White settlers responded by shooting several natives who hadn't been involved in the Pejepscot incident. Wabanakis responded by burning Thomas Wakely's farm on the Presumpscot River on September 12, killing Wakely and several family members and kidnapping a young girl. Raids also began to the south of Saco, as well: Natives burned two houses owned by the Chesleys in Oyster River as well as Richard Tozier's house at Salmon Falls. It was a season of fear and loss up and down the coast from Pemaquid to Piscataqua.

During this time, Doughty and his family moved south to Wells. In July 1676, he won a court case on a lumber contract he shared with James Oare and Henry Brown.[51] It is likely that Doughty worked and lived with his fellow Scots during the late fall and winter of 1675 through 1677.

Eventually, though, Doughty and his neighbors returned to Saco and began to rebuild, working to recover their losses from the war of 1675. In April 1682—seven years after the raids—the town assessed taxes on "Tho: Doughtys" mill at Saco at five pounds. The only other mill mentioned at Saco, Benjamin Blackman's, was assessed at four pounds.[52] Although the town lists the mill in Doughty's name, it's probable that he was leasing William and Bridget Phillips's large mill at the falls, allowing him to produce a large volume of boards.[53] In 1686, Doughty came before the York County court to confess that he owed Captain Sylvanus Davis—a well-known merchant and militia captain—14,500 feet of merchantable boards. Both the tax assessment and several suits suggest that Doughty was doing a brisk business.

That same year, however, the Catholic King James II appointed Sir Edmund Andros governor of the Dominion of New England. The appointment represented a sea change for Massachusetts Bay, and for many of its residents, an unwelcome one. The newly formed Dominion of New England included nearly all of the present-day northeastern United States: Massachusetts, Maine, New Hampshire, Vermont, Rhode Island, Connecticut, and eventually, New York and New Jersey.

One of the first things Andros did as governor was to present a list of demands. He asked that Puritan meetinghouses in Boston be used for Anglican worship, and when he was told no, he summarily took over Boston's South Church. For Puritans, this was popery thinly disguised. Moreover, New England colonists had developed their own representative form of local government involving selectmen and town meetings. Andros limited both town meetings and the power of town officials. He also declared all land titles inconsistent with the English system and thereby void. Colonists were required to apply directly to him for titles to lands already in their possession and to pay "quit rents," both retroactively and going forward, to the English government.[54]

Leaders of Massachusetts Bay Colony were outraged at their loss of power, at the threat to Puritan supremacy, and especially, at the threat to their plantations, homes, mills, and everything they had worked so hard to build over six decades. Many refused to obey the new laws, and those who did comply were rebuked by their peers.

"The generality of People are very averse from complying with any thing that may alter the Tenure of their lands," wrote Samuel Sewall in a letter to Increase Mather in July 1688, "and look upon me very Sorrowfully that I have given way."[55]

Like Sewell, Thomas Doughty chose the safe route. On July 28, 1687, he sent a petition to Governor Andros, asking that he be allowed to retain his property at Saco:

> Whereas yor Petitionr Thos Doughty of Saco in the Province of Main hath had in his Possession a certaine Tract of fresh marsh lying in the little Desart neer Swan Pond which yor Petitionr hath made use of this twenty yeares or there abouts which wth 300 Acres of Upland and the Grist Mill built by yor Petitionr at his sole charge Your Petitionr prayes that yor Excellcie would be pleased to grant a Warrant for the admeasuring the same And yor Petitionr as in duty bound shal ever pray & c[56]

Doughty's letter to Andros is straightforward yet restrained. He makes his case for having resided on and improved the land, though he doesn't say that he purchased, bargained for, or possessed a deed to it. In the spirit of having "made use of" the land "twenty years or there abouts," he asks for the governor's consideration. But the letter is all the more poignant for what it doesn't say. The English government had banished him to New England. Some thirty-seven years later, after struggling to build an independent life, that same government threatened to take it all away. Doughty's is one of dozens of letters from individuals who believed they could be deprived with the stroke of a pen of everything they'd worked hard to build.

Other New Englanders—Cotton Mather, along with "Gentlemen, Merchants, and Inhabitants of Boston, and the Country Adjacent"—were not so restrained. On April 18, 1689, they composed a "Declaration of Grievances" intended to free themselves from Andros's autocratic rule. This declaration is remarkably similar in tone and substance to another, more famous one written some eighty-seven years later:

> Because these Things would not make us miserable fast enough, there was a notable Discovery made of we know not what flaw in all our Titles to our lands; and tho, besides our

purchase of them from the Natives, and besides our actual peaceable un-questioned Possession of them for near three-score Years. . . Yet we were every day told That no Man was owner of a Foot of Land in all the Colony. Accordingly, Writs of Intrusion began everywhere to be served on People, that after all their Sweat and their Cost upon their formerly purchased Lands, thought themselves Freeholders of what they had. And the governor caused the Lands pertaining to these and those particular Men to be measured out for his Creatures to take possession of; and the Right Owners, for pulling up the stakes, have passed through Molestations enough to tire all the Patience in the World.[57]

Referring to their "purchase" of lands from the natives and their "peaceable un-questioned Possession of them," the letter-writers conceal the complexity and controversy behind their acquiring them. Land deals often involved negotiating with, pressuring, and out-maneuvering native sachems, using English-language deeds and English courts as weapons.[58] As we've seen, some colonists claimed rights to land simply by "improving" what they considered to be vacant spaces: clearing, planting, and building structures. Regardless of how they'd acquired property, most white settlers felt justified in their actions, and Puritan clergymen like Cotton provided religious and intellectual validation of their methods. Yet now their ownership was being challenged by the very government in whose name they had worked to secure those lands. All "their Sweat and their Cost" was being dismissed by a king and governor who were insensitive and out of touch.

In late 1688, Andros's authority was eroded by England's Glorious Revolution. After two brief skirmishes, the Catholic James II was forced to flee to France, abdicating the throne to his son-in-law, the Protestant William of Orange and his wife Mary. Back in New England, colonists revolted themselves; Andros was pursued and arrested by a group of Bostonians led by former Massachusetts Bay governor Simon Bradstreet.

The Bostonians held Andros for ten months before sending him to England for trial. One of the main complaints against him was the perceived effort to weaken representative government in Massachusetts. But New Englanders' bitterest resentment involved land: "The despair this people were brought to when instead of defending them in their just Right and Properties those in the late Government fought to turne them out of their Lands and possessions upon which under God they had their dependence for a necessary Livelihood."[59] New Englanders proved that they weren't going to relinquish lands they had come to consider their own without a fight.

Once in England, Andros was never brought to trial; Massachusetts agents in London never formally signed charges against him. Perhaps they felt that they had accomplished their purpose by returning him to England and airing their grievances with the king and his advisors.

Northern New England in the seventeenth century was, in many ways, a land of plenty. Abundant fish, fowl, and game, dense forests, and fast-flowing rivers spelled opportunity, even for immigrants who came to America with no baggage and little hope. Thomas Doughty took advantage of this bounty and transformed himself from a prisoner and servant to a landholder, lumberman, miller, and business owner. Yet even though land was easier to come by in New England than in Scotland, he couldn't know how difficult it would be to hang onto. Gaining his freedom and building a livelihood was the defining ambition of his early years in America. But holding onto the land that he had worked hard to clear and develop was the struggle that defined the second half of his life. It was a battle as challenging as any he had faced to date.

Chapter Seven

A CHILDE
UNLAWFULLY BEGOTTEN

The Nights are still cold and long, which May cause great Conjunction betwixt the Male and Female Planets of our sublunary Orb, the effects whereof may be seen about nine months after.
— John Tulley,
An Almanack for the Year of Our Lord MDCLXXXVIII

IN 1661, two close friends of Thomas Doughty, Peter and James Grant, found themselves in a quandary. The Grants were summoned to court in Kittery, Maine, for failing to return to their wives in Scotland: "Wee present Peter Grant a Scotchman for not returneing home to his wife. Wee present James Grant a Scotchman for not returneing home to his wife,"[1] states the court record. Like Doughty, the Grants had served in the Scottish Army during the Wars of the Three Kingdoms and were taken prisoner during battle. Peter was with Doughty at Dunbar in 1650 and endured the infamous Death March to Durham Cathedral, banishment to New England, and six years of servitude. James may have been either at Dunbar or at Worcester. Regardless, both Grants had been sent to New England against their wills. Paradoxically, an arm of the English government, which had banished them in the first place, was now ordering them to return home.

Peter Grant's movements before the court case are hard to pin down. He first appears on the tax rolls at Oyster River in 1659.[2] But his name also appears among those employed at the Hammersmith Iron Works, on the list of contributors to the Scots Charitable Society in Boston, and among those residing at Unity Parish.[3] He may have served with Thomas Doughty as a servant to Valentine Hill or been affiliated with Richard Leader at the Great Works. James Grant may have also been one of Hill's servants at Oyster River. Neither returned to Scotland, despite the court order. In fact, there is no evidence that any of the Dunbar prisoners ever again saw the country of their birth. That was, after all, the idea: Cromwell wanted all Scottish soldiers capable of mounting an insurrection or rebellion out of his hair. The best way to accomplish his design was to transport them to the Americas.

But the Grants' neighbors in Maine wanted them gone, too. In 1652, Massachusetts Bay Colony annexed the province of Maine: a change that caused considerable controversy. Suddenly, the formerly Anglican colony fell under Puritan laws. And according to those laws, married individuals who left spouses behind in the British Isles were considered threats to the morals of the community. A Massachusetts law enacted in May 1647 states:

> Whereas divers persons, both men and women, living within this jurisdiction, whose wives and husbands are in England, or elsewhere, by means whereof, they live under great temptation here, and some of them committing lewdness and filthiness here amongst us, others make love to women and attempt marriage, and some have attained it. . . . For the prevention of all such future evils . . . all such married persons as aforesaid, shall repair to their said relations by the first opportunity of shipping, upon the pain or penalty of twenty pounds.[4]

On paper, at least, the Grants became the poster boys for the behavior magistrates were trying to prevent. They managed to skirt the law, perhaps because Maine was more permissive than Massachusetts, or because laws were harder to enforce there. Maine was clearly the frontier; its population was more scattered and more diverse, and law and religion simply didn't have the same teeth in such a place. Moreover, the written law is one thing; enforcing it upon your neighbor, a flesh-and-blood human being, is another.

Why didn't the Grants simply board a boat and return home? Getting by in seventeenth-century New England was struggle enough; adding the cost of a transatlantic passage was prohibitive for most.[5] Many were inclined to stay anyway; the passage was not just expensive, it was dangerous and grueling. And even though the Scots had arrived as prisoners, once they achieved their freedom in New England, opportunities were generally better there than in Scotland. Life on the New England frontier wasn't easy, by any means, but wild game and fish were still abundant and there was a need for labor throughout the colonies. Perhaps most important, land was cheap and available; Peter Grant had taken advantage of this in October 1659 by purchasing a piece of land at present-day South Berwick, then the Parish of Unity.[6]

So the Grants stayed on, despite the court's admonition. And some time after being called to court for abandoning his Scottish wife in 1661, James married a local woman named Joane. While the records reveal no date for the marriage, it must have occurred between 1661 and 1664, when Peter was again called into court: "Wee present Peter Grant & Joane Grant the wife of James Grant deseased for liveing In one house togeather, hee oweneing of her as his wife & they being not married."[7] The Grants' neighbor, Richard Abbott, brought the scandal to the court's attention. In Puritan New England, you didn't keep this kind of information to yourself; minding your own business was considered complicity in sin.

It was a strange turn of events. Ordered to return to his wife in Scotland in 1661, James stayed on and inexplicably married Joane soon afterward. Then, around 1663 or 1664, he died. Some genealogists have speculated that he was captured or killed by Native Americans, but conflicts with native communities didn't arise until 1675; others, that he became a mariner and left his second wife behind, marrying a third time in Boston; others, that he returned to Scotland. But at least three James Grants arrived in New England as prisoners on the *John and Sara*, and two of the three ended up in York County, Maine. Despite the confusion caused by the numerous James Grants, we have no reason to dismiss the court record that clearly states that James, the husband of Joane, is "deseased" by 1664.

Chances are, James and Peter Grant were brothers, or close relatives, and lived together with Joane in a single household until James's
death. In New England, households were typically composed of family and extended family; if the family was well-to-do, the household
included servants and others. Simple economics dictated most of
these arrangements. It was also common—and sometimes manda-
tory—for single persons to live with family members, or with other
respected families in the community. This practice was intended to
dampen the threat that single men supposedly posed to the community's morals.

So Peter lived with his brother, or blood relative, and wife. After
James's death, he continued to live with Joane, perhaps for convenience, perhaps for family reasons:

> Whereas Itt appears by Peter Grants acknowledgement of
> his keepeing Company with Joane Grant In soe familiar man-
> ner as If they had been lawfully married which they never were
> nor Could bee, because the Grants wife is yett alive for any
> thing that is known to the Contrary, & the sd Joane Grant
> being now bigg with Child, It is ordered by the Court as fol-
> loweth: In reference to Peter Grants presentment for his living
> with Joane Grant a Widdow Incontinently, being by his own
> acknowledgement never lawfully married to her, & shee being
> by him with child as not denyed, It is ordered that the sd Peter
> Grant for his offence herein shall either pay tenn pounds In
> to the Treasury or to have tenn lashes given him on the bare
> skine.[8]

Joane arrived in court obviously pregnant. Peter did not deny that
the child was his. Yet records show that Peter never legally claimed
the child, later named Elizabeth. Nor were Peter and Joane charged
with fornication: the legal term for conceiving a child out of wedlock.
Rather, they were charged with living "incontinently": that is, co-
habiting without being married. It seems the magistrates had some
doubt as to the child's paternity, too.

Scandalous as the situation may have seemed to their neighbors,
it likely developed out of necessity as much as convenience. Domestic
life in seventeenth-century New England entailed a long list of exhausting activities: cultivating, plowing, and harvesting crops, hunt-

ing, tending domestic animals, cutting and curing cord after cord of firewood for cooking and heating, drawing water, brewing, cooking, churning, spinning, weaving, and the list goes on. Losing one member of a household would be trauma enough; breaking up the household partnership entirely would've constituted a true hardship for both parties, but especially for the pregnant Joane.

Moreover, Maine was a lonely place. It's true that several Dunbar and Worcester Scots lived close to one another and supported each other in times of trouble. It's equally true that neighbors meddled in others' business. Richard Abbott, who turned the Grants in, was not a member of the tight-knit Scottish community. But the province was still remote, forested, and sparsely populated, and the winters were cold, dark, and very, very long. It was—and still is—a challenge to live alone in such a place. Settlers were undoubtedly anxious to pair up, as the rapid remarriages of widows and widowers throughout New England demonstrate.

Although the court sentenced Peter to pay ten pounds or receive ten lashes for living with Joane, he requested and was granted a stay. Two months later, he was back in court, appealing his case with Thomas Doughty by his side:

> Peter Grant & Tho: Doughty do Ingage them selves In a bond of 20li that the sd Grant shall prosecute his appeale to the next County Court & the sd Grant & Doughty do Ingage In a bond of 20li that further Peter Grant shall take meete care to mantayne the Child of the sd Joane Grant soe soone as shee is delivered.[9]

Together, Grant and Doughty engaged in a bond of twenty pounds. Most likely, the two put up their land holdings as surety should Grant fail to show at the next court session or to provide for the infant not yet born. Because Doughty proved willing to shoulder part of his friend's obligation to the court, Peter Grant likely avoided a whipping or a larger fine, which he would have been hard-pressed to pay.

Doughty and Grant had both ended up in Oyster River, New Hampshire, in the late 1650s. Although Grant was living on the Maine side of the Newichawannock (or Salmon Falls) River when called to court, Doughty still lived in Oyster River, New Hampshire.

Yet he showed up in court to support his friend. The following year, Peter returned the favor, serving as security for Doughty on a contract with Eliakim Hutchinson to operate the Great Works sawmill.[10]

Doughty's presence—and his willingness to shoulder some responsibility for Grant's behavior—seems to have helped. Magistrates appear to have suspended the whipping and fine for Grant. But they threatened more consequences should Peter continue to live with Joane:

> For preventing any further evill betweene the sd Peter and Joanee Grant by there frequent unlawfull Comeing together . . . hereby theere shall bee and is an Act of seperation made betweene them, after publication whereof if they shall bee at any tyme found frequently or unseasonably togeather . . . each person shall either forfitt tenn pounds to the County Treasury or bee lyable to such other Censure as the Law in such Cases doth provide.[11]

The court is quite clear, ordering Peter and Joane to immediately separate or be subject to further punishment. Of course, the magistrates seem to have forgotten or forgiven the court order of three years earlier that Peter Grant return to his wife in Scotland.

Inexplicably, two months after the court ordered Peter Grant and Joane to separate, they married.[12] This series of events is astonishing, particularly given the court record, and questions loom large for the local magistrates and their motives. Did they believe that Peter was the father of Joane's child? Did the court simply change its mind and insist that Peter marry Joane to legitimize their cohabitation? If not, how could the marriage take place so soon after the court ordered the couple to live separately? And what about Peter and Joane? Did they have a genuine affection for each other? Did Peter feel it was his duty to support his relative's widow? Or did they simply disobey the court's order?

All of these events seem to fly in the face of local laws and the authorities' ability to enforce them. Obviously, Puritan law, though strict in word, was much more lenient in action, and in Maine, particularly so. Courts and local officials did try to regulate behavior, but they often weren't successful. And in some cases, like the Grants, they appear to have chosen the lesser evil. Without doubt, the sur-

viving court documents are merely the tip of the iceberg; Grant must
have engaged in significant negotiations with local magistrates.

But who were these magistrates? Typically, they were wealthy and
prominent citizens: large landowners or businessmen, many of whom
also served as officers in the local militias. In the Grants' case, they
were Edward Rishworth, a representative from Maine to the Massachusetts General Court; the prominent Captain Daniel Gookin,
from Cambridge, superintendent of all "praying"—or Christian—
Indians for New England; Major William Phillips, a miller and the
largest landowner in Saco; George Munjoy, a large landowner in
Casco (present-day Portland); Ezekiel Knight, an early settler, town
commissioner, and associate justice from Wells; and Roger Plaisted,
one of the earliest settlers in Newichawannock (South Berwick), also
a representative to the General Court from 1663 to 1667. Although
they served multiple terms as magistrates, few, if any, of these men
had any legal training or background. In many cases, the wrongdoers
appearing before them were their immediate neighbors: individuals
whom they saw every Sabbath, who served under them in the local
militia, and with whom they regularly carried out business transactions.

York County magistrates seemed particularly concerned about
support for the offspring of unmarried couples. This consideration
may have been a large part of their motive in allowing Peter and
Joane Grant's case to run its irregular course. In 1667, another of the
Dunbar Scots, Andrew Rankin, was accused of fathering Martha
Merry's illegitimate child. Two other Scots, Robert Junkins, a former
servant of Valentine Hill with Doughty, and another James Grant
engaged in a bond of one hundred pounds to support Rankin. The
court ordered Rankin to "mantayne that Child" and thus "to free the
Town of Yorke from all charges which may accrew from the Mainte-
nance thereof."[13] Rankin and Martha Merry later married; marriage,
after all, was considered the best possible solution to fornication.[14]

It's easy to dismiss the Grants' case—with multiple wives and
questionable paternity—as highly unusual. But although settlers having wives in America and abroad was both scandalous and unlawful,
it wasn't unheard of. In October 1651, the York County Court
granted Margery Randall a divorce from a William Noreman because
he had a wife still living in England:

> Whereas it apperes that William Noreman had maried two wives which were both alive . . . said Noreman shall hence forth be banished out of this province & is to depart thence within 7 dayes . . . & in case the said Noreman be found after that tyme in this jurisdiction, he shall forthwith, according to law, be putt to death.[15]

For bigamy, Noreman was banished from Maine, and the consequences of his lingering sounded dire indeed. But he didn't seem to take the warning too seriously. He simply moved fifty miles away to House Island in Portland Harbor, where, in 1663, he sold a quarter of the island and the house upon it to magistrate George Munjoy.[16]

F ive years after the Grant drama, Thomas Doughty found himself in court over family matters. In January 1670, he had married Elizabeth Bully, probably the daughter of Saco fisherman Nicholas Bully.[17] Doughty was thirty-nine years old. And while no birth record for Elizabeth appears in Saco, she was likely much younger than Thomas—in her mid to late teens—at the time of her marriage.[18]

It was unusual for Doughty to have remained single until he was thirty-nine. But like all Scottish prisoners, he had not been permitted to marry while bonded to Valentine Hill. Two of his closest Scottish friends and business partners, James Oare and Henry Brown, lived together in one household and remained single throughout their lives. Although there's no evidence for it, one or both of these Scots may well have left spouses behind in Scotland.

But Thomas's and Elizabeth's union was controversial for other reasons. In the York County Court records of July 5, 1670, the couple were fined five pounds for "haveing a childe unlawfully begotten."[19] This was their first child, also named Elizabeth, born on February 14, 1670,[20] less than a month after their marriage. Doughty, the record says, "ownes the presentment." After paying the fees, he was dismissed with "an admonition."[21]

Their case is somewhat different from one heard across the Piscataqua in Portsmouth just a few days earlier:

> Wm Durgin & his wife prsented for Comitting of fornication before marriage Confest Sentence to be forth with whipt

to ye Number of 10 stripes a peece or redeeme it by a fine of 50s a peece & fees, they engaged to pay the fine.[22]

Here, the same transgression is called "fornication before marriage," and although Durgin and his wife are given the same fine,[23] they are threatened with a whipping if they cannot pay it.

In Maine, and in some other parts of New England, the typical fine for fornication—that is, conceiving a child outside of marriage— was fifty shillings, or two pounds, ten shillings,[24] which each guilty party had to pay. Whipping was viewed as a particularly humiliating punishment, and class status was often the determining factor. Those without property, or the capacity to pay fines, had no choice but to endure physical punishment. Wealthier individuals, however, weren't subject to the whipping, unless their transgressions were serious. According to the Massachusetts Body of Liberties: "nor shall any true gentleman, nor any man equal to a gentleman be punished with whipping, unless his crime be very shameful, and his course of life vicious and profligate."[25]

Although their fines were the same, the formal charge for Doughty and his wife Elizabeth wasn't the standard "fornication" that the Durgins were charged with but rather the softer, "a childe unlawfully begotten." Nor were they offered a whipping. Perhaps, because Doughty had come to own land and a business, magistrates viewed him as more of a gentleman. Or perhaps Doughty's ready admission that he and Elizabeth had violated the law inspired the court to apply the euphemism "unlawfully begotten" in place of "fornication." At least one magistrate in the case—John Wincoll—had had lumber contracts with Doughty. Magistrates' familiarity with Thomas's character and contribution to the community may have been an additional factor in the Doughtys' favor.

Conceiving a child out of wedlock was a common offense in early New England. Fornication was the most common crime mentioned in New England's court records during the seventeenth century. In Essex County, Massachusetts, more than 150 couples were convicted of premarital sex between 1640 and 1685.[26] Unmarried couples, as well as those who married fewer than nine months before the birth of a child, could be charged with the crime—although as Else Hambleton has pointed out, fines for births occurring thirty-two weeks or more after marriage were rare.[27]

We will never know the exact circumstances of the Doughty marriage. Was Thomas forced to marry Elizabeth? Did he take advantage of a much younger woman? Were they already betrothed and simply conceived the child in anticipation? Many things are possible.

The truth is, marriages in colonial New England rarely took place rapidly. Publishing banns was required, and without them, couples were forbidden to marry. They could announce their intentions at three consecutive meetings at the local meetinghouse or post a notice on the meetinghouse door over the two weeks preceding the marriage. This law was yet another attempt to ensure that marriages didn't take place in secret and that neither the bride nor groom was already married to someone else.[28] In fact, Maine magistrates themselves were called to court for marrying couples who hadn't given notice: "Wee present Major Nicho: Shapleigh for Marriing Mr. Michell & Miss Gunnison before publication Contrary to the laws of the Countrey."[29] In 1670, Captain Francis Raynes was also fined for marrying a couple before they had published their intent.[30] Still, as we've seen, bigamous marriages weren't avoided altogether.

In the Doughtys' case, a late marriage—one month before the birth of their first child—suggests that theirs was a union of necessity, or that one of the two, Thomas or Elizabeth, resisted. The marriage may have also caused strain in the Bully family. Elizabeth was not mentioned in her father's will.[31] Nicholas Bully gave the bulk of his assets—including some two hundred acres along the Saco River—to daughters Ann and Grace,[32] never mentioning Elizabeth. He also bequeathed three pounds to his granddaughter Sarah. While it's possible that Elizabeth had received her portion of Nicholas Sr.'s estate at the time of her marriage, it's equally possible that her marriage to Thomas was a controversial one, which is why there is no mention of her in the will.[33]

No matter how young or naïve Elizabeth was when she married, the community likely didn't see her as the victim of an older man. In seventeenth-century New England, women were sometimes seen as "willing" if the sexual encounter resulted in pregnancy.[34] And they were often viewed as more responsible than the man involved.

Take the case of Jane Jackson. Jane was the wife of Walter Jackson, another former Scottish prisoner from the Battle of Worcester, who was Thomas Doughty's neighbor in Oyster River. Jane was charged with committing fornication with Andrew Wiggin:

100 The Involuntary American

> Jane ye wife of Walter Jackson prsented for Comitting of
> fornication, sentence of Court that she be forthwth whipt to
> ye Number of 10 stripes or pay a fine of 4l Walter Jackson en-
> gaged to pay the fine of 4l in 2 m° & fees of Court 28 6d.[35]

To prevent her from being whipped, Jane's husband Walter
stepped in and paid the fine. And then the Jacksons countered the
fornication charge with one of their own: that Wiggin impregnated
Jane Jackson while she lived with him: "sd Wiggin then to answr ye
charge Lade to him in begetting watr Jacksons wife with child while
she Lived wth him."[36]

It might seem reasonable that Jane was called to court for fornication, especially since she had been living with a man not her husband. But at the next court session, it became clear that she was living
with Wiggins out of necessity:

> Waltr Jackson petitioning the Court when Last held at
> Dover concerning ye wrong Mr Andrew Wiggins had done
> to his wife in begetting her with child while she Lived wth sd
> Wiggin as his servant made did yn bind sd Wiggin to this
> Court of Adjourm to answr sd complaint — This Court upon
> Examynac'on of ye same doe not find sd Andw Wiggin
> Guiltie of ye same, doe there-fore acquit & discharge him.[37]

Jane Jackson, we learn, was Andrew Wiggin's live-in maid. And
although the word "rape" never emerges, the Jacksons' petition suggests that's what happened. Clearly, Wiggin had power and advantage
over Jane as her master; saying no to his advances would have likely
meant choosing between a job and poverty. The fact that Jane was
living with Wiggin indicates that she and her husband were already
hard-pressed to support themselves. Moreover, Wiggin was from a
distinguished family. His father, Thomas Wiggin, was one of the
founders and governor of the Province of New Hampshire. Andrew
himself was married to the daughter of Massachusetts Bay governor
Simon Bradstreet and poet Anne Bradstreet, and granddaughter of
Massachusetts Bay governor Thomas Dudley.

Still, it's astonishing that the court held Jane Jackson entirely responsible for the pregnancy, and Wiggin suffered no penalty. If the
child had been her husband's, Jane would not have been charged with
fornication. So the magistrates tacitly agreed that Wiggin was in-

volved, yet they chose not to charge him. Magistrates were understandably reluctant to charge individuals with adultery or rape since both were capital offenses.[38] But this case also demonstrates two truths seen time and again in colonial court records: first, that well-connected individuals in the community typically won their cases, particularly when their adversaries were members of the working or servant classes; and second, that women often bore unequal responsibility for sexual crimes. In Maine and New Hampshire during the seventeenth century, numerous cases of fornication involve a woman only, without a partner.[39]

How does this reflect upon Elizabeth Doughty, Thomas's young wife? Her community, and most likely even her family, saw her as culpable for conceiving a child before marriage, regardless of the age difference between her and her husband. And the fact that Doughty married her, then "owned" the presentment in court and chose to pay the fine, could suggest several things: that he had been pressured into the marriage; that he believed it was the right thing to do; that the couple had already decided to marry but simply rushed into consummation of the union; that they truly cared for one another. Whatever the case, when they arrived in court together as new parents, Doughty had become more than Elizabeth's lover and husband; he had taken on the role of her protector.

Despite their inauspicious beginnings, both the Grant and Doughty marriages became less noteworthy—at least as far as legal records go—after their initial difficulties. The Grants were called to court again in 1669 "for using profane spechis in theyr common talke as in makeing answer to severall questions, ther answer is the divell a bett." Puritan laws took speech very seriously. Massachusetts Bay's General Laws of 1641 proscribed lying, blasphemy, cursing, slander, and swearing.[40] And neighbors were encouraged to report on others' transgressions. Thomas Withers reported the Grants to the magistrates, and his word alone was enough to bring them before the court.[41]

Peter Grant was called to court once again in 1680 for "lyeing drunke in the high way," (as witnessed by James Emery and Thomas Abbott)[42] another common offense, and in 1691 for "profaning the Sabbath," when he, his two sons, and another person shot a deer on Sunday.

Peter and Joane Grant had seven children: William, James, Alexander, Daniel, Grizzel, Mary, and Hannah.[43] And by the time of his death, Peter was proprietor of a homestead and more than sixty acres of land along the Salmon Falls River. His will divided his property among his seven children. Elizabeth, the child with whom Joane was pregnant before they married, wasn't mentioned. Peter also bequeathed to his wife "all my moveables . . . as also the hole use of my homeSteed housing barns Lands & Orchards and dwelling place During her Naturall Life."[44] It was common for a man to leave land and houses to his children while stipulating certain rights to his widow during her lifetime. But Peter's generosity in giving Joane full use of his assets clearly conveys his affection and his desire that her future be protected. Grant, it seems, wasn't the scoundrel that Maine's legal records might suggest at first glance.

Although the Doughtys' marriage also began inauspiciously, they, too, appear to have had a solid one. Thomas and Elizabeth lived together for more than three decades and raised seven children: Elizabeth, Margaret, Joseph, Benjamin, Patience, James, and Abigail. The two of them were called into court only one more time: in July 1675 for failing to attend church.[45] This was the second most common transgression among seventeenth-century colonists after "fornication." And it's not surprising. Roads were few, rivers had to be crossed, people fell ill, and the weather in all seasons presented serious challenges.

Not all marriages went as smoothly. The court records include many, many instances of husbands and wives living apart. Divorces were sometimes granted, particularly for transgressions like bigamy—as we've seen with William Noreman—adultery, abandonment, and failure of a husband to provide for his family. And verbal abuse typically merited an appearance in court. Philip Chesley, Doughty's former neighbor in Oyster River, was called to court numerous times for domestic disturbances, including "thretning his wife to break hir necke if shee would not goe out of the Doars and other thretning speechis."[46] Neighbor William Beard told the court that Chesley's wife sought shelter at his house out of fear. Two other neighbors, William Roberts and William Williams, testified that Chesley called "God to witness that he would never have any more sosiety with hir with many other vows."[47] Chesley was forced to post £40 bond and to pay all court charges accruing from his multiple presentments.

While corporal punishment was permitted within the family unit, husbands weren't allowed to whip their wives unless they had been attacked first: "Every married woman shall be free from bodily correction or stripes (whipping) by her husband, unless it be in his own defense upon her assault," stated article 80 of the Massachusetts Body of Liberties. The courts simply didn't tolerate physical abuse, regardless of which spouse was dishing it out:

> Henry sherburne for beating his wife severall times, owned by him Sentence to pay a fine of 20s & fees 2s 6d & to be bound in a bond of 5l to be of ye good behavr entred below The wife of Henry sherburne for beating her husband & breaking his head owned in Court, Sentence to pay a fine of 20s & fees 2s 6d to be bound in 5l bond to be of ye good behavr.[48]

If the accused couldn't pay the fine, more humiliating punishments were prescribed: "Wee present Mis Saraih Morgan for strikeing of her husband. The delinquent to stand with a gag in her Mouth halfe an houre at Kittery at a Publique Town meeteing & the cause of her offence writ upon her forehead, or pay 50s to the County."[49]

Marriage in seventeenth-century New England was not a private relationship between spouses. It was an institution designed to reflect and uphold morality and public order—to encourage individuals to conform to social and religious expectations. Even in their most private moments, New Englanders' lives were to serve as examples to their peers. And to help maintain the social order, citizens were expected to note and report the transgressions of their neighbors. Because Maine was sparsely populated, its residents benefited from a somewhat freer atmosphere than those of the more settled areas like Boston. Thomas Kemble, the merchant who sold the Worcester Scots into servitude at Boston in 1651, offers an example. Kemble returned from a long voyage in 1656 and was observed kissing his wife "publicquely" at their doorstep in Boston on a Sabbath. He was sentenced to spend two hours in the stocks for "lewd and unseemly behavior."[50]

Still, residents of Maine were often called to task for their behaviors at home, and their neighbors dutifully reported their infractions. The laws of Massachusetts Bay tried to establish order, even in outposts like Maine. But in reality, when laws were flouted, magistrates were forced to be creative. Sometimes that involved prescribing lesser charges and punishments, retracting their initial sentences, or looking the other way.

What little we know about the Doughtys' domestic life comes from Thomas's appearances in the public record. We know that he ran a sawmill at Saco, that he built a house and grist mill nearby which he operated for twenty years, that he served on several grand juries, and served as Saco town treasurer, or "clerk of the writs." He seems to have taken an active role in Saco town matters and to have found his niche there. And despite losing a £1,200 lawsuit to Eliakim Hutchinson for breach of contract at the Great Works mill in 1671, Doughty appears to have suffered few serious financial or social repercussions.

We know much less about Elizabeth, his wife. She doesn't appear in court records after answering to the charge of not attending church. Like women of her time, she wasn't eligible to serve in a public capacity, and as a married woman, she could inherit but not purchase land, nor could she engage in contracts or make business agreements. In the sole surviving seating list of the women at the Saco meetinghouse made by selectmen in 1674, Elizabeth Doughty does not appear, though other members of her extended family do.[51] On paper, at least, she is largely invisible.

Apart from a smattering of vital and court records, the lives of most seventeenth-century women in New England are lost to history. But women in early New England weren't powerless victims, as historian Laurel Thatcher Ulrich pointed out in *Good Wives: Image and Reality in the Lives of Women in Northern New England 1650-1750*. They were in charge of household tasks, child-rearing, nursing, caretaking, and they often handled business transactions when their husbands were away. Although Elizabeth Doughty cannot speak for herself, the diary of Mary Cooper, a Long Island farm wife from a century later, suggests that the lives of colonial women were filled with much work and little rest:

> Wee are much hurred drying appels.
> I am much tired cookeing and washing dishes.
> A very grevous storme of rain and snow. It has beene a tiresom day to me. It is now bed time and I have not had won minuts rest today.

I am drying and ironing my cloths til allmost brake of day.
O, I am tired almost to death waiteing on visseters. My feet
ach as if the bones was laid bare. Not one day's rest have I had
this weeke.[52]

Apart from the circumstances of her marriage, Elizabeth caused
little controversy in her day-to-day life. She bore seven children who
survived to adulthood during challenging and often chaotic times.
That is no small feat, particularly since she served as their mother,
nurse, cook, housekeeper, spinner, weaver, seamstress, gardener, and
primary educator. And it's fair to say that the tremendous volume of
work she performed in or about the home enabled her husband to
build a profitable milling operation, to fulfill his civic duties as town
treasurer and member of the local militia, and to enjoy a long life.

Chapter Eight

ETHNIC WARS

Governor of Boston . . . we can fight as well as others but we are willing to live pesabel. We will not fight without they fight with us first.—William Woum Wood, Hen Nwedloked, Winakeermit, Moxes, Essomonosko, Deogenes, Pebemoworet, Tasset, John, Shyrot, Mr. Thomas

IN 1605, French explorer Samuel de Champlain sailed south along the coast of Maine. Intrigued by what he saw at the mouth of the Saco River, he sketched a map that shows the river ("Chouacoit," in his French transliteration), marshes, islands, and a substantial Native American settlement with a fort, cultivated fields, and "cabins" among the fields. Champlain referred to the local natives as the "Almouchiquois," and wrote that not only were their cornfields the first he had noticed but that these natives lived in permanent homes along the river. [1]

Some twenty years later,[2] English explorer Christopher Levett noted blithely that the very same land was "fit for planting corn and other fruits, having heretofore been planted by the savages, who are all dead."[3] The indigenous population, from Massachusetts to the Kennebec, had been devastated by so-called "virgin soil epidemics" in a span of a dozen years: [4] a catastrophe so great that it was obvious even to short-term visitors.

Native communities had no immunity against certain pathogens introduced to America by European fishermen, traders, and explorers. As families and entire communities fell sick from these contagious diseases, few were well enough to hunt, carry water, or feed themselves. "They fell down so generally of this disease as they were in the end not able to help one another; no, not to make a fire nor to fetch a little water to drink, nor any to bury the dead," wrote William Bradford, describing an epidemic among a native community on the upper Connecticut River.[5] Scores of individuals died of disease or malnutrition, and many communities ceased to exist.

The natives' demise left open the door for white settlement in the Saco River basin, which began about 1630. The river continued to serve the diminished western Wabanakis as a main highway from the coast to the interior, and as a critical source of food during the seasonal migrations of herring, salmon, eels, sturgeon, and bass.

The scattered European residents of the province of Maine lived peacefully with the Saco community of Almouchiquois during the early seventeenth century. But tensions began mounting in the third quarter of the century as the forests receded inland under the axe, the river and its tributaries were dammed for mills, natives' favored planting fields were annexed by settlers, and the values of the two cultures clashed.

By the 1670s, the Saco settlement was a thriving port with bustling fishing and lumbering operations. Winter Harbor, at the mouth of the river, was "a noted place for Fishers" with "many stages" for processing fish, wrote John Josselyn around 1678. "Saco adjoyns to this, and both make one scattering Town of large extent, well stored with Cattle, arable land and marshes, and a Saw-mill."[6] The mill Josselyn mentions was likely William Phillips's large lumber mill at the falls. We know he had a grist mill near that site, as well. Thomas Doughty owned a smaller grist mill and possibly a small sawmill upstream, near the confluence of the Saco with Swan Pond, but he undoubtedly worked closely with Phillips, and likely operated Phillips's mill for a time.

In the fall of 1674, the natives of southern New England, particularly the Wampanoags and Narragansetts, were growing increasingly frustrated with their English neighbors. Plymouth Colony had used questionable treaties, deals, and court decisions to wrest strategic parcels of land from them. And the suspicious deaths of two natives, the Wampanoag leader Wamsutta, brother of Metacom (also known as Metacomet or Philip), and John Sassamon, a native closely allied with the English and involved in land deals, set everyone's nerves on edge. Colonists feared that the Indians, especially Metacom, were plotting a war against them.

The response of Massachusetts Bay governor Leverett was to ban the sale of shot and powder to Indians throughout the colony, which included Maine. The native communities of Maine depended heavily on game during the winter months and had grown used to having muskets, shot, and gunpowder to hunt with. The ban, coming as it did during the second-coldest winter recorded in North America in the last six centuries,[7] was particularly severe. Madockawando, whom William Hubbard, the Puritan historian, called "chief Sagamore of all the Indians about Pemaquid and the Penobscot,"[8] requested that his people be allowed to keep their weapons, since they had done the English no harm. Hubbard documented the sachem's protest, conveying the anger and dismay the Native leader must have felt: "Madochewando asked them what [he and his people] should do for Powder and Shot, when they had eat up their Indian Corn, what they should do for the Winter, for their hunting Voyages; asking withall, whether [the English] would have them dye, or leave their Country, and go all over to the French?"[9] Madockawando's prescient comment suggested that English colonists' fears were forcing the Wabanakis to ally with the French.

Fear of the natives and the potential harm they could do to settlements up and down the New England coast caused the leaders of Massachusetts Bay to take a hard line. They determined to treat eastern native communities as a unit, punishing the Penobscots out of fear of the Narragansetts, Wampanoags, and other communities to the south and west, when it was obvious that they sought to stay out of the conflict.

A few white voices demurred: "I do not find by Anything that I Can discerne that the Indianes East of us are in the least our Ennimies," wrote Thomas Gardner of Pemaquid, who commanded local militias. "[They] only fly for fear from Any boats or English thay se & good reason for they well Know it may Cost them their Lives if the wild fishermen meet with them."[10] As Gardner pointed out, many

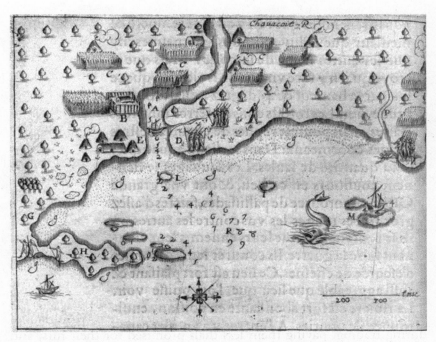

Sailing through Saco Bay in 1605, Samuel de Champlain drew this map showing
a lively Native American community at the mouth of the Saco River. Champlain's
"Chouacoit" shows a fortress, cornfields, a longhouse and wigwams, or wetus.
Winter Harbor, present-day Biddeford Pool, is labeled "H" at lower left. (*Library
of Congress*)

of the eastern native communities had already chosen to move away
from the coast to avoid confrontation with whites. And while Wabanaki fur trappers were displeased with the trading practices of some
Englishmen—particularly Thomas Purchase at Pejepscot (Brunswick),
William Hammond at Nequasset (Woolwich), and Richard Waldron
at Cocheco (Dover)—there is no evidence that natives were scheming
to ally in an all-out ethnic war against the English.

To the south, the situation was growing more tense by the day. In
June 1675, violence broke out in Plymouth when a local court sentenced three Wampanoags to hang for murdering John Sassamon,
whose lifeless body was found near a pond. Importantly, that pond,
as scholar Lisa Brooks has pointed out, was "at the center of a heated
land claim," involving Sassamon and Plymouth settlers Benjamin
Church and Thomas Southworth.[11] Shortly thereafter, a band of

Wampanoags attacked the village of Swansea, setting fire to the town and killing several inhabitants. The English retaliated, attacking the Wampanoag town of Mt. Hope and killing many. These events launched an all-out war between the Wampanoags—with Metacom (King Philip), as their leader—the Narragansetts, the Nipmucks, and the Pocumtucks, against white settlers and their native allies: the Mohegans, the Mohawks, and the so-called "praying Indians" who had converted to Christianity.

To the east, disputes were more localized, came to a head more slowly, and once started, took longer to contain. Three months after the war began in earnest in Massachusetts, a group of Ammoscoggins sacked Thomas Purchase's trading post at Pejepscot while he was away, taking rum and other goods, but most tellingly, powder, shot, and weapons. Purchase's wife and daughters were home at the time of the raid but weren't harmed. The raid likely wasn't directly connected to the strife to the south. Rather, it probably resulted partly from the governor's weapons ban, and even more directly, as retribution for Purchase's business practices: plying Indians with alcohol during trading, paying them less than promised for their furs, and charging exorbitant amounts for goods they needed. One member of the Anasagunticook community complained that he had paid Purchase £100 for water from Purchase's well.[12] He may have exaggerated, but the sentiment was clear: Purchase made no effort to treat native traders fairly.

In Maine, the English caused the first casualties. After the Pejepscot raid, as white settlers were attempting to secure cornfields near Purchase's house, they noticed several Wabanakis at the door of another house nearby. Without asking questions, the settlers shot and wounded one and killed another. A third escaped. Those individuals happened to be Penobscots, not Ammoscoggins. A second raid occurred soon after; Wabanakis attacked the Wakely farm at Falmouth, killing six family members, carrying off a young girl, and setting fire to the house and barn. The attack was not simply about revenge; it also demonstrated the Wabanakis' increased frustration with encroachment. John Wakely's farm was among the first built on the north side of the Presumpscot River near John Phillips's sawmill; both encroached on lands where Wabanaki leaders Warrabitta and her brother Skitterygusset and their extended family had lived, farmed, and fished.[13]

Farther south, the Sacos might not have become involved in the conflict at all, but for an incident in late summer of 1675. English sailors came upon a native woman with a small child in a canoe, and in a brutally racist prank, decided to flip the canoe to see if native children, like wild animals, could swim at birth. The infant sank to the bottom of the river. Distraught, the mother dived and finally recovered the child, escaping back to her village. But the next day, the child died. The woman and child were the wife and son of Squando, the powerful sachem or priest of the Sacos. Squando lived along the lower Saco River, was influential among several native communities, and had, until the canoe incident, gotten along well with his white neighbors. But white settlers, including Thomas Doughty, were moving deeper into the Saco watershed, bringing unwanted changes.

Squando decided to ally with the hostile Ammoscoggins and the Pequackets, who inhabited the headwaters of the Saco. Together, they launched several brutal attacks in quick succession against settlements from Scarborough to Oyster River during September 1675.[14]

At the time, only about six thousand European colonists lived in Maine,[15] scattered sparsely along a hundred miles of coastline from Kittery to Pemaquid. The province could only field some seven hundred men through the local militias. Saco's comprised one hundred men,[16] including Thomas Doughty, under the command of Majors William Phillips and Brian Pendleton. Phillips owned the large mill complex on the south side of Saco Falls[17] and large tracts of the surrounding land. His home, surrounded by a tall palisade fence, served as the local garrison. Major Pendleton's garrison lay at Winter Harbor, current-day Biddeford Pool, some six or seven miles downstream on Saco Bay.

Local militias met up six or eight times per year to perform training exercises. Militiamen were required to bring their muskets, to use them competently, and to follow the orders of their superiors or risk fines and other punishments. Officers like Phillips and Pendleton were chosen for their wealth and social status, not their knowledge of military tactics. "Freemen," or smaller landowners like Thomas Doughty, comprised the rank and file.

Doughty was no longer the youthful recruit he'd been twenty-five years earlier in the Scottish Army. He was forty-five, and he now had a wife and three children under the age of eight. Moreover, the circumstances of war, and the enemy he and his neighbors were facing, could not have been more different from Cromwell and his Ironsides. However brief, Doughty's experience of war at Dunbar simply didn't translate.

The Wabanaki possessed infinitely deeper knowledge of the local terrain than the colonists, and because northern New England's heavily forested interior struck fear into the hearts and minds of white settlers, it provided excellent cover. Though their guns and ammunition were limited, the Wabanaki were unpredictable by the standards of European warfare. They were elusive, refusing to fully engage or to meet the colonial soldiers face-to-face. One Rhode Island settler described them as "wild Deare in the Wilderness," who "will Never stand to maintaine any fight, but come upon some of our out plantations & burne some of the remote houses & kill one or two & take there scalps and get away that our souldiers can rarely find any of them."[18] Former soldiers like Doughty learned quickly that marching in formation, pushes of pike, and firing volleys would be ineffectual against their current rivals. Marksmanship, flushing out a hidden enemy, and learning to conceal or barricade themselves were more appropriate to New World warfare.

Nor was religion a primary catalyst in this First Indian War; instead, land and conflicting visions for that land were paramount. The English vision proposed dammed rivers bustling with sawmills, cleared fields, and individually owned properties carefully delineated by fixed boundaries. The native vision proposed free-flowing streams for migrating, spawning fish; deer yards; deep forests and rotating agricultural fields with flexible boundaries; and shared sense of belonging and responsibility. The question was: could Native Americans and European settlers continue to trade and live in close proximity without stark cultural differences over land and water rights continually boiling over into armed conflict?

Soon after the raids at Pejepscot and Falmouth, violence spread south. Yet not all natives were belligerent toward their white neighbors. A Wabanaki named "Scossaway" warned residents near Saco Falls of an impending attack, so some left for Major Pendleton's at Winter Harbor. Fifty others made it to the Phillips's garrison on Sep-

In the Provinces of Maine and New Hampshire during the 1600s, European settlements hugged the coastline. Natives lived in, around, and beyond these areas, as they had before the Europeans arrived. Indigenous communities cannot be easily demarcated; the names here are meant to provide a broad sense of the Native peoples inhabiting New England's eastern frontier. Those communities were diverse, integrated, and often overlapping. (*Map by Andrew Comas*)

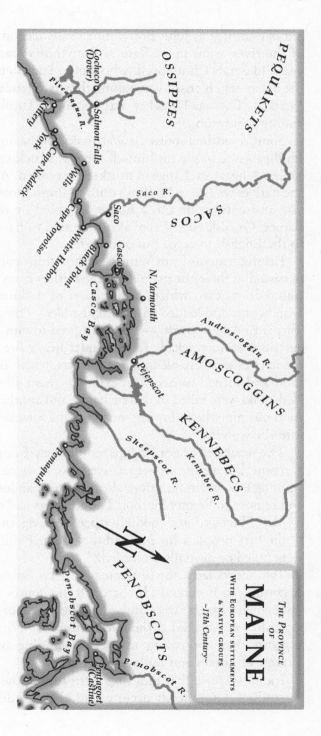

THE PROVINCE OF **MAINE**

WITH EUROPEAN SETTLEMENTS & NATIVE GROUPS

~*17th Century*~

PEQUAKETS

OSSIPEES

SACOS

AMOSCOGGINS

KENNEBECS

PENOBSCOTS

Cocheco (Dover)

Piscataqua R.

Kittery

Salmon Falls

York

Cape Neddick

Wells

Saco R.

Saco

Cape Porpoise

Winter Harbor

Black Point

Casco

Casco Bay

N. Yarmouth

Androscoggin R.

Pejepscot

Sheepscot R.

Kennebec R.

Pemaquid

Penobscot Bay

Penobscot R.

Pentagoet (Castine)

tember 18, just as John Bonython's residence, on the opposite bank of the river, went up in flames. Bonython's granddaughter, eight-year-old Sarah Churchwell, who would later figure prominently in the Salem witch crisis, was among those who escaped to the Phillips garrison. Thomas Doughty and his young family were most likely among them, too.

Soon, a sentinel spotted a Wabanaki combatant, and when Major Phillips came to see for himself, he was struck in the shoulder by a bullet. A heavy exchange of musket fire ensued. About an hour later, the natives set fire to Phillips's outbuildings: those inside watched as saw and corn mills and a house occupied by tenants went up in flames. Outside, the Wabanakis were said to have called mockingly to the English to come put out the fire.[19]

Reinforcements from Winter Harbor didn't come. And the natives persisted in their efforts to drive the settlers from the garrison. They found an ox cart, which, under cover of darkness, they barricaded with boards and loaded with combustibles—"birch rinds pitchwood Turpentine and powdr"—and attempted to ram a hole through the garrison's stout stockade fence. Under heavy fire from the garrison, the natives were unable to guide the cart, which became stuck in the mud and turned to one side, exposing them all to musket fire. Six Wabanaki were killed in this exchange and another fifteen wounded. At about nine the following morning, the attackers finally withdrew into the woods.

The wounded Major Phillips sent for help from Major Pendleton's garrison, but again, no help arrived. So, because the colonists were running low on ammunition, all agreed to abandon Phillips's garrison and remove to Winter Harbor. The attackers had managed to kidnap a "Mrs. Hitcock," and to kill five people navigating up the Saco, but of the fifty people who endured the raid at Phillips's garrison, none were killed or mortally wounded.[20]

Two weeks later, the settlement at Saco Falls was gutted by fire. According to Reverend Hubbard, all the houses that lay "above the Fisher-mans Stages" were burned.[21] The stages, or shacks for processing fish, were located at the river's mouth at Winter Harbor, which suggests that everything upriver—including both Phillips's and Doughty's homes and mills—were burned.

It's no surprise that mill sites were among the first to be "fired." Sawmills did not merely occupy land, they cut deeply into the landscape and into the core values of Wabanaki culture. They destroyed forests, diminished habitat for wild game, and dammed rivers, stopping annual runs of salmon, alewives, herring, and shad. Wabanakis depended heavily on the ecosystems that mills altered, and they watched as mills crept further inland along rivers and streams. Moreover, the Wabanaki knew that colonists depended heavily on the mills; without them, ships, settlements, and garrisons were virtually impossible. It's unlikely that Thomas Doughty fully understood this dynamic when he first came to New England. But now he was forced to recognize that even his small operation at Swan Pond was an affront to his native neighbors.

The Saco Falls raid was frightening enough to force Thomas and Elizabeth Doughty to flee with their three small children: six-year-old Elizabeth; Margaret, who was probably four; and Joseph, two. Yet Winter Harbor proved no more secure than Saco. Its only advantage was its location on Saco Bay, which enabled rapid escapes by sailboat. An expeditionary force from Dover, Portsmouth, and Kittery, under the command of Major Richard Waldron of Cocheco, was ordered to reinforce the troops at Saco and Scarborough. Waldron was the regional commander and a person of significant stature in Piscataqua and the entire northern frontier. A Puritan, he owned a prosperous sawmill and trading operation at Cocheco, held the favor of the Massachusetts Bay government, and served as a government magistrate.

Waldron could be a formidable enemy, ruthless in dealing with those who challenged his authority. In 1662, the inhabitants of Dover petitioned to have three Quaker women removed from the community for preaching and suggesting practices antithetical to Dover's Puritan First Church. Waldron responded by invoking the Cart and Whip Act, a legal, but brutal, punishment:

> To the constables of Dover, Hampton, Salisbury, Newbury, Rowley, Ipswich, Wenham, Linn, Boston, Roxbury, Dedham ... every one of you are required ... to take these vagabond Quakers ... and make them fast to the cart's tail, and driving the cart through your several towns, to whip their naked backs, not exceeding ten stripes apiece on each of them, in each town; and so to convey them from constable to constable, till they are out of this jurisdiction.[22]

Waldron's order was issued on December 22, in especially frigid weather. According to a contemporary account, "Now in a very cold Day, the Deputy Walden at Dover, caused these women to be stripp'd naked from the Middle upward, and tied to a Cart, and then whipt them."[23]

In the wake of the Wabanaki raids on Saco and Scarborough, Waldron moved east with his troops to assist the terrified settlers. But he and his forces carried out their mission reluctantly. As he wrote in a letter to his superiors at Boston:

> Neither My self nor Capt Davis nor any pty I sent out tho in those pts I had 120 Souldiers could ever see an Indian. Therefore . . . the little hopes wee had of meeting with ye enemy who As soon as ever they discovered a pty of Souldiers in one place fled to another & by Reason of ye Vast Inconveniences Attending a march in that Country ocationed by many rivers Marshes & c. I thought it most prudente to Contracte ye people into as small a Compasse as may be in those towns & there make some fortifications to defend themselves.[24]

Waldron left sixty soldiers stationed among the three settlements of Falmouth, Scarborough, and Saco—barely sufficient to maintain the garrisons. He brought the remaining forces back with him to Wells, York, and Kittery, instructing them to "garrison themselves for yr own defence." Doughty and his family likely departed for Wells at that time.

Doughty's two close friends and fellow Dunbar prisoners, James Oare and Henry Brown, lived together at Wells. Doughty had partnered with Oare in several lumber contracts, and Oare and Brown, along with a Worcester Scot named Robert Stewart, ran a sawmill at Wells, near the head of tide of the Cape Porpoise River, today known as the Mousam. In 1675, this mill—and perhaps another nearby—belonged to millwright Henry Sayword, of York.[25]

Doughty and his family may have stayed at a Wells garrison, or may have moved in with Oare and Brown for a time. It's probable that Doughty rented a small dwelling at Wells from Sayword or someone else. Just prior to the end of the war in 1677, the Wells

Militia Committee awarded "Thomas Dowtey" a little over £3 as: "Common Arrers ffor Souldiers Charges of the Late warre Granted and Allowed by the Comittee of Millitia of Wells from the first Begininge of the Late Indian warre vnto the first September 1677."[26] The same notice awarded Oare and Brown a single payment, as though for a household, suggesting the payments were for billeting soldiers.

During 1675, attacks and raids continued up and down the coast. The severity and proximity of the attacks caused constant anxiety for the colonists. At Oyster River, they cut particularly close to the bone for Doughty. Natives burned two houses belonging to the Chesleys, Doughty's former neighbors. They burned five or six more houses in the area, including the house and corn-filled barn of Captain John Wincoll, a mill owner to whom Doughty had supplied lumber. William Roberts, from whom Doughty had purchased his first piece of land, and his son-in-law were both killed during the raids.[27] And "a good old Man whose Name was Beard" was also killed; attacking Indians "cut off his Head and set it upon a Pole in Derision."[28] This man was likely William Beard, brother to Thomas Beard, the carpenter under whose direction Doughty and other servants had built Valentine Hill's sawmill at Oyster River.

On October 9, "The Body of Winter-harbour Houses were fired by the Enemy; three Men slain, and one Woman carried away."[29] Shortly thereafter, Major Brian Pendleton abandoned the effort to maintain a garrison there.

One week later, Newichiwannock, the site of Doughty's failed attempt to run the Great Works Mill, was attacked. Roger Plaisted and George Broughton wrote a desperate missive to Colonel Waldron at Cocheco from nearby Salmon Falls on October 16:

> These are to inform you, that just now the Indians are engaging us with at least one hundred Men, and have slain four of our Men already . . . Sir, if ever you have any Love for us, and the Country, now shew yourself with Men to help us, or else we are all in great Danger to be slain, unless our God wonderfully appear for our Deliverance. They that cannot fight, let them pray; Nought else, but I rest, Yours to serve you, Roger Plaisted, George Broughton.[30]

Waldron and his reinforcements didn't show. Plaisted survived the attack but was killed the next day as he and twenty soldiers left the garrison to bury the dead from the previous day's raid.

"These Outrages thus daily committed, filled all the Plantations about Pascataqua with Fear and Confusion," wrote Hubbard, describing how it must have felt to be under the constant threat of violence. "Scarce any Place, where there was not either Reason for some to complain of the Loss of their Friends, or burning of their Houses. . . . All the Inhabitants in those Parts in general, were alarmed to stand upon their Guard."[31]

The brutality of the attacks was recounted with hair-raising detail throughout frontier towns and villages, which heightened colonists' anxiety and encouraged them to see their former neighbors as "savages." Not only was Beard's head placed on a pole at Oyster River, at Cape Neddick, the Wabanakis "dashed out the Brains of a poor Woman that gave suck," wrote Hubbard, and then "nayled the young Child to the dead Body of its Mother, which was found sucking in that rueful Manner, when the People came to the Place."[32] But atrocities were practiced on both sides. When fishermen brought two native captives from Maine to the constable in Marblehead, women leaving a Sabbath meeting refused to let them or their captors pass. Instead, deposed one of the fishermen, "with stones, billets of wood, and what else they might, [the women] made an end of these Indians. . . . We found them with their heads off and gone, and their flesh in a manner pulled from their bones."[33]

On the eastern front, the natives took the upper hand; between June and November 1675, the Wabanakis killed or captured some 150 colonists between the Kennebec and Piscataqua.[34] But both sides in the struggle had abandoned their crops to wage war, so the impending winter promised shortages all around. Colonel Waldron wrote to Boston that "psons being fforced to fforsake yr Plantations and leave their Corn & Cattle to ye enemy doth portend Inevitable want & c. to ensue unless god by his extraordinary providence doe prevent."[35] At that time, some twenty English families who had lived along the coast from Falmouth to Saco left Maine for Salem.[36] Doughty, his family, and his friends Brown and Oare stayed on at Wells.

By December, the raids on both sides had stopped. "The Snow being found generally in those Woods four foot thick on the tenth of December," as Hubbard remembered, forced an English expedition to abandon its effort to roust the Ossipees and Pigwackets from the interior.[37]

Circumstances for the combative Indians were probably very dire, also. They had harvested little corn, they had spent much of their precious powder and shot in warfare, and they had little with which to procure game during the long winter ahead. So in January 1676, facing the prospect of a prolonged winter, they agreed to meet with Major Waldron at Cocheco to discuss an end to the hostilities. According to Hubbard, "The depth of the Snow, and Sharpness of the Cold were so Extream, that the Indians in those Parts were so pinched therewith, that being hunger-starved, they began to sue for Peace."[38] Any agreement from that meeting appears to have been temporary.

Farther south, the war continued, but it wasn't going well for King Philip's legions. By the summer of 1676, some three thousand Native American men, women, and children had been lost. The English had sold hundreds more captives into slavery. On August 2, the English captured Metacom's wife and young son, whom they sold into slavery in Bermuda. Metacom himself was at last killed on August 12, 1676, and his severed head—along with those of two other native combatants—was displayed at Plymouth Fort for all to see. Revenge and brutality were common currencies for natives and colonists alike.

Many of the native survivors of the southern war, hoping to escape English justice, left to find sanctuary among New Hampshire's Pennacooks. Native communities in Maine and New Hampshire were divided; some remained hostile, while others, like the Pennacooks, had remained neutral.

By September 1676, attacks on the northern frontier had also waned. Nevertheless, the Massachusetts government engaged Waldron, along with Captains William Hathorne, Joseph Sill, and Charles Frost to find and capture all the hostile Indians hiding among nonbelligerent communities. On September 6, 1676, Major Waldron invited the Pennacooks to a feast at Cocheco under the guise of peace negotiations. A large number arrived, including many from the Wamesit, Narragansett, Nipmuc, and Wampanoag communities. But only twenty were armed, so Hathorne, Sill, and their men easily surrounded them. Waldron then addressed the group, telling them "what must be done" but assuring them that the "Innocent should not be damnified."[39] He then proceeded to take "80 fighting men & 20 old men" and "250 women & children" into custody. Waldron appears to have sent most to Boston for judgment—including nearly all 250 women and children. He did, however, recruit ten of the captives to fight for the colonists and sold several others into slavery. According to Puritan historian Hubbard, of those sent to Boston, seven or eight individuals were hanged. The rest, including many women and children, were "sent into other Parts of the World, to try the Difference between the Friendship of their Neighbours here, and their Service with other Masters elsewhere."[40] Once again, the English resorted to selling undesirables into slavery abroad as a solution to problems they faced at home. For the Wabanaki, the incident at Cocheco represented the kind of betrayal for which Waldron became infamous—an action which they never forgot.

The Massachusetts government appears to have had great faith in Major Waldron's ability to manage both war and peace. They continued to trust him with peace negotiations on the northern front. He met with native representatives twice during 1677, and both meetings resulted in further violence.

On July 1, 1677, the Kennebec sachem Deogenes Madoasquarbet wrote to Governor John Leverett to express the Kennebecs' point of view. They had brought white prisoners to peace talks with Waldron for a prisoner exchange, but once again, he betrayed them:

> governor of boston this is to let you understand how Major Walldin served us we cared 4 prisners abord we would fain know whither you did give such order to kill us for bringing your prisners is that your fashing to com & mke pse & then kill us we are afraid you will do so agen Major Waldin do lye we were not minded to kill no body Major Waldin . . . gave us drink & when we were drunk killed us if it had not a bin for this falt you had your prisners long ago . . . Major Waldin have bin the cause of killing all that have bin kiled this sommer.[41]

Madoasquarbet argued that, rather than working for peace, Waldron had in fact prolonged hostilities by his double-dealing with the natives. Waldron likely had some doubts about the Wabanakis' sincerity; but the natives, in turn, had plenty of concrete reasons for not trusting Waldron.

It took representatives from New York and Governor Andros, whom the Wabanaki saw as more neutral and diplomatic, to iron out a peace agreement on the northern frontier. In July and August 1677, Andros's commissioners Anthony Brockholls, Matthias Nicholls, and Caesar Knapton met at Pemaquid with Kennebec leaders Moxus and Madoasquarbet. Massachusetts agreed to let the New Yorkers negotiate in their place, and the Kennebec sachems worked hard to bring the reluctant Squando of Saco into the agreement. The parties agreed to cease raids and violence and to exchange prisoners on both sides.

The terms of the prisoner exchanges were dictated at a later meeting at Casco in April 1678. There, Major Nicholas Shapleigh of Kittery and Captains Champernowne and Fryer convened with Squando and other sachems to ratify the Treaty of Casco. The treaty stipulated that captives on both sides were to be turned over without ransom, and that white settlers could return to the homes and towns they had been driven from during the war. They could not, however, expand their settlements. And each white family was required to provide the natives with a peck of corn annually, except for Major Phillips of Saco, who was required to contribute a bushel. White settlers likely viewed this demand as a form of "rent" or "tribute" to the Wabanaki. But as Lisa Brooks has pointed out, corn contributions were standard features of both deeds and treaties and were similar to the annual contributions that native families were expected to make to their own communities. By demanding that the settlers contribute annual quotas of corn, the treaty acknowledged that they belonged to a collective community and had responsibilities toward it, as did their native counterparts.[42]

As a result of the war, 260 white settlers in Maine either lost their lives or were carried into captivity by the Indians, never to return.[43] Mills, trading posts, homes, barns, and other structures up and down the coast were burned, cattle and livestock slaughtered, and livelihoods interrupted or destroyed. The cost to native communities is largely unknown, though it's clear they lost many to combat and to malnutrition during the long winters. Still, say scholars Emerson Baker and John Reid, "The Wabanakis effectively won the northern extension of King Philip's War and remained a serious military threat for decades afterwards."[44]

Yet, according to Hubbard, the northern war need not have been
fought at all, had the government of Massachusetts made a greater
effort to monitor and control colonist-native relations in Maine:

> It is reported by some of the Inhabitants of Kennibeck,
> lately fled, or rather driven from thence, that about five Years
> since some English-men were slain by the Amoroscoggin In-
> dians up Pegypscot River, that runs into Kennibeck; but it was
> concealed by the wicked Traders of those Parts, for fear of dis-
> covering their wicked Manner of trading with the Heathen;
> which if it had been duly enquired into when it was first done,
> much of what followed might have been prevented.[45]

Without doubt, the English settlers' "wicked Manner of trading"
drove a wedge between white and native communities. But other issues added to the tensions. Certainly, increasing incursions of settlers
into the Wabanaki's most prized hunting, fishing, and agricultural
areas created tensions, as did the Massachusetts Bay government's decision to treat the eastern natives as hostile and to confiscate their
guns. Early on, Thomas Gardner had warned that the violence on
the eastern front was caused "by our owne Acctings," and that "Indianes in these parts did never appear dissatisfied until their Armes
wear Taken Away."[46]

Another letter from ten sachems to Governor Leverett expresses
their grievances and their understanding that English bias against
them was a catalyst for the conflict:

> gov of boston this is to let you understand, how we have
> bin abused. . . . if the wolf kill any of your cattel you take away
> our gons for it . . . if we brek a tobarko pip they will prisson
> us becaus there was war at naragans you come here when we
> were quiet & took away our gons & mad prisners of our chief
> sagamore & that winter for want of our gons there was severall
> starved we count it kild . . . now we hear that you say you will
> not leave war as long as on engon is in the country we are
> owners of the country & it is wide and full of engons & we
> can drive you out but our desire is to be quiet.[47]

English courts, the letter implies, were particularly harsh on the Wabanaki simply for being "Indian." But the missive points to an issue
much larger than weapons or court cases: English settlers' pervasive

ethnic bias. The sachems complain that the Massachusetts Bay government views them not as discrete communities or as individuals but as a monolith: a stubborn obstacle in the way of English domination. On the eastern front, the ethnic war was one of the Puritan's own design.

Thomas and Elizabeth Doughty and their children managed to survive the First Indian War by moving from Saco to Wells, some twenty miles south. There, they had friends who helped them find shelter and work. It couldn't have been easy; families from as far north as Pemaquid had converged on Wells and Kittery, and food was extremely scarce. But while Saco and towns to the north burned, Wells remained secure.

Once the Treaty of Casco was signed, many white settlers, including the Doughtys, were optimistic enough to return to lands they'd formerly inhabited and rebuild. For the next decade, the Wabanaki and whites in the Saco region managed uneasy, but mostly peaceful, relations.

For the Doughtys, it was a busy decade. In 1678, Elizabeth's father, Nicholas Bully, died in Boston, failing to mention or acknowledge Elizabeth in his will. Elizabeth's life at the time was more than likely consumed with her own nuclear family. In the span of five years, from 1678 through 1682, she gave birth to four children—Benjamin, James, Patience, and Abigail—for a total of seven.

Thomas's lumber business continued to grow, as local court and town records show. In 1678, he once again began working for himself.[48] In 1682, he was billed five pounds in taxes on his sawmill at Saco, money that was to support the cost of maintaining Fort Loyal at Casco, including arms, ammunition, men, and provisions.[49] Clearly, the late war and the prospects for future conflict remained on the minds of Maine's white inhabitants.

Doughty also faced—and initiated—several lawsuits that suggest business was brisk. In 1678, he sued Henry Sayword, withholding more than twenty thousand feet of boards; in 1685, he was ordered to pay Richard Palmer of York the equivalent of eight English pounds in merchantable boards; and in 1686, he confessed in court that he owed Captain Sylvanus Davis 14,500 feet of merchantable boards.[50]

Although they had once again begun living as neighbors, Native Americans and colonists continued to have uneasy relations. In August 1681, magistrates at Wells expressed alarm at the growing incidences of drunkenness among the Indians. Contrary to law, whites had been proffering spirits to natives, which the court record declared was "greatly to the dishonour of god & hazarding of the lives & Estates of his Majestys subjects." Authorities were so alarmed that they threatened draconian punishment for anyone found guilty of giving liquor to natives:

> If any person or persons shall presume to sell or give, or lett any Indean have any rume, brandy, spirits or any strong Lyquors, wine, strong beare . . . or any kind of strong drinke, directly or Indirectly, they shall forfitt their whoole Estate . . . & the person or person to bee keept in pryson, without baile or Manprise, for one whoole yeare.[51]

Magistrates knew only too well that alcohol had helped fuel the First Indian War, at least on the eastern front. Traders like Thomas Purchase had used spirits to weaken natives' bargaining power, and military men like Major Waldron had used them to gain an advantage in conflict negotiations. The Wabanaki resented these tactics mightily. In the wake of the war, English authorities had become more fearful and more diligent in seeking to prevent such abuses.

Yet there were other sources of friction. Magistrates at the same court session noted the "bould Attempts of the Indeans in killing & wounding of severall Cattle this present weeke at Wells, which gives us good grounds to suspect that they intend some further Mischeefe." More than likely, the Indians were protecting their cultivated fields from intruding cattle. Nevertheless, the court prescribed that: "all Traine souldgers, & others of the Inhabitants are required every Lords day, to Carry their armes, with Ammunition to the Meeteing house for their defence & safety." Ordering colonists to carry their weapons to Sabbath meetings shows just how concerned local magistrates were for the community's safety.

The tension abated for a while, but it didn't go away. By 1685, English-Wabanaki relations had again grown contentious. In August of that year, magistrates convened a special court session at Saco to deal with "the frequent drunkenness of the Indeans, which have been seene to ly Drunke almost at every doore." After "diligent Inquiry," they couldn't pin the problem on any specific members of the community. So authorities vowed that "those houses nearest Adjaycent to any Indeans lying in any such drunken Capacity, shall be Accounted the very places where those Indeans have received there Lyquors," and that the owners would be punished. The court also declared "that not any powder shall be traded by any English with the Indeans, more then law alloweth, upon poenulty the law expresseth." Their subsequent pronouncement is even more chilling:

> It is ordered by this Court, that not any person or persons whatsoever shall desert the towns or Garrisons, upon forfeiture of their Estates to the Towne . . . unless they have liberty under the hands of Cheefe Commander & the Militia of sd Townes.[52]

Relations between colonists and natives were at a flashpoint. If Saco's white settlers had to be ordered not to desert their homes, military responsibilities, or the local garrison, it suggests that some had already done so, and others were openly considering doing the same. Clearly, for some families, the lack of security at Saco had become untenable, and the only thing preventing them from fleeing south were threats and admonitions from local officials. Saco residents like the Doughtys were faced with a stark choice: forfeiting their properties to the town, or potentially losing those properties—and their lives—to Wabanaki ire.

Maine court records during the 1680s show that, despite the hostilities during King Philip's War, colonists and Wabanakis in frontier settlements continued to trade with, and live close to, one another. But the late war meant that minor incidents could no longer be dismissed as simple misunderstandings between white and native individuals; instead, they became like sparks and tinder with the potential to rekindle another disastrous war.

In May 1688, the towns of Saco and Cape Porpoise (Kennebunkport) unified, and selectmen, constables, and clerks were chosen. "Thos. Doubty" was appointed town treasurer, which suggests his stature and reputation in town were growing. But that is the last record we have confirming Doughty's presence in Saco. Indeed, from that meeting to the year 1717, no vital records or town meeting minutes for Saco or Cape Porpoise survive.

That vacuum belies a series of catastrophic events for Doughty and the vast majority of white settlers in Maine. It began a year earlier, when Governor Andros decided that the land beyond the Kennebec belonged, not to France, but to England. Andros ordered the Frenchman Jean-Vincent, Baron de St. Castin, to abandon the fort and trading post at Pentagoet, near the mouth of the Penobscot. A year later, in the spring of 1688, Andros arrived by ship to enforce his order. St. Castin fled into the woods, and Andros and his men sacked St. Castin's home on Penobscot Bay.

But St. Castin was well connected. A French nobleman and army officer, he had married Pidianske, also known as Marie-Mathilde: the daughter of Penobscot sachem Madockawando. St. Castin was adopted into the Penobscot community and became influential among native communities nearby. He began to muster support among those communities for joint French and Indian raids on English settlements up and down the coast.

The natives needed little coaxing. They had already begun to complain that English settlers were ignoring promises made under the Treaty of Casco. Settlers had expanded their territory, particularly near North Yarmouth; they were failing to pay their promised annual contributions of corn; and they were allowing their livestock to trample and devour the Indians' crops.

In September 1688, Saco once again became a flashpoint for these disagreements. Netombonet, the successor of Squando, and Robin Doney, another local native, complained that white settlers were blocking the Saco River with large nets, seizing a key source of food for the natives: at least a dozen species of migrating fish. When cattle invaded the natives' fields and began eating their corn, the Indians shot them.

Benjamin Blackman, the local justice of the peace who had built a mill on the Saco's east side, was persuaded that the problems could be eliminated by simply rounding up a few Wabanaki troublemakers. He managed to capture fifteen to twenty, including Robin Doney and Hopehood, who had fought the English in King Philip's War, and sent them to Boston for punishment.[53] Governor Andros, who took a more conciliatory position toward the natives than had Governor John Leverett and Massachusetts Bay, freed the twenty natives, believing that Blackman and the Maine colonists had used them too severely.

Even so, Wabanaki reprisals began. At Sheepscot, the natives destroyed houses and a garrison; farther south, at Winter Harbor and Cape Porpoise, Indians kidnapped the Barrow and Busey families.[54] Natives also burned the mills at Mousam, destroying the livelihoods of Dunbar Scots Henry Brown and James Oare, though the two Scots survived.[55]

One year later, events in England stirred yet another conflict in the colonies. The Glorious Revolution removed James II, an unpopular king and convert to Catholicism, in favor of the protestant William of Orange and James II's protestant daughter Mary. William and Mary were crowned in February 1689. The news encouraged colonists in Boston, who, in April, launched the Boston Revolt to remove Sir Edmund Andros as governor of the Dominion of New England. Former Massachusetts Bay governor Simon Bradstreet replaced Andros.

Tensions between the English and the French-Wabanaki allies continued to simmer. But soon, the incidents became part of a larger conflict, waged in both Europe and America. In May 1689, England, under King William III, and the League of Augsburg declared war on France, under Louis XIV. France was trying to expand its power, seeing a potential advantage with the uncertain future of the Spanish throne. In America, England had been trying to get a leg up on the lucrative fur trade with Native Americans, which French colonists had largely dominated. Long-term disagreements over land and Indian loyalties composed a bitter brew. The English colonies of New England and New York along with the Iroquois plotted against the French and their native allies, including the Wabanaki.

Some colonists remained optimistic, believing the unrest would remain localized. On June 7, 1689, some native women at Cocheco asked to stay at Major Waldron's garrison for the night. The request wasn't unusual; natives had lived in and around Piscataqua alongside white settlers for decades and were regulars at Waldron's trading post. The Waldron family likely knew the women well and so permitted them to enter. But while the family slept, the women opened the gates to allow Wabanaki men inside. These men had not forgotten

Waldron's treachery a dozen years earlier, nor his double-dealing with them as a trader and judicial magistrate. The Wabanaki entered the house and awakened the eighty-year-old Waldron, who picked up his sword and tried to fight them off. But he was subdued and tied to a chair placed upon a table. The intruders instructed his family to prepare dinner. Several natives slashed Waldron across the chest with their knives, stating "I cross out my account," in apparent retribution for unfair trading practices. Finally, as he fainted from loss of blood, one Wabanaki held Waldron's own sword under him as he fell over and died.

The natives burned Waldron's mill as well as five houses at Cocheco, killed twenty-three inhabitants, and took another twenty-nine captives, whom they marched to Canada.[56] One of these was Waldron's daughter, a Mrs. Lee, who was later rescued and offered intelligence to Benjamin Church and his forces.[57]

In July, another skirmish took place at Saco. Wabanaki warriors shot four young men tending to their horses. When an armed group of twenty settlers went out to bury the men, the Indians attacked again and were driven into the woods. But they returned shortly afterward with reinforcements and killed six more settlers, forcing the rest back into their fort.[58]

Thomas Doughty and his family were once again caught in the midst of the violence, and they had seen and experienced enough. They made the difficult decision to move farther afield to Massachusetts proper, where they joined scores of refugee families who had already abandoned Maine altogether.

At nearly sixty years of age, Doughty was once again forced into exile; this time, he was compelled to leave behind the home, mill, and business that he and his family had struggled to build, rebuild, and hold onto for more than twenty years, through Native attacks, changes in government, and challenges to ownership. Brought to the New England frontier against his will, he now had to abandon it in the wake of violence incited by forces beyond his control. Even on the remote frontier it was impossible to escape the larger disputes that roiled Europe and America in the late seventeenth century: England vs. France; Protestantism vs. Catholicism; and the struggles brought on by colonization, testing whether peoples of vastly different cultures could hope to coexist.

Chapter Nine

REFUGEES

Hell is empty and all the devils are here.
   —William Shakespeare, *The Tempest*

THE DOUGHTYS had been prudent, or lucky, to leave Maine when they did. The year 1690 proved a grim one for the New England frontier. In March, Joseph-François Hertel de la Fresnière led a band of sixty French and Wabanakis, whom Cotton Mather described as "Half Indianized French or half Frenchified Indians," to attack Salmon Falls, New Hampshire. They burned homes and mills, killed thirty-four, and captured fifty-four, mostly women and children, marching them through thick woods and snow to Canada.

Among the captives was former Dunbar prisoner John Key, who had lived—and possibly served—at Oyster River with Thomas Doughty and eventually settled at Newichawannock. Key's five-year-old son James was said to have been killed by the infamous Hopehood, or Wohawa, son of Kennebec sachem Robinhood, whose bitter resentment of white colonists may have been stoked when he served as a slave at Boston.[1] The older members of the Key family made it all the way to Quebec, where they remained prisoners at least until 1695.[2]

In May, Hertel and Baron de St. Castin led a much larger force of four hundred to five hundred French and Wabanakis to attack Fort Loyal at present-day Portland. The one hundred English remaining[3] at the fort were vastly outnumbered and were forced to surrender after a five-day siege. New Englanders to the south found the news especially distressing, since most of those who surrendered willingly after being promised quarter by the French were killed and left unburied on the spot. A small number were marched to Canada.

Yet the tragedy might have been prevented. John Hathorne and Jonathan Corwin—two influential magistrates who would figure prominently in the Salem witch trials—had traveled to Maine in April. Their job had been to assess defenses and recommend to the Massachusetts government how best to defend Maine's coastal settlements against French and Wabanaki forces. Shortly after they returned to report their findings, Captain Simon Willard, who had been stationed at Fort Loyal with sixty soldiers, received orders to depart, which he did: on the day before the attack.[4] By drawing off troops at Fort Loyal, the Massachusetts Bay government itself was at least partly to blame for the disastrous loss of life, loss of the fort, and the virtual abandonment of the Maine coast north of Wells. By November 1690, only four English colonial towns remained in Maine: Wells, York, Kittery, and the Isles of Shoals.

When they first moved to Massachusetts-proper, the Doughty family probably settled at Boston or Malden.[5] Thomas was sixty years old, Elizabeth, his wife, was in her late thirties, and their children ranged from seven to twenty years old. After August 1690, the large family lapsed into obscurity, at least as far as written records go, for nearly a decade. Their disappearance is symptomatic of people fleeing conflict, regardless of era. Losing their homes or properties is traumatic, but refugees typically also sacrifice livelihoods, social status, independence—their very identities. With little of value left, they rarely appear in court, probate, or even vital records, becoming, simply, the forgotten.

The Doughtys' disappearance corresponds with an especially turbulent time, dubbed by Cotton Mather "Decennium Luctuosum," or "Mournful Decade." Though Boston and nearby towns were more secure than Maine, life wasn't easy, especially with refugees pouring in from the east. Most of these families had left behind homes, occupations, and in many cases, the graves of family members killed in raids. Since land was already at a premium in the towns near Boston and Salem, most refugee families had little recourse but to work for others or to rely on their charity. Servitude was often the only recourse for youths who had lost one or both parents.

As refugees flooded south, Massachusetts militias sent soldiers north and east to the frontier. News of conflict and deaths dominated the public discourse. Despite the loss of Fort Loyal, some news was hopeful. In May, Major General Sir William Phipps sailed to Port Royal, Nova Scotia, with eight ships and eight hundred men, and found the Acadians as unprepared as the English at Fort Loyal had been. Phipps and his ships easily won and went on to destroy the French fort at the mouth of the St. John River. As part of the spoils of that trip, Phipps brought back a servant: the daughter of Baron de St. Castin and his Wabanaki wife, Pidianske. [6]

Emboldened by that success, Phipps and the Massachusetts government launched another expedition in October, this time to Quebec. Phipps sailed up the St. Lawrence and was to be supported by a land force of English and Iroquois from Connecticut and New York. The land contingent would be commanded by Fitz-John Winthrop, marching by way of Albany and Montreal. But Winthrop was delayed by lack of supplies, infighting, and disease. So he sent a much smaller force, led by Captain John Schuyler, northward. Schuyler managed to just reach the outskirts of Montreal before having to turn back.

Phipps met similar obstacles. Smallpox began spreading through his ships almost as soon as they departed Boston. Phipps's fleet arrived at Quebec and began bombarding the city, but they soon ran out of ammunition. He dispatched a small land force, but they found the city well-protected by its situation upon a hill and by French soldiers who had arrived from Montreal after Schuyler's failed attempt on that city. Eventually, Phipps's diminished force and hobbled ships were forced to withdraw, though they did manage to ransom some English captives before leaving. Said a member of the expedition: "Not ye Enimy but ye Almighty God himself did . . . frustrate our design . . . the Holy God send diseases (a malignant feaver & ye Small pox) into our Army."[7]

Phipps's and Fitz-John Winthrop's failures cast a pall over English colonies up and down the coast. To pay for the expedition, Massachusetts Bay had issued bonds that were to be repaid with plunder obtained by sacking Quebec, which was never taken. New York gGovernor Henry Sloughter noted that

> The whole country from Pemaquid to Delaware is extreamely hurt by the late ill managed and fruitless expedition to Canada, which hath contracted fourty thousand pounds debt and about a thousand men lost by sickness and shipwrack and no blow struck for want of courage and conduct in the Officers, as is universally said and believed.[8]

Back in Massachusetts, the same smallpox epidemic that had overtaken Phipps's fleet was raging on land. It afflicted 320 in Boston alone—a significant outbreak for a town of some 7,000—and was moving eastward: "It now unhappily spreads in several other places," stated New England's first newspaper, *Publick Occurrences, both Forreign and Domestick*, "among which our Garrisons in the East are to be reckoned some of the greatest sufferers."[9] The eastern frontier just couldn't catch a break; the Doughtys were indeed fortunate to have escaped when they did.

The newspaper also reported at length about the ongoing war in New York and Maine. But a second issue was never printed. Editor Benjamin Harris wrote that the English had mistreated French captives, and he published rumors about incest within the French royal family. Governor Bradstreet and his council weren't pleased; they banned the publication after the first edition.

Although eastern Massachusetts was largely outside the combative zone, its inhabitants channeled the fear and hysteria that their neighbors to the north and east experienced. The Reverend John Emerson related to Cotton Mather a series of events in Gloucester during summer of 1692. Residents of the town heard noises "as if men were throwing stones against the barn," and on several occasions saw individuals "who looked like Frenchmen" and "which look'd like an Indian, having on a blue coat," lurking about the houses, garrison, and swamps. After several skirmishes with these evasive individuals, the men from Gloucester failed to capture or kill a single one, so they requested help. Major Appleton of Ipswich sent sixty men to assist, but they, too, failed to shoot or capture any of the intruders. Mather's informant concluded "that *Glocester* was not alarumed last summer for above a fortnight together by real *French* and *Indians*, but that the *devil* and his agents were the cause of all the molestation which at this time befel the town." The notion that the devil was responsible for the many strange events occurring in the colony was taken seriously, and literally, by many New Englanders. Mather himself concluded that the "prodigious war" itself was in large part the work of "spirits of the invisible world upon the people of New-England."[10]

This atmosphere—epidemics, increasingly cold and volatile weather,[11] a summer drought,[12] attacks on frontier settlements, and the simmering anxiety caused by ongoing war—created fertile conditions for the most infamous event of the 1690s: the Salem witch crisis, during which scores were accused and twenty individuals were found guilty of witchcraft and executed. The center of the crisis was Salem Village, the rural area lying beyond the port of Salem Town. Andover, Amesbury, Gloucester, Topsfield, and other towns were involved, too. Because some two hundred individuals were accused of witchcraft in just eight months, the crisis touched virtually everyone in one way or another and consumed everyday life throughout Massachusetts, even in the midst of war.

While numerous disastrous events converged to bring about the witch hysteria, it was, at least in part, inspired by a refugee crisis.[13] A large proportion of those afflicted and accused had ties to Maine, either having lived there or having served in the militias. Even the judges had connections: most either owned land or had invested in sawmills in Maine or New Hampshire,[14] and, like the Doughtys, had sustained heavy financial losses as their lands became worthless and their mills went up in smoke.

Thomas Doughty and his family weren't directly involved in the witchcraft crisis, but it was all around them. Few families at the time could escape knowing both accusers and accused and becoming caught up in the panic. In fact, Doughty hailed from a culture where such events were even more prevalent. Scotland established witchcraft as a capital offense in 1563, and over the next 170 years, some 4,000 people, 84 percent of whom were women, were tried. Nearly one-third of those came from Lothian, the Lowland region where Doughty was likely raised.[15]

Two major witchcraft episodes had occurred in Scotland during Thomas's lifetime: from 1628 to 1631, just as he was born, and just before the Battle of Dunbar, from 1649 to 1650. The parallels of the latter episode to Salem are striking. Amid unusually cold weather, poor harvests, an outbreak of the plague, and an impending war, the ruling Kirk Party determined that God's wrath, not coincidence or bad luck, was behind the unfortunate events. So they passed the Witchcraft Act of 1649 and encouraged local church officials and congregations to actively seek out witches. This campaign resulted in some six hundred accusations and more than three hundred executions. If the Scots reaped any benefits at all from their loss at the Battle of Dunbar and Cromwell's occupation of Scotland, it was that witch hunts subsided, at least for a time.

Some forty years later, Thomas Doughty witnessed another such crisis—this time, an ocean away in Massachusetts. Once again, war, epidemics, and extreme weather formed the backdrop—or the impetus—for the upheaval. Men of influence were largely responsible for the war. But refugees and servants, those at the bottom of the social ladder, would become key catalysts for the witch crisis. Many were young girls traumatized by the Indian Wars in Maine. At least two were immediate neighbors of the Doughtys in Saco.

The crisis began when the Reverend Samuel Parris's nine-year-old daughter Betty and niece Abigail Williams were taken with "fits." The girls began to behave oddly: their limbs and bodies appeared to contort involuntarily; they felt sharp pains, like pinches or pinpricks, sensations of being choked, and at times, they couldn't talk. Tituba, the Parris's servant woman of native origin, said to be from "New Spain," was the first to be questioned about the girls' afflictions. When pressed by the examiner—Nathaniel Hawthorne's second great-grandfather, John—about what had caused Betty and Abigail's strange behavior, Tituba told quite a story: "The devil came to me and bid me serve him," she stated. He sometimes looked "like a hog and sometimes like a great dog," and she added that he "had a yellow bird," and "more pretty things that he would give me if I would serve him." The devil, she contended, had forced her to do evil to others under the threat of death, and she and two other witches performed evil acts at neighbors' houses. When asked how they got from house to house to perform their evil acts, Tituba answered that she and her companions would "ride upon stickes and are there presently."[16]

Once Tituba testified, other key accusers came forward. At least five of these young women were refugees from Maine; three of them were now servants in other families' households.

Abigail Hobbs, a rebellious teenager who likely lived through at least one Wabanaki attack at Falmouth, was accused and accuser both, naming seven others as witches. Perhaps most important, she linked events in Salem to the Maine frontier. When asked by examiners John Hathorne and Jonathan Corwin whether she had ever seen the devil, Hobbs volunteered that she had seen him once, "at the Eastward at Casko-bay." Given their own disastrous experiences on the frontier and their role in the Fort Loyal tragedy, Hathorn and Corwin likely felt bedeviled themselves. They had plenty of reason to find Abigail's testimony credible.[17]

Sarah Churchwell, from Saco, survived the attack on the Phillips garrison in 1675 along with the Doughtys, and like them, her family lost everything in the series of raids that year. Forced to flee to Marblehead, the Churchwells struggled financially. To help ease the family's difficulties, Sarah signed on as the servant of the elderly George Jacobs, Sr. She not only confessed as a witch herself—saving her own neck—but named six others, including Jacobs, her master.

Mercy Lewis lost both of her parents in a Wabanaki raid on Falmouth. She was a servant, first for the Reverend George Burroughs, and second, for Thomas Putnam of Salem Village. Thomas was the father of the afflicted Ann Putnam, Jr., who, at age 12, leveled more accusations than any other individual. Mercy Lewis was obviously traumatized by the loss of her parents and the goings-on in the Putnam household; she accused two men who had both resided in Maine—the Reverend George Burroughs, who was hanged, and John Alden, a merchant, sailor, and soldier who escaped—of practicing witchcraft.

Mercy Short, a fifteen-year-old orphaned servant, had been ransomed by Sir William Phipps at Quebec. Mercy had survived the brutal Salmon Falls raid of 1690, during which her father, mother, brother, and sister were killed. She and five other siblings were marched to Canada during the cold, wet New England spring. She witnessed—and likely recounted for Cotton Mather—the brutality of that march, including Hopehood's killing of young James Key; the torture of Robert Rogers; and the agony of Mary Plaisted, a mother forced to watch as her Wabanaki captor took her infant by the heels and swung the child against a tree. Under the protection of Mather, Short's accusations against individuals were never divulged.

Susanna Sheldon was also a refugee. She and her immediate family had survived the raid on the family garrison at Black Point on October 10–13, 1675, during which her uncle was killed. Susanna was two years old at the time. Her family moved from Black Point to Salem Village in 1688, as tensions with the Wabanakis began to boil over a second time. Her brother Godfrey joined the Salem militia and was killed in Maine during the summer of 1690. Her father William died in Salem in December 1691. Susanna's statements helped further twenty-four legal complaints against individuals including George Burroughs and the wealthy merchant from Jersey, Philip English.[18]

Several among the accused also had connections with Maine, particularly the Reverend George Burroughs, charged with being the ringleader of the witches. Burroughs's career illustrates the ongoing connections between Salem and the eastern frontier; he had ministered at Salem, as well as Casco, Black Point, and Wells, Maine.

John Alden, Jr., son of the Mayflower couple John Alden, Sr. and Patricia Mullins, was the son-in-law of Saco's wealthiest landowners, Major William and Bridget Phillips, whom Doughty knew well.

Doughty also had connections with the Towne sisters, Sarah Towne Cloyce, Mary Towne Easty, and Rebecca Towne Nurse, perhaps the most well-known of the accused witches. Peter Cloyce, with whom Doughty had served in the Wells militia[19] and on the infamous Woodman grand jury, had moved from Maine to Massachusetts during the First Indian War in 1675. There, he met and married the widow Sarah Towne Bridges and settled in Salem Village. Her sister, Rebecca Towne Nurse was arrested and charged with witchcraft on March 23, 1692. When Sarah attended church the following Sunday, the Reverend Samuel Parris, whose daughter and niece were suffering with fits, declared that witchcraft had "broken out here." Incensed at the likely reference to her sister, Sarah left the meetinghouse and slammed the door. On April 11, Sarah herself was accused. Shortly thereafter, her sister Mary Towne Easty was arrested. Of the three Towne sisters, Sarah Cloyce was the only one to escape the gallows.

Witchcraft trial judges and associates had also suffered financial losses on the eastern frontier, but most were wealthy and weren't left destitute. Samuel Sewall, an associate of the court, owned sawmills at Salmon Falls that were destroyed in the 1690 raid. John Hathorne owned land in Maine, and Jonathan Corwin owned a sawmill at Cape Porpoise (Kennebunkport), managed by his brother-in-law and Hathorne's brother, Eleazar Hathorne.[20] When Saco and Cape Porpoise merged in 1688, Thomas Doughty was elected treasurer, and so he undoubtedly knew both Corwin and Eleazar Hathorne. Troubles on the frontier didn't keep Corwin from continuing to invest in Maine. As late as 1692, Corwin purchased a two-hundred-acre farm in Wells from Doughty's close friend, James Oare.[21]

The witch hysteria, which had begun in early spring of 1692, continued throughout the long, parched New England summer. In recounting one of the darkest days of the crisis, August 19, diarist and court associate Samuel Sewall shows that seeds of doubt had begun to germinate:

> This day [in the margin: Dolefull Witchcraft!] George Burrough, John Willard, Jno Procter, Martha Carrier and George Jacobs were executed at Salem, a very great number of Spectators being present. Mr. Cotton Mather was there. . . . All of them said they were inocent, Carrier and all. Mr. Mather says they all died by a Righteous Sentence. Mr. Burrough by his Speech, Prayer, protestation of his Innocence, did much to move unthinking persons, which occasions their speaking hardly concerning his being executed.[22]

The hangings were well attended, and well communicated by word-of-mouth afterward. By all accounts, the Reverend George Burroughs had given an especially moving speech just before his execution, which piqued the consciences of some among the "very great number" who came to witness the spectacle. Sewall tried to dismiss others' doubts as the response of "unthinking persons." Still, they must have made an impression, or he wouldn't have felt compelled to record them in his diary. Clearly, those seeds of doubt were spreading.

Shortly thereafter, the crisis began to fade. In early October, accusers and confessors began to recant their statements. Thomas Brattle, a wealthy, educated Boston merchant and member of the Royal Society, wrote a widely circulated letter charging that justice wasn't being equally served. Most individuals had been convicted simply upon accusation, he argued, while Mrs. Thatcher, the mother-in-law of Judge Corwin, had not. And while some of the accused spent months in prison, Hezekiah Usher, a wealthy merchant accused by Susannah Sheldon, was allowed to stay in a private house and eventually escape out of the province. Brattle also criticized chief judge William Stoughton, Massachusetts deputy governor, whom he said was "very zealous in these proceedings," and "impatient in hearing any thing that looks another way."[23]

On October 3, 1692, the most influential man in New England, Increase Mather, the father of Cotton Mather and the man who had had enormous influence in the makeup of the Massachusetts Bay government under its new charter, delivered a sermon entitled "Cases of Conscience Concerning Evil Spirits." That sermon questioned the use of spectral evidence in the trials and called for restraint: "to take away the life of any one, meerly because a *Spectre* or Devil, in a Bewitched or Possessed person does accuse them, will bring the Guilt of Innocent Blood on the Land." And, he contended, "It were better that Ten Suspected witches should escape, than that one Innocent Person should be Condemned."[24] But Mather's sermon had come too late for the twenty already put to death.

On October 12, Governor Phipps ordered a halt to both arrests and trials. Phipps was closely allied to the Mathers, but he had another motivation, as well: his wife, Lady Mary Phipps, had recently been accused as a witch, too.[25] Like many of those involved, the Phippses had deep connections to the Maine frontier: Sir William had not only led a naval attack on Acadia, he was born and raised in Nequasset (present-day Woolwich, Maine). Lady Mary Phipps was the daughter of Roger Spencer, a merchant and landowner in Maine who had been given the right to erect a sawmill at Saco Falls in 1653.

The specters themselves eventually began to dispute the rectitude of the convictions. On November 14, seventeen-year-old Mary Herrick confessed belatedly that, in addition to others, she had seen the specter of Mary Easty, who had been hanged on September 22. Herrick claimed that, on the eve of her execution, Easty's specter told her: "I am going upon the Ladder to be hanged for a Witch, but I am innocent, and before a 12 Month be past you shall believe it."[26]

One final episode occurred in the fall of 1693. Margaret Rule, another Saco refugee, had moved with her family to Boston in the 1680s.[27] There, Margaret had argued with a neighbor: a woman who had once been jailed for witchcraft. After the confrontation, Margaret experienced pinches, pinpricks, and contortions. Her Boston neighbor and pastor, Cotton Mather, took her under his care, urging the girl and her family not to press charges against the neighbor but to pray. She did. And her symptoms eventually disappeared. It was becoming clear to many New Englanders that death by hanging had been too potent a medicine for curing the society's ills.

As numerous scholars have argued, the witch crisis was symptomatic of a society under stress from war, loss of life and property, displacement, and climatic extremes. The Doughtys and their neighbors in Maine had suffered the brunt of these traumas. Many internalized the violence they witnessed, and while some, like Thomas and his family, seemed able to quietly go about rebuilding their lives, others, especially vulnerable girls and young women, struggled. Their afflictions and accusations took on greater weight as influential members of the community—Increase and Cotton Mather, Governor William Phipps, Samuel Sewall, John Hathorne, and Jonathan Corwin among others—were themselves challenged to make sense of the deluge of violence and loss.

The influx of families from the east exerted tremendous pressure on Salem and surrounding towns. In 1680, well before the beginning of the Second Indian War, Salem's selectmen noted that the town had sustained "greate losses by the [first] indian warr, togather with considerable losse since, and thereby many poore widows & fatherless children [now live] amonghts us."[28]

Land had become extremely scarce, too: from the arrival of hundreds of refugees, and from the dividing of family farms among the offspring of original owners. Farms in Essex County were growing smaller by the day. During the 1660s, the average Salem Village farm comprised 180 acres; by 1690, the average had fallen to 124 acres, and it continued to shrink throughout the decade. [29] Expanding outward to unsettled areas was largely unthinkable, given the ongoing war.

One exception involved the newly settled Salem End: present-day Framingham. In the wake of the witchcraft crisis, some members of affected families did move away from Salem Village to Salem End. Peter and Sarah Cloyce were among the first to leave in 1693, and several children and members of their extended family followed them. The new town was peopled with Cloyces, Bridges, Townes, and Nurses. By century's end, Salem End had attracted more than fifty former residents of Salem Village. [30]

In 1700, at the age of seventy, Thomas Doughty found opportunity once again, this time in Salem. He'd ultimately lost his home and land in Saco. But somehow, at the turn of the century, the aging Doughty put up seventy-odd pounds to purchase 200–250 acres on the far western edge of Salem—just south of the Salem Village boundary—from James Menzies, a Boston merchant. [31] Doughty's new land extended into Lynn, encompassing much of Humphrey's Pond (present-day Suntaug Lake). Today it lies mostly within the town of Peabody.

It's not clear where the money for this purchase came from. Yet, through experience, Doughty knew that land was critically important. So even though he'd sold and lost land on the New England frontier, it's likely that he and his family were laboring hard throughout the Mournful Decade to accumulate enough assets to purchase more, with the hope that, this time, they could hang onto it.

Land, it appears, was the consuming obsession of Doughty's life. Owning property conveyed both independence and social status; it helped ensure one's capacity to build a livelihood. But Thomas Doughty's connection with the land ran deeper still. He had experienced what it meant to be both an exile and a refugee; his relationship

Opposite: Property parcels in the Cedar Pond region of Salem in early 1700. An Essex deed shows that, on October 4 of that year, Thomas Doughty purchased James Menzies's property on the far southwestern side of Salem, surrounding Humphrey's Pond. Map by Sidney Perley appears in "The Cedar Pond Region, Salem, in 1700," *Essex Historical Collections*, 51(1915):23.

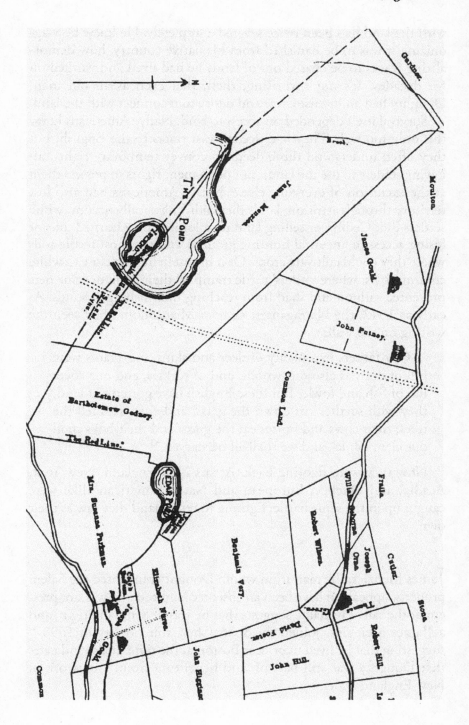

with the land had been twice severed completely. He knew how agonizing it was to be banished from his native country, how demoralizing it was to be chased out of lands he had lived and worked on for decades. It's not surprising, then, that even as an old man, Doughty had an intense drive and desire to reconnect with the land.

Survival itself depended on access to land. Native Americans knew this only too well. They had deeded vast tracts to the English, but they often understood those deeds to convey temporary rights, allowing settlers to use the lands, not permanent rights to possess them at the exclusion of everyone else.[32] Native Americans had also lost territory through attrition; lands they didn't physically occupy, white settlers did. Ceding or selling land to colonists, they learned, meant losing access to ancestral hunting grounds and the most fertile soils where they could cultivate crops. Or it meant living too close to white communities, where settlers' cattle trampled their corn, or seine nets prevented salmon and shad from reaching their fishing grounds. As early as 1642, the Narragansett sachem Miantonomo had seen the writing on the wall:

> Our fathers had plenty of deer and skins, our plains were full of deer, as also our woods, and of turkies, and our coves full of fish and fowle. But these English have gotten our land, they with scythes cut down the grass, and with axes fell the trees; their cows and horses eat the grass, and their hogs spoil our clam banks, and we shall all be starved.[33]

Now they were fighting back. Across New England, New York, Acadia, and Quebec, European and Native American alike were caught up in the same battle: fighting to retain land they saw as their own.

James Menzies, the man from whom Doughty purchased the Salem property, appears to have been an absentee landlord and was not present at the sale. His name suggests that he was of Scottish origin, and a "James Meinzies" joined the Scots Charitable Society in 1695,[34] suggesting that he lived in or near Boston at the time. It also indicates that Doughty was still part of, and benefiting from, a network of New England Scots.

The witchcraft hysteria eight years earlier may well have influenced Menzies' desire to sell. The men who served as his attorneys in the land transaction were Captain John Lloyd of Rumney Marsh, who had commanded a post at Saco in 1689 and was among those accused of witchcraft, and Stephen Williams of Roxbury. John Nurse, the son of Rebecca Nurse, who had been convicted and hanged, was a witness to the sale.

Curiously, less than a year after the purchase, Thomas Doughty sold one hundred acres of this land to John Nurse.[35] Even though Nurse had witnessed Doughty's purchase of the land from Menzies in October at seventy pounds, in March he purchased the smaller parcel from Doughty at eighty pounds plus twenty head of cattle: more than Thomas had purchased the entire 200–250 acres for. John Nurse may have already owed money to Doughty. It's also likely that he needed the extra land. His father, Francis, like Thomas Doughty, had enhanced his standing in the community by purchasing three hundred acres of farmland in Salem Village in 1678.[36] But Francis divided his land among eight sons and daughters and their spouses in 1694, shortly before his death.[37] John, therefore, likely inherited a small parcel from his father, and perhaps a small parcel through his wife, Elizabeth Very, just east of Cedar Pond. The extra acreage that Doughty offered may have been valuable to him.

Yet John Nurse had other motives to be willing to pay much more than Doughty paid for less than half the acreage. Thomas Doughty was seventy, and everyone knew that his oldest son, Joseph, stood to inherit the land at his death. In fact, in 1707, Joseph would marry John Nurse's daughter, Elizabeth. So it's probable that Elizabeth was already betrothed to Joseph Doughty, and the deal was made with the couple's future in mind. Doughty and Nurse may have been, in effect, combining their assets into a package so that the young couple would have a good start.

Though they were relatively new to Salem, the Doughtys didn't find it peopled with strangers. Thomas's wife Elizabeth, especially, had many connections in Salem: most of them refugees from the Indian Wars. After the first Wabanaki raid on Saco in 1675, Simon Booth, Elizabeth's brother-in-law, and Humphrey Case, a tavern-keeper, moved from Saco to Salem: "driven ffrom there habetations by the Barbarios heathen,"[38] according to town records. Peter Henderson, who married Elizabeth's niece, Abigail, moved from Saco to Salem the following year. Sometime between 1681 and 1683, John Henderson married Elizabeth's sister-in-law, the widowed Ellen Booth Bully, sold his land in Saco, and moved to Salem.[39] New England remained an intimate community; in Salem, the Doughtys were surrounded by many of the neighbors and relatives they had known in Saco.

By 1700, Thomas Doughty had left behind lumbering and milling for farming, for the land deed refers to him as "husbandman." But he hadn't forsaken his belief that the key to survival lay in obtaining, owning, and selling land. There is little question that Thomas was thinking of his family's future when he purchased the parcel in Salem. He knew his days were numbered and wished to leave his large family with some semblance of security. Land was the best insurance there was.

In fact, one year after the purchase, Thomas Doughty, "yeoman," found himself short on cash. He used his land to obtain a loan from the influential Major William Browne, a wealthy Salem merchant. Doughty put up "about 100 acres of upland and swamp" as collateral on a twenty-four-pound loan, which he was to repay at twenty-five pounds, ten shillings one year later. A note in the margin of the deed from Browne's two sons indicates that the loan was, in fact, repaid.[40]

Doughty's transition from "husbandman" to "yeoman" in the land records illustrates another benefit of purchasing land: improving one's social status. And despite the vicissitudes of his experience—from soldier to prisoner to servant to miller to husbandman to yeoman—the change in title reflects the slow but steadily upward trajectory of his status and the urgency with which he resisted the status quo.

Thomas Doughty lived on his Salem farm for five years before his death in 1705. Existing records say nothing about how or why he died, though seventy-five was quite old for the time—old enough to die of natural causes. He was more fortunate than most of his Dunbar comrades; he died, not on a battlefield, or in a prison, a garrison, or in the woods between Pisacataqua and Quebec. Nor was he buried at sea. He died on land he had purchased and worked: land that belonged to him.

But although he'd left his family a home and property, he hadn't left behind a will. That meant that his estate would devolve to his oldest son. An inventory of Thomas's belongings was made the following June. But his estate wasn't fully settled until a dozen years later, on May 17, 1717. In part, that was because, while eldest son Joseph was able to remain in Salem on the Doughty farm, his landless siblings were forced to scatter, seeking opportunities elsewhere.

Two years after Thomas's death, in 1707, a spate of marriages occurred in the family. In March, Patience Doughty married Benjamin Follett of Salem. In April, third son James married Mary Robinson of "Quamscuk," or present-day Exeter Falls, New Hampshire. And in December, eldest son Joseph married Elizabeth Nurse, granddaughter of Rebecca Nurse.

Thomas and Elizabeth's second daughter, Margaret, had already settled in Malden, marrying Edmund Chamberlain in 1703. In 1710, Chamberlain fought at the Siege of Port Royal—during which the English wrested Acadia from the French and their Wabanaki allies once and for all. Chamberlain was wounded in the battle and died shortly after arriving home, plunging Margaret, his widow, into poverty. In a letter to John Burrill, Speaker of the Massachusetts Legislature, John Greenland of Malden wrote:

> These may jnform you: that: we have a poore woman liveth jn our Town: whose name is margret Chaimberlin : : her husband having ben sent To port: royal upon ye late expedition: and came home: again alive: Tho very weakly: and soon dyed Aftar his return:: now Sr ye Cause is thus this woman never Resaived her husbands wages: Tho she might have had it: if she would have Administer on her husbands estate:: but the estate beeing so very little and ye charge would be Great she dare not doe it.[41]

Like Margaret, many refugees continued to suffer losses from the ongoing wars, even after abandoning the frontier. Ultimately, however, the legislature granted Margaret her husband's military wages and the town of Malden voted to forgive her tax bill.[42]

Eldest daughter Elizabeth, the "childe unlawfully begotten," married Thomas Thomes, also of Exeter, New Hampshire, sometime before 1712. In June of that year, youngest daughter Abigail signed Thomas's probate documents as "Abigail Doutey of Lynn," suggesting that she may have taken work as a servant of a Lynn family. Five years later, she married Robert Edmunds.

Thomas Doughty, it seems, had been the glue holding the family together.

Thomas Doughty moved at least seven times in his adult life: from Scotland to Oyster River (Durham) to Newichawannock (South Berwick) to Doughty Falls (North Berwick) to Saco to Wells, back to Saco, to Boston or Malden, and to outer Salem (present-day Peabody/Lynn). His journey was inspired by a variety of causes: war, forced political exile, violence on the frontier, and the search for economic stability and security. He was not alone. Some lost their homes; some reclaimed them; some moved elsewhere. And although some families managed to retain the homesteads of their earliest ancestors in America, many began to disperse, rather than to divide those properties into smaller and smaller units as their families expanded over time.

The French and Indian wars drove British subjects back toward Salem and Boston from the eastern and western frontiers: Maine, New Hampshire, the Connecticut Valley. But the push to resettle those outlying areas continued in fits and starts throughout the early eighteenth century. In fact, families from across Massachusetts Bay and Plymouth Colonies show a distinct pattern of spreading and scattering, absorbing new lands toward New England's interior and further reaches.[43] The Doughty family represents a microcosm of those population trends.

After Thomas's death in 1705, oldest son Joseph and his wife, Elizabeth Nurse, remained in Salem on ninety-eight acres of the land that Thomas had purchased in 1700. They passed this property on to successive generations of Josephs and Thomases, who adopted the surname spelling of "Douty."

Doughty's other children were forced to look elsewhere for opportunity, becoming, in a sense, economic refugees. Patience Doughty and her husband Benjamin Follett moved to Windham, Connecticut, taking Thomas's widow, Elizabeth, and second son, Benjamin, with them. Elizabeth, her daughter Patience, and son-in-law Benjamin Follett appeared as communicants at the Windham Congregational Church in 1726.[44] Elizabeth would have been in her early 70s.

By 1716, Doughty's eldest daughter, Elizabeth, her husband, Thomas Thomes, and Doughty's third son, James and his wife had moved back to Falmouth, Maine, near the waterfront of present-day Portland. While the destruction of Fort Loyal in 1690 left Falmouth devastated, it was reincorporated in 1719, and Thomas Thomes was chosen as constable. The legislature provided the impetus to settle some fifty families on vacant land along the peninsula (present-day downtown Portland), and a committee was formed to lay out lots. Thomes built a home in Clay Cove, near present-day Commercial Street. James Doughty settled near the intersection of Middle and Exchange Streets, where he worked as a shoemaker.[45] He had eight children who adopted the surname spelling "Doughty"; their descendants have continued to live and work along the coast of Maine for generations.

During the winter of 1718–1719 at Falmouth, the Thomes and Doughtys encountered a wave of new immigrants: "About three hundred souls, most of which are arrived from Ireland." These were among the first Scots-Irish, or Ulster Scots, who would eventually settle in great numbers along the Maine coast.[46] Presbyterians of Scottish origin, the Ulster Scots had been lured by James I—and his successors—away from the Scottish Lowlands to the Irish province of Ulster early in the seventeenth century with the offer of land. The scheme was intended to ease population pressure on the Lowlands, seize territory from Irish landowners in Ulster, and displace them with Protestants, who would help keep the rebellious Catholics in line. But by century's end, Ulster Scots were coping with successive crop failures, religious discrimination, increasing rents, and a diminished linen trade, which had supported many families. Many determined to make their way to America.

The Ulster Scots' first winter at Casco Bay was difficult indeed: "Not one Half have provisions near sufficient to live upon over the Winter, & so poor as they are not able to buy any," states a petition for assistance to the Massachusetts Bay Colony government. "& none of the First inhabitants so well furnished as that they are able to supply them." The Doughtys and Thomes were likely among those "first inhabitants" struggling to build their own lives on the frontier. Fortunately, the government responded: "Ordered: that One Hundred Bushels of Indian Meal be allowed & given to the Irish People mentioned in the petition."[47]

Thomas Doughty was among the earliest wave of immigrants to settle in America. Despite strong resistance from native peoples, his generation and his progeny continued to reach deeper and deeper into the American continent like the receding, rebounding waves of the incoming tide. Regardless of what propelled them in the first place, those waves of humanity would never stop.

Chapter Ten

& FURTHER SAYTH NOT

I have always thought the actions of men the best interpreters of their thoughts.

—John Locke

THE NARRATIVE of individuals risking everything and coming to New England seeking freedom to worship and economic opportunity has been a powerful founding myth for the United States. While it accurately describes an important group of early colonists, it offers a narrow view of seventeenth-century society. Thomas Doughty's New England was different: it was a diverse and often unruly society whose inhabitants experienced the extremes of liberty and oppression.

Extending across cultures, Doughty's life journey reflects a seventeenth-century Atlantic world in which the climate was changing physically, politically, and socially. Throughout the century, unusually cold, wet weather in Scotland triggered famine and epidemics. These were especially acute during Thomas's formative years. The Reformation inspired a proliferation of religious sects, which in turn inspired power struggles in England, Scotland, and Ireland among Presbyterians, Anglicans, Puritans, and Catholics, and between Royalists and Parliamentarians. Trade, colonization, and migration caused disparate cultures and values to collide. These changes affected rich and poor alike and swept unsuspecting laborers like Doughty into servitude and slavery abroad, wresting them from their families, cultures, and homelands.

Doughty began his journey as a young man with few prospects or choices, compelled to do others' bidding as a laborer, conscript, soldier, prisoner, and bond servant. Yet when viewed in the whole, his life illustrates an important seventeenth-century trend toward greater self-determination: at least for individuals of European heritage. Once freed from bondage, Doughty was able to purchase and sell land, move freely throughout New Hampshire and Maine, build a business, and have a voice in town politics. It's doubtful that he could have done as much had he stayed in Lothian.

Like him, many oppressed individuals escaped their bonds, and, amid strife and conflict, found modest opportunity on New England soil. But Doughty was white. His Scottish background was a liability at first, but it ultimately made his independence possible and attainable. Individuals of color were on a different trajectory. Increasingly, kidnapped Africans supplanted lower-class white Europeans as bonded laborers. Rather than owning property, they remained the property of others. And as white colonists expanded their numbers and their territory in New England, Native Americans were squeezed into smaller and smaller parcels of the lands they once roamed freely. Native peoples' capacity to determine their own futures was increasingly subject to the strictures of white society. Their livelihoods—cultivating crops, hunting, and fishing—were fenced, dammed, and otherwise hemmed in, or out. They endured questionable land and trade deals and were frequently denied justice in English courts. Although they went to war to resist these changes, Native Americans' choices continued to diminish.

Religious freedom, too, was relative. During much of Doughty's life on the eastern frontier, Maine and New Hampshire fell under Massachusetts Bay, and therefore, Puritan, control. But unlike Massachusetts proper, the eastern provinces comprised a community that included Puritans, Anglicans, Quakers, Antinomians, and others.

Doughty's master, Valentine Hill, was a Puritan. The man who had once owned Hill's land, John Wheelwright,[1] was an Antinomian. Like Anne Hutchinson, Wheelwright had been banished from Massachusetts proper for his religious beliefs. Richard Leader, who reestablished the Great Works sawmill, was a Muggletonian[2]—a member of a small sect founded by two self-declared Christian prophets. William Phillips's third wife Bridget was not only the daughter of Antinomian Anne Hutchinson, she was a practicing Quaker. Phillips built a large mill complex at Saco Falls, but he may have chosen to live there in part so his wife could attend Quaker meetings at Scarborough or Kittery.[3]

Though the eastern frontier was in many ways more diverse than Boston or Salem, magistrates still tried to enforce strict adherence to Puritan religious practices. Sometimes they succeeded; often, they didn't. Quakers, for example, found both sanctuary and persecution on the frontier. Bridget Phillips owned land in Maine and continued to thrive even after her wealthy and influential husband died.[4] Thomas Doughty probably leased the Phillips's sawmill at Saco Falls from her: a business transaction that likely benefited both. Yet the three women who dared to hold Quaker meetings in Dover in 1662—Ann Coleman, Mary Tompkins, and Alice Ambrose—were tied to carts half naked, whipped, and paraded through the wintry streets as they were led out of the province by order of Puritan magistrate Richard Waldron.

Some New Englanders spoke out against religious intolerance, but most of those lived beyond the Puritan sphere of influence. Roger Williams, founder of Rhode Island and a religious exile from Massachusetts Bay, observed in 1644 the damage being done in New England and abroad in the name of religious conformity and theocracy:

> God requireth not a uniformity of religion to be enacted and enforced in any civil state; which enforced uniformity (sooner or later) is the greatest occasion of civil war, ravishing of conscience, persecution of Christ Jesus in his servants, and of the hypocrisy and destruction of millions of souls.[5]

While some parts of New England—the eastern frontier and Rhode Island—were more accepting than others, the religious tolerance and separation of church and state that Williams envisioned was still an exile's pipe dream.

Men and women of Thomas Doughty's class had little time or inclination to contemplate the larger moral questions that Williams, or the Winthrops, or Anne Hutchinson did. It's probable that Thomas was highly religious, that he believed in God, heaven and hell, the devil, and, like his contemporaries, witches. Those were not abstractions, not metaphors, but facts. He fought in a religious war on behalf of Presbyterianism, but his participation may have resulted more from coercion than conscience. Once in New England, he demonstrated no partiality nor rebelliousness toward Puritanism. He was called to court once for failing to attend Sabbath meetings; he likely mended his ways because he knew what it took to get ahead. But his life shows a greater dedication to work, family, and self-preservation than to any particular religious doctrine.

In Doughty's New England, trade and commerce were as important as piety: perhaps even more so. Religious and political conflict were the ostensible reasons for his being sent to America, but the labor and profit needs of wealthy industrialists were equally well served. Even clergymen had business dealings involving prisoners, bond and chattel slaves. The Reverend John Cotton wrote to Cromwell, assuring him that the Dunbar prisoners sold into servitude were being well treated in New England, though it's doubtful that he visited Hammersmith to learn the truth. His grandson, Cotton Mather, minister of Boston's Second Church, held slaves and pretended to justify the practice through religion: "Christianity directs a Slave . . . to satisfy himself, That he is the Lords Freeman, 'tho he continues a Slave."[6] Slaves, according to Mather, could comfort themselves with the notion that, though slavery was sanctioned on earth, it was absent in heaven. To accomplish work in New England—whether commercial, agricultural, or intellectual work—one needed slaves and servants. It was a rare educated or well-to-do New England family that didn't own or employ servants or slaves of some sort.

Mercantile interests in Massachusetts Bay were front-and-center, almost from the start. The Hammersmith Iron Works was the brainchild of John Winthrop, Jr., son and namesake of the colony's leader and governor. Valentine Hill, a Puritan and close friend of Winthrop, Sr., footed the bill for a meetinghouse at Oyster River but invested more heavily in two sawmills which supplied his merchant ships with lumber to transport and sell to English settlements throughout the

Atlantic basin. The labor was supplied by his Scottish bond servants. Despite his unusual religious beliefs, Richard Leader, another purchaser of Scots prisoners and a trader of kidnapped Irish servants, was tolerated as manager of the iron works because of his knowledge of the ironmaking process. When he fought with the iron works shareholders, he was welcomed in Maine and rewarded with vast tracts of woods by the town of Kittery.

Trade was the engine of New England's success as a colony and the source of many of its difficulties. Commerce fostered slavery, though admittedly, not on the scale of the southern or Caribbean colonies. It also changed the very face of the New England landscape. Trade felled the forests, dammed the rivers, and caused heated conflicts among English and French colonists and Native Americans. It wasn't by coincidence that frontier trading posts were among the first buildings to go up in smoke; those fires signaled larger conflagrations to come. Trade was behind the growth of wealthy towns and settlements like Piscataqua, Newburyport, Ipswich, Gloucester, Salem, and especially, Boston. It contributed to the prominence of New England families, including those of Eliakim Hutchinson, William Phillips, Brian Pendleton, Valentine Hill, Richard Leader, John and Richard Cutt, and Richard Waldron. Local court records throughout New England are filled with suits and settlements involving trade disputes. Thomas Doughty often found himself in court—as plaintiff and defendant—because of lumber deals gone awry.

Doughty fully embraced the mercantile ethos, seeking opportunities to trade in land and lumber wherever he could. He not only built his livelihood on trade, he rubbed shoulders with some of the wealthiest merchants in New England. To him, trade offered a means of supporting his family, of getting ahead, of ingratiating himself to the powerful, of elevating his status.

Although there was plenty of money to be made on the eastern frontier, life wasn't secure. Residents, like their counterparts in the Connecticut Valley, paid a price for living at the outer edges of English influence. Many, like Doughty, managed to rebuild during the uneasy peace that succeeded the King Philip's War. But eventually, nearly all of those who made out handsomely by building and investing in Maine lands and businesses during the seventeenth century lost everything in the conflicts that followed. Even York, the second-southernmost community in the province, was virtually leveled by fire in January 1692, as French and native combatants killed or carried away fifty to a hundred settlers, including former Dunbar prisoners of the Scotland settlement.

Hostilities between the English and the Wabanakis, with their French allies, continued with Queen Anne's War. This was part of a much larger conflict known as the War of Spanish Succession, pitting global powers France and Spain against England, soon to become Great Britain. In the New England theater, natives attacked Groton in 1694 and Deerfield in 1704. Though he remained secure in Salem, Thomas Doughty never lived to see an end to the ethnic and territorial hostilities that drove him from Saco.

As a result of these conflicts, northern New England was subject to waves of settlement and resettlement on behalf of white colonists. But not until the end of Queen Anne's War in 1712–1713 did large numbers of English subjects return to Maine. Among those were Doughty's eldest daughter, Elizabeth, and his third son, James. Both took advantage of land grants offered to help resettle Falmouth, which later became Portland, the province's largest city.

But who was Thomas Doughty? That question remains hard to answer succinctly. For us, his character emerges only as the sum of his heritage, experiences, and actions.

After laboring for fifty-five years in New England, Doughty left behind an estate worth roughly £190 and debts amounting to £79.[7] It wasn't a fortune, but in comparison to his Scottish peers in New England, it was comfortable.[8] Except for his land—which by 1705 had shrunk from over two hundred to ninety-eight acres—the details of his estate point to a very modest standard of living, filled with the essentials of everyday rural life in early America: four oxen, two cows, two calves, cooking utensils, two beds, three chairs, two spinning wheels, and "timber chaines & other old iron."

Thomas also left his name on Doughty Falls on the Great Works River in North Berwick, Maine. And he left behind a large family; seven sons and daughters survived him, and many of those would

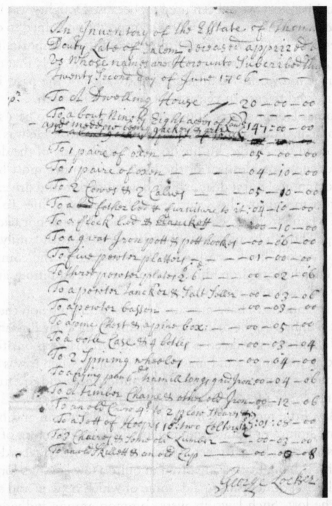

Detail from the probate inventory, estate of Thomas Doughty, March 12, 1706. (*Records of the Massachusetts Supreme Judicial Court Archives, New England Historic Genealogical Society*)

have children of their own who helped to settle Maine, Massachusetts, and Connecticut.

As with so many immigrants in early colonial America, Thomas Doughty's most important legacy was his staying power. Holding one's ground and surviving against the odds was the determining factor for building the America we know today. It's not, perhaps, the very positive story we've been used to, because Doughty was brought to America against his will, and his transportation helped to displace peoples who had been there for millennia. But it's important to understand Doughty's place—and our place—in precisely that context, for that is the world we inhabit. "History is not the past; it is the present," said twentieth-century writer James Baldwin.

Thomas Doughty was, above all, a survivor. And to be a survivor in turbulent times takes discretion and self-control. He was not the man to lead the charge; his life does not exhibit any of the defiance, rebelliousness, or idealism of the kind that inspires most histories and biographies. But it does exhibit determination and drive: relentless effort to improve his security and his station in life. To survive on the Maine frontier, Doughty had to be forward- not backward-looking. Though he undoubtedly missed his Scottish family, home, and native soil, he determined to fully engage in the community where fate chose to drop him. He also had to be ambitious and constantly on the lookout for opportunity.

Yet he appears to have measured his risks carefully: on the battlefield at Dunbar, on the march to Durham, on the New England frontier. He had the good sense to throw down his weapon, to avoid provoking his captors and master, and to know when it was time to abandon Saco once and for all. This cautiousness and careful calculation no doubt preserved his life more than a few times.

Today, little remains of his work. The mills he ran and built are gone; no homes or homestead remain. Only a smattering of official records attest to his existence. What do those written records tell us about him? Doughty was involved in quite a few lawsuits for timber not delivered or debts not paid, some of which he won and some of which he lost. Such lawsuits were common among individuals involved in business dealings, and they are more indicative of industriousness than dishonesty. Doughty was called to court a handful of other times: once, for fighting with a notoriously belligerent neighbor; once for being "in drinke"; once for conceiving a child out of wedlock; once for failing to appear at court on behalf of someone for whom he'd made bond; and once for failing to attend church. When seen in the context of his peers, Doughty's transgressions are unremarkable. In fact, they read like a list of the most common cases in early colonial courts. Had Massachusetts Bay magistrates not had to adjudicate business disputes, fighting, drunkenness, fornication, and skipping church, they would have had little to do.

In several cases, Doughty arrived in court and "owned," or admitted to, his debts and transgressions before magistrates had the chance to admonish him. It may be that he was contrite; it may be that he knew that approach was effective at disarming disapproval. In the Salem witch trials, the accused learned quickly that confession was an effective means of avoiding the gallows. At the very least, Doughty's owning of his indiscretions suggests a willingness to move on quickly.

Thomas Doughty left behind no record of his thoughts, and in the few places where his statements were recorded, they exhibited a remarkable neutrality and matter-of-factness. They evidenced no longing for family or homeland, nor even the slightest reference to his Scottish origins. They betrayed no bitterness, resentment, or despair for any of the hard turns his life took; nor did they ever ask for pity or special consideration. Take his letter to Governor Andros, requesting that he be allowed to keep his land and mill in Saco:

> Whereas yor Petitionr Thos Doughty of Saco in the Province of Main hath had in his Possession a certaine Tract of fresh marsh lying in the little Desart neer Swan Pond which yor Petitionr hath made use of this twenty yeares or there abouts which wth 300 Acres of Upland and the Grist Mill built by yor Petitionr at his sole charge Your Petitionr prayes that yor Excellcie would be pleased to grant a Warrant for the admeasuring the same And yor Petitionr as in duty bound shal ever pray & c.[9]

This brief petition describes the plot of land that Doughty seeks to retain, emphasizing how long he has held it and how he has improved it. The letter's ending offers polite conventions of the day: respectfully acknowledging Andros's authority and suggesting that a favorable decision would earn Doughty's gratitude.

Although probably transcribed by the same hand, a letter to Andros from another former Dunbar prisoner and Doughty's neighbor in Saco, Patrick Denmark, reveals an entirely different personality:

> The petition of patrick Denmarke senir of Saco humbly sheweth that yr petitionr having lived many yrs in said towne

& now having a Great Charge of Children but Could never procure any land by reason of his one povertye & others high Demands to this day Hee therefore humbly prayes yr Excellencys graunt of one hundred acres of vacant Lands about three miles to the Westward of Saco rivr neare the way to Wells with ten acres of meadow ground also vacant adjoyning thereunto.[10]

Denmark approaches his argument differently, seeking to appeal to Andros's empathy. He "humbly" requests that Andros grant him a hundred acres in Saco, not because he has improved them but because they lie "vacant," because he has never been able to afford purchasing property, and because those acres would help him to support his "Great Charge of Children."

Only two additional documents quoting Doughty himself survive. He gave two depositions regarding Valentine Hill, his onetime master, and it is equally difficult to extract attitude or emotion from them. In 1670, he and James Oare acknowledged that Valentine Hill was "their master."[11] And in 1700, at age seventy, he deposed:

Abought Forty years Ago or More I Lived with Vallantin Hill whom ye Said Hill was In Possesion of ffive hundred Accres of Land Ajacent to his Mill . . . which Land ye Said Hill Peassably Lived on without any Mollestation by any porson or porssons, with the ffresh Meddow at Whelwrights Pond . . . [Hill] Built A hows ther and keept Cattell & spent the Hay ther, Many years, and ye said Hill afterwards hired ye said Doubty to Cutt and Make A way to that Meddow and was to give him Ten pounds for Making the way and the said Hill honestly sattisfyed him for the same and further sayth not.[12]

This statement, like his others, is remarkably straightforward. And although much of that is a result of context—the court had no doubt requested a concise statement about Valentine Hill—it is consistent with what we know of Doughty. From everything we can gather, he was a man of few words and contained emotion.

Still, what Thomas Doughty's statements do not say speaks volumes. We know what he experienced, but, the truth is, we don't know how it felt to him. In writing about his journey, I've sought to engage the reader's complicity in filling those gaps with homesickness, pain, triumph, humility, sadness, and outrage. In that way, this story is not Thomas Doughty's altogether. Some of it is ours. His experiences dictate the narrative arc; his movements, the chapters; and his perspective—the position from which he experienced events—provides the lens through which we view historical events. But the emotions are ours. In that way, this is a shared journey.

The journey ends in a gas station parking lot on busy U.S. Route 1 in Peabody, Massachusetts. In that parking lot sits a tiny cemetery, set off from the sea of blacktop by a weathered wooden fence. A small sign informs the visitor that this is the Douty Cemetery, established in 1816. Within this thirty-by-thirty-foot space are nineteen headstones, three of which bear the surname "Douty." Henry Douty, the first person to be buried here—or at least, the first person to be buried here in a plot that retains its marker—died in 1816. Though no existing vital records point to his parentage, probate records confirm that Henry is Thomas Doughty's second great-grandson.

The Douty Cemetery lies on land that Thomas purchased in 1700 and that was passed on to his son Joseph. No headstones for Thomas or Joseph are found here. Yet in early New England, graves were not consistently marked. Some had wooden markers, long since rotted or vanished; some had plain, uncarved stones; some had no marker at all. Many graves were known to the living by their locations with regard to trees, stone walls, hillocks, and other topographical features. This information was passed on from one generation to the next until lost to memory. Nevertheless, it's a good bet that Thomas Doughty, along with his eldest son Joseph, his grandson Joseph Jr., his great-grandson Thomas, and other members of their families found their final resting places near this spot, on land where they worked and lived until their deaths.

For the living, the lack of a gravestone can be unsettling. What life is too obscure or unworthy to pass without the merest acknowledgment? That concept, in a way, was the motive behind this book: to acknowledge Doughty's existence and to insist that he was as real as Oliver Cromwell, John Winthrop, Cotton Mather, Onesimus, Anne Hutchinson, Mary Rowlandson, Madockawando, Squando, and the world they inhabited together. His life also helped to shape that world and the one we've inherited, even if his contribution can't be measured.

Thomas Doughty never learned to write—never composed a will—and today, lies somewhere in or near that small cemetery in Peabody, Massachusetts, in an unmarked grave. It's possible that he dreamed about some sort of monument to his time on earth. But given what we know of his character, that seems unlikely. It's more reasonable to believe that he went to his grave knowing, simply, that nothing more needed to be said: his life would speak for itself.

Notes

INTRODUCTION

1. Bernard Bailyn, *The Peopling of British North America: An Introduction* (New York: Alfred A. Knopf, 1986), 8.

2. Lack of records make it impossible to estimate child mortality in Scotland alone, and rates could vary widely from region to region and year to year. But there is some scholarly agreement that, during the 1600s, up to a third of English children died before reaching age fifteen. See Hannah Newton, "The Dying Child in 17th-Century England," *Pediatrics* 136 (August 2015). Accessed 10/12/17 at: http://pediatrics.aappublications.org. See also, Lynda Payne, "Health in England (16th-18th c.)," Children and Youth in History, Item #166, http://chnm.gmu.edu/cyh/items/show/166 (accessed 10/12/17).

CHAPTER I. PASSAGE

1. William Bradford had described the pilgrim's arrival at Cape Cod: "Besides, what could they see but a hideous and desolate wilderness, full of wild beasts and wild men—and what multitudes there might be of them they knew not." See *Of Plymouth Plantation, 1620-1647,* ed. Samuel Eliot Morison (New York: Alfred A. Knopf, 2011), 62.

2. Formerly referred to as the English Civil Wars.

3. The Council of State controlled England's political affairs after King Charles I was executed.

4. Some 9,000 Scots had been taken prisoner at Dunbar; 5,100 had been released, and 3,900 had begun the march to Durham. The English Committee of the Council of State for Irish and Scottish Affairs requested that Hesilrige send 2,000 to Ireland, 900 to Virginia, and 150 to New England. See September 19, 1650, and October 28, 1650, in *Calendar of State Papers, Domestic Series, 1650*, ed. Mary Anne Everett Green (London: Longman & Co., 1876). In his answer to the Council on October 31, 1650, Hesilrige admits that he simply no longer had the numbers, and that of the 1,400 or so remaining prisoners, only 600 were healthy. See "A letter from Sir Arthur Hesilrige, to the honorable committee of the Councel of State for Irish and Scotish affairs at White-Hall, concerning the Scots prisoners," National Library of Scotland.

5. Durham University Archeology Department studies confirm that bodies were thrown naked into pits. Richard Annis, senior archeologist, presentation at Saugus, Massachusetts, on October 25, 2016. Sir Arthur Hesilrige details the dates of the Scots' movements, deaths during the march and in the cathedral, and the numbers of prisoners dead and alive as of October 31 in "A letter from Sir Arthur Hesilrige, to the honorable committee of the Councel of State for Irish and Scotish affairs at White-Hall, concerning the Scots prisoners," National Library of Scotland.

6. November 11, 1650, *Calendar of State Papers, Domestic Series, 1650*, ed. Mary Anne Everett Green (London: Longman & Co., 1876).

7. See November 7 and 8, 1650, in *Calendar of State Papers, Domestic Series, 1650*.

8. Charles Edward Banks, "Scotch Prisoners Deported to New England by Cromwell, 1651-52," in *Proceedings of the Massachusetts Historical Society*, LXI (Oct. 1927-Jun. 1928), 12, states that an "order to sail was dated November 11," but he doesn't cite the source. He also notes the unusual chronology, whereby on November 11, the Council of State requested 150 prisoners from Hesilrige in Newcastle, even as 150 Scottish prisoners lay aboard ship in the Thames. Banks and other scholars have uncovered evidence of only one group of 150 Scots shipped to New England.

9. Information on how these prisoners changed hands and were transported comes from Banks, "Scotch Prisoners Deported to New England by Cromwell," 4-29. For information on Becx and Foote, and their stipulation that the prisoners be "well and sound and free from wounds," see September 19, 1650, in *Calendar of State Papers, Domestic Series, 1650*.

10. The ship may have been built in Boston by Benjamin Gilliam, a shipwright, who sold a quarter of a ship of that name to John Leverett. See Banks, 11.

11. Ian K. Steele, *The English Atlantic, 1675-1740: An Exploration of Communication and Community* (New York: Oxford University Press, 1986). Steele studied 132 voyages between London and Boston during the late seventeenth and early eighteenth centuries.

12. Thomas B. Macaulay, *The History of England from the Accession of James II* (London: Longman, Brown, Green and Longman's, 1849), I: 652.

13. Leo Francis Stock, ed., *Proceedings and Debates of the British Parliaments Respecting North America* (Washington, DC: The Carnegie Institution of Washington, 1924), I: 249.

14. Thomas Bellows Wyman, *The Genealogies and Estates of Charlestown: in the County of Middlesex and Commonwealth of Massachusetts, 1629-1818* (Boston: David Clapp and Son, 1879), II: 990.

15. See *The Journals of Henry Melchior Muhlenberg*, trans. Theodore G. Tappert and John W. Doberstein (Philadelphia: Muhlenberg Press, 1942), I: 30. Daniel Francis Pastorius, "Compare the ship that bore them hither with Noah's Ark: Francis Daniel Pastorius describes his impressions of Pennsylvania, 1683." History Matters website. Accessed 07/27/15 at: http://historymatters.gmu.edu/d/7439.

16. *The Journals of Henry Melchior Muhlenberg*, I: 30.

17. Diary of John Harrower, 1773-1776, *American Historical Review*, 6 (no. 1, Oct. 1900): 74.

18. Ibid., 74.

19. Daniel Francis Pastorius, "Compare the ship that bore them hither with Noah's Ark: Francis Daniel Pastorius describes his impressions of Pennsylvania, 1683." History Matters website. Accessed 07/27/15 at: http://historymatters.gmu.edu/d/7439.

20. Diary of John Harrower, 74.

21. *Gottlieb Mittleberger's Journey to Pennsylvania in the Year 1750 and Return to Germany in the Year 1754*, translated by Carl Theo. Eben (Philadelphia: John Jos. McVey, 1898), 20.

22. Ibid., 24.

23. Ibid., 23.

24. *The Journals of Henry Melchior Muhlenberg*, I: 32.

25. *Mittleberger's Journey to Pennsylvania*, 21.

26. In *Ironworks on the Saugus* (Norman: University of Oklahoma Press, 1957), E.N. Hartley estimates a mortality aboard the *Unity* of around 10 percent (see p. 45). Banks, in "Scotch Prisoners Deported to New England by Cromwell," estimates "The usual toll of scurvy must have taken at least ten per cent of the total number" (p. 19) of prisoners from the Battle of Worcester, deported a year after the Dunbar prisoners. Colin Palmer, *The First Passage: Blacks in the Americas 1502-1617* (Oxford: Oxford University Press, 1995), estimates mortality on board slave ships from Africa to the Americas at 10–15 percent during the eighteenth century (see p. 38). In *A Path in the Mighty Waters: Shipboard Life & Atlantic Crossings to the New World* (New Haven: Yale University Press, 2015), Stephen R. Berry contends that "Between 1700 and 1775, death rates aboard slave ships ranged between 8 percent and 24 percent, depending on a variety of such factors as the point of embarkation, destination, and the amount of time spent on the ship. . . . The European averages in the same period never equaled that of the African trade. Mortality rates aboard vessels ferrying German emigrants averaged between 3 percent and 5 percent over the course of the eighteenth century. . . . The transatlantic voyage was more deadly than life on shore, but its toll did not equal that of the slave trade." (236-37).

27. See *A Collection of Papers Relating to the Iron Works at Lynn*, Baker Library Special Collections, Harvard University, 103.

28. No precise lists exist for how the Scots were disposed of in 1650–1651. But various sources give us a relatively clear idea. For an accounting of Scots at the iron works and the Great Works sawmill in Maine, see Suffolk County Court Files, case #225; Banks, 13-14; and Stephen P. Carlson, *The Scots at Hammersmith* (Saugus, MA: Eastern National Park & Monument Association, 1979), 5. For the Scots who worked with Valentine Hill at Oyster River, see *Historical Memoranda Concerning Persons and Places in Old Dover, N.H.*, John Scales, ed. (Dover, NH, 1900), I: 145, 340. See also: Craig Stinston, "Oyster River Scots," June 3, 2018, Scottish Prisoners of War Society, www.scottishprisonersofwar.com/oyster-river-scots-by-b-craig-stinson.

29. See Banks, "Scotch Prisoners Deported to New England by Cromwell," 13. Banks concludes that Becx and Foote must have made around £1,500 from the sale of Scots, but he fails to account for the death of some 10 percent of the prisoners aboard ship. Calculating the worth of £1,000 in today's dollars is a thorny

and controversial proposition. Still, it's important for emphasizing that trafficking in slaves and servants was a profit-making activity. The "six-figure" estimation was reached using the Measuring Worth calculator (www.measuringworth.com). According to that tool, the "commodity value," "labour value," and "income value" of one thousand pounds in 1650 all resulted in six-figure amounts for 2017 British Pounds.

30. William Bradford wrote that he and his peers reasoned that if they "were in a place where they might have liberty and live comfortably," they would "practice [their religious devotion] as they did." See *Of Plymouth Plantation*, Samuel Eliot Morison, ed. (New York: Alfred A. Knopf, 2011), 24. In "A Model of Christian Charity," John Winthrop exhorted his peers to "do justly, to love mercy, to walk humbly with our God," with the promise that they could build a truly pious society: "[God] shall make us a praise and glory that men shall say of succeeding plantations, 'may the Lord make it like that of New England.' For we must consider that we shall be as a city upon a hill. The eyes of all people are upon us."

31. While no statistics exist for the proportion of servants who came to New England by force during the earliest years of colonization, Stephen R. Berry has written that "In the period 1700-1775, the largest category of European immigrants to enter British North America was indentured servants." See *A Path in the Mighty Waters,* 20. Berry does not differentiate among those who came as voluntary indentures versus those who came by force. Nevertheless, Berry and other historians seem to agree that the servant class comprised the largest number of arrivals.

CHAPTER 2. RELIGIOUS WARS

1. From "KING CHARLS HIS SPEECH Made upon the SCAFFOLD At *Whitehall*-Gate, Immediately before his Execution, On Tuesday the 30 of *Ian.* 1648 With a Relation of the maner of his going to Execution. *Published by Special Authority.*" London: Printed by Peter Cole, at the sign of the Printing-Press in Cornhil, near the Royal Exchange. 1649. Accessed online 5/24/18 at: http://anglicanhistory.org/charles/charles1.html.

2. Letter CXXVI, September 2, 1650. Thomas Carlyle, *Oliver Cromwell's Letters and Speeches: with Elucidations* (London: Chapman and Hall, 1846), II: 201.

3. The Covenanters sought to preserve Presbyterianism as the official religion throughout Scotland.

4.There were sharp political and religious divisions within Scotland. Some Scots formed a Royalist army in support of the king, led by James Graham, Marquis of Montrose. To complicate matters more, Montrose had earlier sided with the Presbyterian Covenanters.

5. William Scott Douglas, *Cromwell's Scotch Campaigns 1650-51* (London: Elliot Stock, 1898), 29.

6. John Hodgson, "A Large Relation of the Fight at Leith Neere Edenburgh," in Henry Slingsby and John Hodgson, *Original Memoirs Written during the Civil War: Being the Life of Sir Henry Slingsby and Memoirs of Captain Hodgson.* (Edinburgh: James Ballantyne & Co., 1807), 214.

7. Alexander MacKenzie, *The History of the Munros of Fowlis with Genealogies of Principal Families of the Name: to Which Are Added Those of Lexington and New England* (Inverness: A & W MacKenzie, 1898), 238.

8. *History of Scots Affairs from MDCXXXVII to MDCXLI* (Aberdeen: Spaulding Club, 1841), I: 235–36.

9. Contemporary accounts of the Battle of Dunbar and the movements leading up to it have a decidedly English perspective. An English soldier, John Hodgson, wrote later of his experience during the campaign; an English weekly of the time, *Mercurius Politicus*, offered updates on the conflict; and Cromwell's copious personal correspondence provide most of the details that historians have used to reconstruct the events of that summer. No firsthand accounts from Scottish participants or eyewitnesses have survived, though in the aftermath, the Scottish press did offer some coverage.

10. Hodgson, "A Large Relation," 207.

11. Ibid., 208.

12. Short for "defencible," this term simply means "able to bear arms."

13. Anwen Caffell, "Palace Green Library Excavations 2013 (PGL13), Human Remains." Department of Archeology, Durham University, July 2014. See Table 1: Summary of osteological and paleopathological results (skeletons). Retrieved 05/30/17 at: https://www.dur.ac.uk/resources/archaeology/pdfs/PGL13_Human _Bone_Report.pdf.

14. Nearly all accounts of the battle mention the wet and windy weather. See, for example, contemporary accounts: *Mercurius Politicus* and John Nicoll, *A Diary of Public Transactions and Other Occurrences,* mentioned below. Recent scholars agree: Peter Reese, *Cromwell's Masterstroke: Dunbar 1650* (Barnsley, UK: Pen and Sword Military, 2006), 81; Stuart Reid, *Dunbar 1650: Cromwell's Most Famous Victory* (New York: Osprey, 2004), 58; John D. Grainger, *Cromwell Against the Scots: The Last Anglo-Scottish War, 1650-1652* (East Linton, Scotland: Tuckwell Press, 1997), 47.

15. *Mercurius Politicus*, September 12-19, 1650, 227.

16. Hodgson, *Memoirs*, 143.

17. John Nicoll, *A Diary of Public Transactions and Other Occurrences, Chiefly in Scotland, From January 1650 to June 1667* (Edinburgh: Bannatyne Club, 1836), 27.

18. "They having fasted, as they themselves said, near eight days," wrote Hesilrige to the Council of State concerning the Scots prisoners on October 31, 1650.

19. See Anwen Caffell, Palace Green Library Excavations 2013: Human Remains, (July 2014 DRAFT), Department of Archeology, Durham University, espec. p. 52. Accessed 05/30/17 at: https://www.dur.ac.uk/resources/archaeology/pdfs/PGL 13_Human_Bone_Report.pdf.

20. A. Gibson and T.C. Smout, "Scottish Food and Scottish History, 1500-1800," in R.A. Houston and I.D. Whyte, Eds., *Scottish Society 1500-1800* (Cambridge: Cambridge University Press, 1989), 73.

21. Geoffrey Parker, *Global Crisis: War, Climate Change & Catastrophe in the Seventeenth Century* (New Haven: Yale University Press, 2013), 675.

22. James Balfour, "Annales of Scotland," in *The Historical Works of Sir James Balfour* (Edinburgh: 1824) III: 409.

23. Samuel Gardiner, *History of the Commonwealth and Protectorate, 1649-1656* (London: Longmans, Green & Co., 1903), I: 290.

24. C.H. Firth, "The Battle of Dunbar," *Transactions of the Royal Historical Society,* New Series, 14 (1900): 35-36.

25. Nicoll, *A Diary of Public Transactions and Other Occurrences,* 27.

26. Numbers of soldiers on each side have been long disputed, though all agree that the Scots Army was significantly larger than Cromwell's. Stuart Reid estimates that the Scots fielded 14,000 men to the English Army's 11,000. See *Dunbar 1650,* 39-41. Peter Reese estimates the English Army at 12,000 versus 21,500 for the Scots. See *Cromwell's Masterstroke,* 40.

27. Firth, "The Battle of Dunbar," 41, n. 3. In 1650, "hutt" referred to a temporary shelter.

28. Ibid., 45, n. 5.

29. Numbers of Scottish prisoners come from Sir Arthur Hesilrige, "A Letter from Sir Arthur Hesilrige, to the Honorable Committee of the Councel of State for Irish and Scotish Affairs at White Hall, Concerning the Scots Prisoners," October 31, 1650. National Library of Scotland.

CHAPTER 3. DEATH MARCH

1. Kirsteen Paterson, "Child soldiers' remains found in mass grave of troops captured at Battle of Dunbar," *National,* September 2, 2015. Accessed 9/3/15 at: http://www.thenational.scot/news/child-soldiers-remains-found-in-mass-grave-of-troops-captured-at-battle-of-dunbar.7130.

2. Christopher Gerrard, "Prisoners of War: Durham and the Fate of the Scots in 1650," talk delivered at Berwick Academy, South Berwick, Maine, 11/2/16.

3. Janet Beveridge, "Discovery." In Christopher Gerrard, Pam Graves, Andrew Millard, Richard Annis, and Anwan Caffell, *Lost Lives, New Voices: Unlocking the Stories of the Scottish Soldiers from the Battle of Dunbar 1650* (Oxford: Oxbow Books, 2018), 23.

4. Durham University, Department of Archeology, "The Identification." Accessed 12/3/15 at: www.dur.ac.uk/archaeology/research/projects/europe/pg-skeletons/find.

5. Richard Annis, "Human Remains Found at Palace Green November 2013," Durham University Department of Archeology, July 2015, 5.

6. David Keys, "Skeletons of Scottish prisoners provide evidence of child soldiers in Britain's civil wars," *Independent,* September 3, 2015. Accessed 9/3/15 at: http://www.independent.co.uk/news/science/archaeology/skeletons-of-scottish-prisoners-provide-evidence-of-child-soldiers-in-english-civil-war-10482793.html.

7. Gerrard et al., *Lost Lives, New Voices,* 55.

8. Annis, "Human Remains," 4.

9. Professor Chris Gerrard, Durham University, correspondence, 5/25/18.

10. All quotations from Sir Arthur Hesilrige, "A Letter from Sir Arthur Hesilrige, to the Honorable Committee."

11. Durham University, Department of Archeology, "The Identification."

12. If the Scots' needs were fully provided for, as Hesilrige argues, then it seems unlikely that they would kill each other over money. Moreover, it is highly unlikely that the prisoners were able to retain anything of value once taken prisoner. The fact that the skeletons uncovered in 2013 were found without clothing or other

artifacts suggests that whatever items they possessed before death were removed before burial and likely repurposed. Also, whereas carved graffiti from other periods (1647 and 1649) was found in the Cathedral, none was recorded in 1650. (Professor Chris Gerrard, correspondence, 5/25/18.)

13. Christopher Gerrard, "Prisoners of War: Durham and the Fate of the Scots in 1650," talk delivered at Berwick Academy, South Berwick, Maine, 11/2/16.

14. Gerrard et al., *Lost Lives, New Voices*, 156-63.

CHAPTER 4: ORIGINS

1. *Provincial Court Cases of New Hampshire*, File 1090, November 2, 1700, New Hampshire State Archives.

2. The evidence that Doughty was a Dunbar Scot is circumstantial but convincing. He appears on a list compiled by George S. Stewart in a 1911 letter to genealogist Elizabeth French on file at the New England Historic Genealogical Society. Stewart's list has never been fully corroborated by any official historical document, but the 112 individuals on it (including Doughty) have been well researched, both by historians and genealogists, suggesting its overall accuracy. In addition, thirty-five of those on Stewart's list are corroborated by a 1653 document showing that the men were property of the Company of Undertakers of the Hammersmith Ironworks on file at Harvard University's Baker Library. We know that Valentine Hill purchased Scots prisoners; Dover town records, deeding Hill four acres "for his Scots," helps to confirm that fact. Thomas Doughty himself deposed twice about Valentine Hill: once with James Oare, where both refer to Hill as their "master," and once indicating that he performed work for Hill in the late 1650s. Doughty, Oare, and several others suddenly appear on the Oyster River tax rolls in 1657-58, precisely when they would have ended their terms of servitude with Hill.

3. George Fraser Black, *The Surnames of Scotland, Their Origins Meaning and History* (New York: New York Public Library, 1962), 217.

4. These Old Parish Records are far from comprehensive. Some parishes began keeping records earlier than others; some were lost or destroyed. And registration was costly, so many people, especially poor families, didn't register important life events. Still, they offer the best information available on seventeenth-century vital statistics. It is also telling that the surname "Doughty" and its variants are not mentioned in Donald Whyte's *Scottish Surnames* nor in David Dorward's *Scottish Surnames,* yet Diane D. McNicoll, *The Surnames of East Lothian Based on the Old Parish Registers of Births & Baptisms for Haddingtonshire* (East Linton: Scottish Families Research, 1999) counts 154 total births and baptisms recorded of that name and its variants in the OPR (see page 151).

5. Robert Louis Stevenson, *The Silverado Squatters* (Boston: Roberts Brothers, 1884), 61.

6. Some scholars believe Scots to be a variant of English; others contend that it has distinct roots, originating with the language of the Angles from Denmark, who arrived in Scotland around 500 AD. See, for example, "Scots History," from the Scots Language Centre: https://www.scotslanguage.com/Scots_History. Still others argue its origins and development are not so easily mapped out. See, for example, the online Dictionary of the Scottish Language: http://www.dsl.ac.uk/about-scots/history-of-scots/origins/.

7. Deborah A. Symonds, "Death, Birth and Marriage in Early Modern Scotland," in Elizabeth Foyster and Christopher A. Whatley, Eds., *A History of Everyday Life in Scotland, 1600 to 1800* (Edinburgh: Edinburgh University Press, 2010), 91. "Small children, especially those of sub-tenants and cottagers, are often invisible in the historical record. Registration of births and deaths by parish clerks, and tombstones, cost money, and early modern kirkyards reflect the lives and monuments of the most substantial members of the parish, not the poor, or the children of the poor."

8. *A Diurnal of Remarkable Occurrents that Have Passed within the Country of Scotland since the Death of King James the Fourth Till the Year MDLXXV* (from a sixteenth-century manuscript) (Edinburgh: 1833), 17. See also *The Surnames of Scotland* (1946) by George Fraser Black (1866-1948), who connects this Duchtie with the surname "Doughty."

9. "Carta con. et mort. per Ballivos de Mussilburgh, de Thomae Duthy, Heremite ordinis Sti. Pauli, primi Heremite de Monte Sinay, et suis successoribus, de una petra terrae territorij de Mussilburgh, pro edificatione unius capellae, in honorum Dei omni potentus et Beatae Mariae de Laureto. Edr. James V. 29 Julij 1534." Quoted in James Paterson, *History of the Regality of Musselburgh: With Numerous Extracts from the Town Records* (Musselburgh, Scotland: James Gordon, 1857), 95.

10. Paterson, *History of the Regality of Musselburgh*, 96-97. Patterson writes that a local land record dated 1523, ten years before Duchtie arrived in Musselburgh with the image, describes "ane croft of land called Halleswalls, lying on the south side of the village of Newbigging, within the liberties of the town of Musselburgh, betwixt the lands some time of Thomas Dughtie on the south of the arable lands of Inveresk on the west." The Dughtie mentioned in the record, Patterson speculates, was probably either the hermit himself or his father, which explains why Dughtie chose Musselburgh as the site for his shrine. As a native, it would have been easier for him to secure a plot of land from the local magistrates.

11. See Audrey-Beth Fitch, "Marian Devotion in Scotland and the Shrine of Loretto," *In A History of Everyday Life in Medieval Scotland, 1000 to 1600*, Edward J. Cowan and Lizanne Henderson, Eds. (Edinburgh: Edinburgh University Press, 2011), 278.

12. W.H. Langhorne, *Reminiscences Connected Chiefly with Inveresk and Musselburgh and Sketches of Family Histories* (Edinburgh: David Douglas, 1893), 116-17.

13. Sir David Lindsay, "A Dialogue of the Miserable Estate of the World, Between Experience and the Courtier," book II, in *The Works of the Famous and Worthy Knight Sir David Lindsay of the Mount* (Edinburgh: Peter Williamson and C. Elliot, 1776), 66.

14. Paterson, *History of the Regality of Musselburgh*, 99-107. See also "The History of Loretto," The Lorettonian Society, accessed 3/4/15 at: http://ol.loretto.com/old_lorettonians/_history_loretto#ch01.

15. Today, a bronze stool in St. Giles commemorates Jenny Geddes's 1637 outburst.

16. Climate change and its political impact in the seventeenth-century have been well documented by Geoffrey Parker in *Global Crisis: War, Climate Change & Catastrophe in the Seventeenth Century* (New Haven: Yale University Press, 2013).

17. David Hamilton, *The Healers: A History of Medicine in Scotland* (Gretna, LA: Pelican, 1981), 45.

18. This inundation began on October 3, 1637. Robert Chambers, *Domestic Annals of Scotland, from the Reformation to the Revolution* (Edinburgh, 1859), II: 113-14.

19. Parker, *Global Crisis*, 333.

20. Parker, *Global Crisis*, 335, and Chambers, *Domestic Annals of Scotland*, II: 122.

21. Parker, *Global Crisis*, 57, 100.

22. Gibson and Smout, "Scottish Food and Scottish History," 73.

23. "Raising Children in the Early 17th Century: Demographics," Plimouth Plantation and the New England Historic Genealogical Society. Accessed 12/18/13 at: http://www.plimoth.org/media/pdf/edmaterials_demographics.pdf.

24. Rosalind K. Marshall, *Childhood in Seventeenth Century Scotland* (Edinburgh: Trustees of the National Galleries of Scotland, 1976), 25.

25. Ibid., 23.

26. Ibid., 24.

27. David McLean, "Lost Edinburgh: The Great Plague of 1645," *Scotsman*, March 24, 2014.

28. George C. Cohn, ed., *Encyclopedia of Plague and Pestilence from Ancient Times to the Present* (New York: Facts on File, 1988), 344-45.

29. D. H. Robertson, M.D., "Notes of the 'Visitation of The Pestilence,' From the Parish Records of South Leith, A.D. 1645, In Connexion with the Excavations of Large Masses of Human Remains During the Drainage Operations at Wellington Place, Leith Links, A.D. 1861-2," *Proceedings of the Society of Antiquaries of Scotland*, IV: 393.

30. See *Register of the Privy Council* (Edinburgh: H.M. General Register House, 1891), X (1613-1616): 671-72. "Forsameikle as the Kingis Majestie having a speciall care and regaird that the trew religioun be advancit and establisheit in all the pairtis of this kingdome and that all his Majesties subjectis especiallie the youth, be exercised and trayned up in civilitie, godliness, knawledge, and learning, that the vulgar Inglishe toung be universallie plantit, and the Irische language, whilk is one of the cheif and principall causes of the continewance of barbarite and incivilitie amongis the inhabitantis of the Ilis and Heylandis, may be abolishit and removeit; and quhair as thair is no measure more powerfull to further his Majesties princlie regaird and purpois that the establisheing of Scooles in the particular parroches of this Kingdom whair the youthe may be taught at least to write and reid, and be catechised and instructed in the groundis of religioun."

31. Bob Harris, "Communicating," in Foyster and Whatley, Eds., *A History of Everyday Life in Scotland*, 167.

32. Christopher A. Whatley, "Work, Time and Pastimes," in Foyster and Whatley, Eds., *A History of Everyday Life in Scotland*, 280.

33. R.A. Houston and I.D. Whyte, "Introduction: Scottish Society in Perspective," in Houston and Whyte, Eds., *Scottish Society, 1500-1800* (Cambridge: Cambridge

University Press, 1989), 12. "Cottars" were farm workers or tenants who occupied cottages in return for their labor.

34. Whatley, "Work, Time and Pastimes," 289.

35. Marshall, *Childhood in Seventeenth Century Scotland*, 19.

36. Adrienne Corliss, "A hoard of 16th and 17th century children's toys," blog in *Irish Archaeology*, February 16, 2013. Accessed 1/22/15 at: http://irisharchae ology.ie/2013/02/a-hoard-of-16th-and-17th-century-childrens-toys/.

37. For a discussion of human trafficking from these and other port cities, see Don Jordan and Michael Walsh, *White Cargo: The Forgotten History of Britain's White Slaves in America* (New York: New York University Press, 2007), 131 ff. See also, Simon P. Newman, *A New World of Labor: The Development of Plantation Slavery in the British Atlantic* (Philadelphia: University of Pennsylvania Press, 2013), 77-79.

38. *Acts of the Privy Council of England, 1619-1621* (London: His Majesty's Stationery Office, 1930), 118.

39. John Winthrop, *The Journal of John Winthrop, 1630-1649*, Eds. Richard S. Dunn, James Savage, and Laetitia Yeandle (Cambridge, MA: Harvard University Press, 1996), 429

40. Ibid., 520–30.

41. *Acts and Ordinances of the Interregnum, 1642-1660*, Eds. C.H. Firth and R.S. Rait (London: Wyman and Sons, 1911), I: 681.

42. *Register of the Privy Council of Scotland*, third series, ed. P. Hume Brown (Edinburgh: H.M. General Register House, 1909), II (1665-1669): 446.

43. Ibid., 503.

44. Information from court proceedings in Williamson's 1762 lawsuit. See Aberdeen City Council, "Green Heritage Trail," 2012, 7. Accessed 2/23/15 at: www.aberdeencity.gov.uk/web/files/LocalHistory/green_trail_leaflet.pdf. See also, *The Book of Bon Accord: or a Guide to the City of Aberdeen* (Aberdeen: Lewis and Smith, 1839), which describes both the kidnapping scheme and the trial proceedings. Douglas Skelton, in *Indian Peter: The Extraordinary Life and Adventures of Peter Williamson* (Edinburgh: Mainstream Publishing, 2007), also details the trial proceedings.

45. Peter Williamson, *French and Indian Cruelty; Exemplified in the Life and Various Vicissitudes of Fortune, of Peter Williamson, A Disbanded Soldier* (York, 1757), 5-6.

46. J. Bennet Nolan, "Peter Williamson in America, A Colonial Odyssey," *Pennsylvania History: A Journal of Mid-Atlantic Studies*, vol. 31, no. 1 (1964), 24-25.

47. Timothy J. Shannon, "King of the Indians: The Hard Fate and Curious Career of Peter Williamson," *William and Mary Quarterly*, third series, vol. 66, no. 1 (January 2009), 17.

48. Peter Williamson, "Aberdeen Slave Child Part 5," *Aberdeen Voice*, June 18, 2011. Accessed 2/22/15 at http://aberdeenvoice.com/tag/peter-williamson/. See also, *The Book of Bon Accord: or a Guide to the City of Aberdeen* (Aberdeen: Lewis and Smith, 1839). The author estimates that "when it is considered that the trade was carried on to an equal extent for nearly six years, it is impossible to estimate the number of unhappy beings carried off at less than six hundred." (pp. 89–90)

CHAPTER 5. PRISONERS, SERVANTS, OR SLAVES?

1. William Wood, *New England's Prospect* (1634), Alden T. Vaughan, ed. (Amherst: University of Massachusetts Press, 1977), 60.

2. *John Josselyn, Colonial Traveler: A Critical Edition of Two Voyages to New England*, ed. Paul J. Lindholdt, (Hanover, NH: University Press of New England, 1988), 18.

3. Edward Johnson, *Wonder Working Providence of Sions Savior in New England (1654)* (New York: Charles Scribner's Sons, 1910), 71.

4. Ibid., 71.

5. See Map of the Town of Boston, 1648, Drawn by Samuel C. Clough, in accordance with information compiled from the records of the colony (April 1919), Massachusetts Historical Society Collections Online. Accessed 11/9/14 at: http://www.masshist.org/database/viewer.php?item_id=1736&mode=small&nmask=16&img_step=6.

6. One contract for the Scottish prisoners survives: that of Alexander Gordon, or "Allexander Gorthing." See Banks, "Scotch Prsioners Deported to New England by Cromwell," 25. For a discussion of indenture, see John Donoghue, "'Out of the Land of Bondage': The English Revolution and the Atlantic Origins of Abolition," *American Historical Review*, October 2010, 948. Donoghue argues for using the seventeenth-century term "bond slave" to describe those who were involuntarily committed to temporary servitude.

7. Samuel Willard, *A Compleat Body of Divinity* (Boston: B. Green and S. Kneeland, 1726), Sermon CLXXIX, 614.

8. *John Josselyn*, 24.

9. Wendy Warren, *New England Bound: Slavery and Colonization in Early America* (New York: Liveright, 2016), 45.

10. See court record of 30 June 1663, *New Hampshire Court Records, 1643-1692* (State Papers Series, volume 40), 183. Also, Everett Hall Pendleton, *Brian Pendleton and his Massachusetts, 1634-1681* (New Jersey, 1950), 171.

11. An Inventory of the goods & Estate of Mr. Robert Cutt of Kittery, July 4, 1676. *Province and Court Records of Maine*, ed. Charles Thornton Libby (Portland: Maine Historical Society, 1931), II: 292.

12. *Suffolk Deeds* (Boston: Rockwell and Churchill, 1897), 9: 336.

13. Will of Simon Bradstreet, cases 2364, 2383, Feb. 20, 1689. *Suffolk County Probate*, 11: 276-82. New England Historic Genealogical Society microfilm.

14. Named for the saint who was himself enslaved.

15. Kathryn S. Koo, "Strangers in the House of God: Cotton Mather, Onesimus, and an Experiment in Christian Slaveholding," *Proceedings of the American Antiquarian Society*, 117: 143-75.

16. *The Adventures and Discourses of Captain John Smith Sometime President of Virginia and Admiral of New England* (London: Cassell & Company, 1883), 51.

17. Margaret Ellen Newell, "Indian Slavery in Colonial New England," in *Indian Slavery in Colonial New England*, ed. Alan Gallay (Lincoln: University of Nebraska Press, 2009), 36–37.

18. John Winthrop describes Pierce's return in *A journal of the transactions and occurrences in the settlement of Massachusetts and the other New England colonies, from the year 1630 to 1644* (Hartford: Elisha Babcock, 1790), 148.

19. Margaret Ellen Newell offers an excellent, in-depth discussion of Indian slavery during and after King Philip's War in *Brethren by Nature: New England Indians, Colonists, and the Origins of American Slavery* (Ithaca: Cornell University Press, 2015). See espec. 143-54. See also Parker, *Global Crisis*, 454, and Nathaniel Philbrick, *Mayflower* (New York: Penguin, 2006), 252.

20. Stephen P. Carlson, *The Scots at Hammersmith* (Saugus, MA: Eastern National Park & Monument Association and the National Park Service, 1976), 15.

21. Letter to Thomas Kemble from Robert Rich, William Green, and John Becx, 11 November 1651, recorded 13 May 1652 in *Suffolk Deeds,* I: 5.

22. Newman, *A New World of Labor*, 80.

23. Linford N. Fisher, "'Dangerous Designes': The 1676 Barbados Act to Prohibit New England Slave Importation," *William & Mary Quarterly*, vol. 71, no. 1 (January 2014), 109-10, 115.

24. See John Donoghue, "Out of the Land of Bondage," 950, and Carla Gardina Pestana, *The English Atlantic in the Age of Revolution, 1640-1661* (Cambridge, MA: 2004), 183–190.

25. Winthrop, *The Journal of John Winthrop*, 573.

26. See meetings of 15 January 1622 and 6 November 1632 in *Records of the Council for New England,* reprinted from the *Proceedings of the American Antiquarian Society* for April 1867 (Cambridge: John Wilson & Son, 1867), 31, 63.

27. *Report on the Records of the City of Exeter* (London: Hereford Times, 1916), 167.

28. *The Register of the Privy Council of Scotland* (3rd series), P. Hume Brown, ed. (Edinburgh: H.M. General Register House, 1908), I: 181.

29. Newman, *A New World of Labor*, 79.

30. See John Donoghue "Out of the Land of Bondage," 960; C.H. Firth and R.S. Rait, Eds, *Acts and Ordinances of the Interregnum*, I: 681; 912; and Peter Coldham, *Emigrants in Chains* (Baltimore: Genealogical Publishing Company, 1992), 46-47.

31. Entry of August 29, 1657, in W. Noel Sansbury, ed., *Calendar of State Papers* (London: Longman, Green, Longman and Roberts, 1860), I: 457.

32. John Donoghue, "Out of the Land of Bondage," 960–61 and 968.

33. John W. Blake, "Irish Transportation to America, 1653-1660," *Irish Historical Studies,* vol. III, no. 11 (March 1943), 278.

34. Peter Coldham, *English Adventurers and Emigrants, 1609-1660* (Baltimore: Genealogical Publishing Company, 1984), 163-64.

35. See article 10, Capital Laws, in the Massachusetts Body of Liberties of 1641.

36. Blake, "Irish Transportation to America," 271-72.

37. Salem Quarterly Court, 26 June 1661. *Records and Files of the Quarterly Courts of Essex County, Massachusetts* (Salem: Essex Institute, 1912), II: 294-95.

38. J.D. Butler, "British Convicts Shipped to American Colonies," *American Historical Review*, vol. 2, no. 1 (October 1896), 21-22.

39. Cotton Mather's "A Good Master Well Served" was published in 1696. Samuel Willard's sermon CLXXIX on servants and masters appeared in *A Compleat Body of Divinity*, published posthumously in 1726, and Sewall's "The Selling of Joseph" was printed in 1700.

40. See Section 88, Massachusetts Body of Liberties of 1641.

41. Section 91, Massachusetts Body of Liberties of 1641.

42. Master Samuel Symonds against Irish slaves William Downing and Philip Welch, June 25, 1661. *Records and Files of the Quarterly Courts of Essex County, Massachusetts*, II: n. 294-95.

43. Peter Williamson, *French and Indian Cruelty; Exemplified in the Life and Various Vicissitudes of Fortune, of Peter Williamson, A Disbanded Soldier* (York, 1757), iii-iv.

44. Donoghue, "Out of the Land of Bondage," 945.

45. Newell, *Brethren by Nature*, 13.

46. Larry Gragg, "A Puritan in the West Indies: The Career of Samuel Winthrop," *WMQ* 50, no. 4 (1993), 774.

47. *Winthrop Papers* (Massachusetts Historical Society, 1947), V: 38.

48. See Company of Undertakers of the Iron Works in New England. Records of the iron works at Lynn, Mass., 1650-1685 (inclusive) (Iron Works Papers). Baker Library, Harvard Business School, 103–4 and ff.

49. Iron Works Papers, 192.

50. Deposition of William Emery, October 27, 1653. *Salem Quarterly Court Records and Files,* II. See note to court session of June 29, 1658, 96–97.

51. Carlson, *The Scots at Hammersmith*, 5.

52. Iron Works Papers, 128, 59.

53. Letter of Undertakers to Giffard, April 26, 1652, in Iron Works Papers, 28, 37-38.

54. Deposition of William Emery, October 27, 1653. *Salem Quarterly Court Records and Files,* II. See note to court session of June 29, 1658, 96-97.

55. Thomas Hutchinson, *A Collection of Original Papers Relative to the History of the Colony of Massachusetts-Bay* (Boston: Thomas and John Fleet, 1769), 235.

56. E.N. Hartley, in *Ironworks on the Saugus*, has come to a similar conclusion: "Nothing in the Company accounts suggests that it provided the generous living and working conditions summarized by Cotton." See note 28, 200.

57. Cotton Mather, *A good master well served. A brief discourse on the necessary properties & practices of a good servant in every-kind of servitude: and of the methods that should be taken by the heads of a family, to obtain such a servant* (Boston: B. Green and J. Allen, 1696), 10.

58. Obidiah Turner, journal entries in James R. Newhall, *Lin: or Jewels of the Third Plantation* (Lyn, MA, 1862), 56, 75, 76.

59. See Hartley, *Ironworks on the Saugus*, 159.

60. See Item of May 23, 1655, in *The Records of the Governor and Company of the Massachusetts Bay in New England*, Nathaniel B. Shurtleff, ed. (Boston: William White, 1854), 3 (1644-1657): 381.

61. *Winthrop Papers*, V: 6–7.

62. *Suffolk Deeds* II: 210.

63. Richard Leader to John Winthrop, Jr., 21 August 1648. In *Winthrop Papers*, V: 248.

64. *Records of the Colony of Massachusetts Bay in New England*, III: 227.

65. Ibid., 257.

66. *Winthrop Papers*, II: 39.

67. John Josselyn, "The Second Voyage," in *John Josselyn, Colonial Traveler: A Critical Edition of Two Voyages to New-England*, ed. Paul J. Lindholdt (Hanover, NH: University Press of New England, 1988), 135.

68. *Province and Court Records of Maine*, I: 152.

69. June 29, 1654. *Province and Court Records of Maine*, II: 28.

70. "McIntire Garrison House at Scotland, York County, Maine," Historic American Buildings Survey (HABS-ME-9), District of Maine, June 23, 1937. Accessed 11/28/15 at Library of Congress http://lcweb2.loc.gov/master/pnp/habshaer/me/me0000/me0083/data/me0083data.pdf

71. Everett S. Stackpole, *Scotch Exiles in New England* (Portland: Maine Historical Society, 1922), 119.

72. See Everett S. Stackpole, *The History of New Hampshire* (New York: American Historical Society, 1916), 1: 76.

73. Banks, "Scotch Prisoners Deported to New England by Cromwell," 14. See also, *Province and Court Records of Maine*, 2:241, which suggests otherwise.

74. Dover Town Records (1: 59) indicate that Hill owned "seven Scotes in the year 1652." But later tax records indicate more Dunbar and Worcester prisoners living in the area. Some of these men may have been purchased by Hill at later dates; others may have worked for him as free employees once their terms of servitude expired elsewhere. Still others may simply have moved to Oyster River to live and work in and among their countrymen. See Craig B. Stinson, "Oyster River Scots," August 23, 2016, www.scottishprisonersofwar.com.

75. Banks, "Scotch Prisoners Deported to New England by Cromwell," 27.

76. Jean A. Sargent, *Valentine Hill: Sparkplug of Early New England* (Laurel, MD: 1981), 8, 18.

77. Richard M. Candee, "Merchant and Millwright: The Water Powered Sawmills of the Piscataqua," *Old-Time New England*, 60 (Spring 1970): 136.

78. Candee, "Merchant and Millwright," 146.

79. Sargent, *Valentine Hill*, 27.

80. Ibid., 29.

81. Everett S. Stackpole and Lucien Thompson, *History of the Town of Durham, New Hampshire* (Durham, NH, 1913), I: 76.

82. April 17, 1657. *Historical Memoranda Concerning Persons and Places in Old Dover, N.H.*, John Scales, ed. (Dover, NH, 1900), I: 48.

83. Candee, "Merchant and Millwright," 132.

84. Gibson and Smout, "Scottish Food and Scottish History," 67.

85. Ibid., 69.

86. Roger Williams, *A Key into the Language of America* (London: Gregory Dexter, 1643), 11–12

87. Lawrence Towner, *A Good Master Well Served, Masters and Servants in Colonial Massachusetts, 1620-1750* (New York: Garland Publishing, 1998), 125.

88. Ibid., 131.
89. *Historical Memoranda Concerning Persons and Places in Old Dover, N.H.*, I: 145, 340.
90. Stackpole, *Scotch Exiles*, 98. See also New Hampshire Court Files, Folder 17101 (1709). The neighbor's name was John Meader.
91. Court of June 30, 1659. *New Hampshire Court Records, 1643-1692* (State Papers Series), 40: 139.
92. New Hampshire Court Files, No. 1090, November 2, 1700. New Hampshire State Archives.

CHAPTER 6. LAND, WOODS, AND WATER

1. See http://scots-charitable.org/about/. The society continues to operate today.
2. They may have spoken Scots Gaelic, Scots, or English.
3. Doughty's land originally belonged to William Roberts, but no record of transfer exists, so we don't know how much he purchased it for. Proof of Doughty's ownership was recorded later, on October 5, 1667, when he sold the parcel to Jonathan Cutt. Again, the record is not clear as to the purchase price. See Doutie to Cutt, item #138, October 5, 1667. New Hampshire State Archives.
4. T.M. Devine, "Social Responses to Agrarian 'Improvement': The Highland and Lowland Clearances in Scotland," In R.A. Houston and I.D. Whyte, eds., *Scottish Society 1500-1800* (Cambridge: Cambridge University Press, 1989), 149.
5. William Cobbett, *Cobbett's Tour in Scotland; and in the Four Northern Counties of England in the Year 1832* (London: Mills, Jowett, and Mills, 1833), 130-32.
6. Charles F. Carroll, *The Timber Economy of Puritan New England* (Providence: Brown University Press, 1973), 78, 83, 86.
7. Ibid., 10.
8. Josselyn, *John Josselyn, Colonial Traveler*, 46.
9. William Cronon, *Changes in the Land: Indians, Colonists, and the Ecology of New England* (New York: Hill and Wang, 2003), 119-20.
10. Ibid., 120-21.
11. Douglas W. MacCleery, *American Forests, A History of Resiliency and Recovery* (Durham, NC: Forest History Society, 2011), 6-8.
12. Benno M. Forman, "Mill Sawing in Seventeenth-Century Massachusetts," *Old Time New England*, vol. 60 (no. 220; spring 1970), 119.
13. James Elliot Defenbaugh, *History of the Lumber Industry of America*, (Chicago: American Lumberman, 1907), II: 38.
14. Charles E.L. Wingate, *History of the Wingate Family in England and America*, (Exeter, NH: 1886), 26.
15. At Dover Court, June 30, 1663. See *New Hampshire Court Records, 1640-1692* (State Papers Series), 40: 179.
16. Ibid., 110.
17. Ibid., 465.
18. Ibid., 468.
19. Court held at Kittery, March 11, 1650. *Maine Province and Court Records*, I: 161.
20. Stackpole and Thompson, *History of the Town of Durham, New Hampshire*, I: 71.

21. Candee, "Merchant and Millwright," 145.

22. The date of the inventory was August 2, 1669. *York Deeds*, ed. William A. Sargent (Portland: Brown Thurston & Co., 1888), II: 69.

23. At the time Maine was under Massachusetts rule.

24. Huchison v. Douty, in *Records of the Suffolk County Court, 1671-1680* (Boston: Colonial Society of Massachusetts, 1933), XXIX: 11.

25. See Doutie to Cutt, item #138, October 5, 1667. New Hampshire State Archives.

26. Candee, "Merchant and Millwright," 134. See also, Edwin A. Churchill, "Mid-Seventeenth-Century Maine: A World on the Edge," in Baker, Churchill et al., Eds., *American Beginnings: Exploration, Culture, and Cartography in the Land of Norumbega* (Lincoln: University of Nebraska Press, 1994), 253.

27. George Wadleigh, *Notable Events in the History of Dover, New Hampshire from the First Settlement in 1623 to 1865* (Medford, MA: Tufts College Press, 1913), 23.

28. Ibid., 25.

29. Ibid., 63.

30. Defenbaugh, *History of the Lumber Industry of America*, II: 65.

31. William Hubbard, *The History of the Indian Wars in New England from the First Settlement to the Termination of the War with King Philip in 1677,* ed. Samuel G. Drake (Roxbury, MA: Elliot Woodward, 1865), II: 75-76. "Rift sawing" entailed cutting logs radially, which produced more waste but made the lumber more stable and long-lasting.

32. Defenbaugh, *History of the Lumber Industry of America*, II: 67.

33. Ibid., 68.

34. George Folsom, *History of Saco and Biddeford with Notices of Other Early Settlements, and of the Proprietary Governments in Maine Including the Provinces of New Somersetshire and Lygonia* (Saco: Alex C. Putnam, 1830), 99.

35. As many scholars have pointed out, land transactions with Native Americans often weren't intended to permanently relinquish native rights to the land; instead, they were often intended as treaties, conveying shared rights and responsibilities. See, for example, Lisa Brooks, *Our Beloved Kin: A New History of King Philip's War* (New Haven: Yale University Press, 2018), 22–23, 41.

36. Folsom, *History of Saco and Biddeford*, 168–69.

37. See Michael Chaney, *White Pine on the Saco River: An Oral History of River Driving in Southern Maine* (Orono: Maine Folklife Center, 1993), Northeast Folklore Series, vol. 29.

38. According to his letter to Governor Andros. See James Phinney Baxter, ed., *Documentary History of the State of Maine* (Portland: Maine Historical Society, 1900), VI: 353.

39. John Cotton, "God's Promise to His Plantation (1630)," ed. Reiner Smolinski, Electronic Texts in American Studies 22. http://digitalcommons.unl.edu/etas/22. John Winthrop, letter to John Wheelwright, ca. March 1638/39 in *Papers of the Winthrop Family*, vol. IV, Winthrop Papers Digital Edition, Massachusetts Historical Society, https://www.masshist.org/publications/winthrop/index.php/view/PWF04d089. Accessed 5/29/18.

40. For Phillips's transaction, see *York Deeds*, II:37. For that of James Oare, see Stackpole and Thompson, *History of the Town of Durham, New Hampshire*, I: 77.

41. See Daniel Remich, *History of Kennebunk from its Earliest Settlement to 1890* (Kennebunk, ME: 1911), 38n.

42. The wooden horse was a military punishment. The offender was strapped to a triangular-shaped wooden post, or to planks nailed together to form a sharp ridge on top. The rider would straddle the sharp ridge of the post, typically with his hands tied behind his back and muskets or other heavy objects tied to his legs to weigh them down to increase the pain and discomfort. The post or planks stood horizontally on four legs and was therefore called a "horse."

43. See *Maine Province and Court Records*, II: 282.

44. In addition to Richard Gibson, Doughty engaged in bonds with, or paid fines for, Peter Grant, Thomas Chicke, and Abraham Collines.

45. Court of June 12, 1666. *Maine Province and Court Records*, I: 262. Magistrates present were "Ed. Rishworth, president, Fran. Champernowne, Ed. Johnson, Fran. Hooke, John Wincoll."

46. See *Maine Province and Court Records*, I: 272.

47. The list of magistrates includes some of the most illustrious merchants and landowners of both Boston and the frontier provinces. Henry Jocelyn (also spelled Josselyn) was the son of Sir Thomas Josselyn, brother of the writer John Josselyn, and a large landowner in Black Point, Maine. William Phillips, a wealthy Boston merchant and the largest landowner in Saco, was a close business associate of Doughty. Edward Johnson was a Puritan printer, historian, and a founder of Woburn. Edward Rishworth was appointed by Sir Ferdinando Gorges to distribute land in Wells and was a long-serving recorder for the York County court. Samuel Wheelwright was Rishworth's brother-in-law and the son of John Wheelwright, the Antinomian who had been banished from Massachusetts Bay along with Anne Hutchinson. Robert Cutt was the brother of John Cutt, first president of New Hampshire (to whom Doughty had sold his first property), and a noted shipbuilder in Kittery. John Wincoll, to whom Doughty supplied lumber, was a captain in the militias and owned a sawmill at Salmon Falls.

48. Court of July 9, 1667. See *Maine Province and Court Records*, I: 286. By "paress," perhaps they meant "peers."

49. Ibid., 286.

50. Court session of June 12, 1666. *Maine Province and Court Records*, I: 272-73. Justices were Francis Champernowne, Edward Johnson, Francis Hooke, John Wincoll, and Edward Rishworth.

51. Doughty won a settlement in court with Oare and Brown on July 4, 1676. See *Maine Province & Court Records*, II: 313.

52. *Maine Province and Court Records*, III: 163. It is likely that Doughty was actually leasing Bridget Phillips's mill at the time, since the tax assessment says the mill is located at Saco Falls. Doughty's own mill, near Swan Pond, may not have been large enough for the volume of work he was engaged in.

53. Colonel William Phillips may have remained in Boston after fleeing the 1675 Wabanaki attack on his garrison. He died in Boston in 1683. The property re-

mained in the hands of Bridget Phillips and the colonel's two sons, Samuel and William, Jr. See *York Deeds*, IV: 20 and VIII: 241.

54. For an articulate and detailed discussion of the land issue, see John Frederick Martin, *Profits in the Wilderness: Entrepreneurship and the Founding of New England Towns in the Seventeenth Century* (Chapel Hill: University of North Carolina Press, 1991), espec. 260 ff.

55. Samuel Sewell to Increase Mather, July 24, 1688. See *The Diary of Samuel Sewell, 1674-1729*, vol. I, 231 in *Collections of the Massachusetts Historical Society*, V (fifth series) (Boston: 1878).

56. James Phinney Baxter, ed., *Documentary History of the State of Maine* (Portland: Maine Historical Society, 1900), VI: 353.

57. Cotton Mather & others, *The declaration of the gentlemen, merchants, and inhabitants of Boston, and the countrey adjacent, April 18th, 1689* (Boston: Samuel Green, 1689).

58. In *Our Beloved Kin: A New History of King Philip's War*, Lisa Brooks argues convincingly that such land deals were a prime catalyst for the war.

59. Instructions for the Agents for the Colonie of the Massachusetts Bay in New England, 24 January 1689/90. In William Henry Whitmore, *The Andros Tracts: Being a Collection of Pamphlets and Official Papers Issued during the Period between the Overthrow of the Andros Government and the Establishment of the Second Charter of Massachusetts* (Boston: Prince Society, 1874), III: 31–32.

CHAPTER 7. A CHILDE UNLAWFULLY BEGOTTEN

1. Inquest, July 1,1661. *Province and Court Records of Maine*, II: 104.

2. Stackpole and Thompson, *History of the Town of Durham*, I: 79.

3. It is possible there were two Peter Grants, since Carlson has Grant in Lynn as late as 1665 and then moving to Hartford, Connecticut, not Maine, after serving at the iron works. See Carlson, 14. See also Stackpole, *Scotch Exiles in New England*, 87, and Banks, 16.

4. Act of May 1647, section 4. See Otto Erwin Koegel, *Common Law Marriage and Its Development in the United States* (Washington, DC: John Byrne & Company, 1922), 60.

5. Banks in "Scotch Prisoners Deported to New England by Cromwell, 1651-52," estimated the cost of a transatlantic trip from England to Boston in 1651–1652 at about £5. Court records from 1664 suggest that Doughty's and Peter Grant's properties combined were worth some £20. While this suggests that either might have been able to save for a transatlantic trip, in New England both had the option of purchasing and owning land. Being able to purchase land in Scotland would have been highly unlikely.

6. Stackpole and Thompson, *History of the Town of Durham*, I: 79.

7. July 5, 1664. *Province and Court Records of Maine*, II: 152.

8. Ibid.

9. September 13, 1664. *Province and Court Records of Maine*, II: 152.

10. See Huchison v. Douty, September 19 and November 9, 1671, *Records of the Suffolk County Court, 1671-1680*, XXIX. Original contract was dated June 1, 1665.

11. September 13, 1664. *Province and Court Records of Maine*, II: 152.

12. *Province and Court Records of Maine*, II: 152 n. states: "This couple married 28 November 1664 according to an attested copy of the Kittery town records, now lost (Suff. Court Files 137175), and Capt. James, their son, was born 23 March 1671-2. The child the bride was big with became Elizabeth, made chief heir as 'Elizabeth Grant, daughter of Joanee wife of Peter Grant' in James Grant's will, 1679, doubtless his half-sister. The husband's will named his seven children, 'them seven,' no Elizabeth."

13. November 12, 1667. *Province and Court Records of Maine*, I: 305.

14. See the Massachusetts Bay law code of 1641. Also, Else Hambleton, *Daughters of Eve: Pregnant Brides and Unwed Mothers in Seventeenth-Century Massachusetts* (New York: Routledge, 2004), 88.

15. *Province and Court Records of Maine*, I: 169.

16. Ibid., 169 n.

17. Some have speculated that Elizabeth was actually the daughter of Nicholas Bully, Jr., who married Ellen Booth in July 1652. See Beatty, *Vital Records of Biddeford, Maine Prior to 1856*. But extant vital records record only two children from that marriage: Abigale and Nicholas, both born in February 1654.

18. Genealogists have speculated that she was as young as sixteen or seventeen, but no extant records prove this. Richard Archer in *Fissure in the Rock* (Hanover, NH: University Press of New England, 2001) states that, on average, 10 percent of women living in New England married before reaching age seventeen; half were married by age twenty, and 90 percent were married by twenty-five. See p. 78.

19. July 5, 1670. *Maine Province and Court Records*, II: 198. Magistrates were: Tho. Danforth, Richard Waldron, Elias Stileman, John Wincoll, ed. Rishworth, Francis Neale.

20. The Julian calendar in use at the time meant that the year didn't officially begin until March 25. So the date of Elizabeth's birth is often recorded as 1669/70. According to the Gregorian calendar, she would have been born February 14, 1670.

21. The vital records are not entirely clear as to dates. In *Vital Records of Biddeford, Maine Prior to 1856* (Camden, ME: Picton Press, 1998), the marriage entry reads "Thomas Doutie maried to Elyzabeth Bullie Jan [Jun?] 24,1669." The transcriber suggests that, given the handwritten record, the date of the marriage could have been January or possibly June, with January being more likely. The same transcription shows "Elyzabeth Dowtie doughter of Thomas borne February 14, 1669-70." The case for a January marriage is stronger for several reasons. According to the Biddeford town historian, the town clerk in 1669-1670 didn't fully close his a's in the handwritten record (correspondence with Charles Butler, town historian, Biddeford, Maine, 10/26/17), so the abbreviations for January and June would be difficult to distinguish. Moreover, June 1669 would have been roughly thirty-one weeks—nearly eight months—prior to the Doughtys' first daughter's birth. It's unlikely that such a schedule would have incurred the standard fine of fifty shillings per person, rather than a reduced fine acknowledging that gestation varied somewhat from individual to individual. In *Daughters of Eve*, Else Hambleton notes only a single conviction in the seventeenth-century records of Essex County, Massachusetts, "in which the pregnancy went longer than 32 weeks" from the date of

marriage (p. 87), suggesting that fornication charges beyond thirty-two weeks were rare. The most likely scenario, then, is that Thomas Doughty and Elizabeth Bully were married on January 24, 1670 (according to our current calendar), less than one month before the birth of their first daughter, on February 14, 1670.

22. June 28, 1670. *New Hampshire Court Records* 40: 258.

23. Under the old system of British currency, there were twenty shillings to a pound. Therefore, the Durgins' paying fifty shillings each amounted to five pounds. Doughty was assessed a fine of five pounds that likely covered both his and Elizabeth's charges.

24. See Abby Chandler, *Law and Sexual Misconduct in New England, 1650-1750: Steering Towards England* (New York: Routledge, 2015), 13. In Plymouth Colony, the fee for fornication was £10 but was reduced to fifty shillings for couples who were betrothed. See John Demos, *A Little Commonwealth: Family Life in Plymouth Colony* (New York: Oxford University Press, 2000), 152 and n.p. 158; Dorothy A. Mays, *Women in Early America: Struggle, Survival and Freedom in a New World* (Santa Barbara, CA: ABC-Clio, 2004), 146; and John D'Emelio and Estelle B. Freedman "Family Life and the Regulation of Deviance," in *Sexualities in History: A Reader*, Eds. Kim M. Phillips and Barry Reay (New York: Routledge, 2002), 148.

25. Article 43, Massachusetts Body of Liberties of 1641. See also, Else Hambleton, *Daughters of Eve: Pregnant Brides and Unwed Mothers in Seventeenth-Century Massachusetts* (New York: Routledge, 2004), 88.

26. Richard Godbeer, *Sexual Revolution in Early America* (Baltimore: Johns Hopkins University Press, 2002), 34.

27. Hambleton, *Daughters of Eve*, 87.

28. Claudia Durst Johnson, *Daily Life in Colonial New England* (Westport, CT: Greenwood Press, 2002), 110.

29. July 1, 1661. *Province and Court Records of Maine*, II: 106.

30. July 5, 1670. *Province and Court Records of Maine*, II: 197.

31. Will of Nicholas Bully, November 1678, Suffolk County, MA, probate case #995.

32. The six Bullie children were Elizabeth, Ann, Grace, Nicholas Jr., Tamsen, and John. Tamsen and Nicholas Jr. predeceased their father.

33. As John Demos has pointed out in *A Little Commonwealth*, parents' capacity to withhold a child's inheritance gave them leverage in dictating whom the child would marry and expressing their approval or disapproval: "One man left his daughter a handsome gift of household furnishings 'att her marriage and if shee please her mother in her match.'" See p. 156.

34. See Godbeer, *Sexual Revolution in Early America*; Katherine Crawford, *European Sexualities, 1400-1800* (Cambridge: Cambridge University Press, 2007); and Abby Chandler, *At the Magistrate's Discretion: Sexual Crime and New England Law, 1636-1718* (Dissertation, University of Maine, 2008).

35. June 25, 1667. In *New Hampshire Court Records*, 40: 224.

36. *New Hampshire Court Records*, 40: 225.

37. September 17, 1667. *New Hampshire Court Records*, 40: 227–28.

38. In the hundred years between 1650 and 1750, 1,843 sexual misconduct trials were conducted in Maine, Essex County, Massachusetts, and Rhode Island. Only

ten of these were for rape. See Chandler, *Law and Sexual Misconduct in New England, 1650-1750*, 10.

39. See cases involving Saraih Smyth, Saphirah Sowards, Ann Greene, and Luce Boaden in *Maine Province and Court Records*, II: 221, 239, 264, and 354, respectively. See cases involving Marie, an Indian woman, Jennet Severne, Sara Pierce, and Grace Roberts in *New Hampshire Court Records*, 40:145, 296, and 390, respectively.

40. Robert St. George, "'Heated' Speech and Literacy in Seventeenth-Century New England." In David D. Hall and David Grayson Allen, Eds., *Seventeenth-Century New England* (Colonial Society of Massachusetts, 1984), 280.

41. July 6, 1669. *Province and Court Records of Maine*, II: 184.

42. *Province and Court Records of Maine*, III: 77.

43. According to his will of 19 October 1709. See *Maine Wills 1640-1760*, ed. William M. Sargent (Portland: Brown Thurston & Co., 1887), 212-13.

44. *Maine Wills 1640-1760*, 212-13.

45. *Province and Court Records of Maine*, II: 308.

46. *New Hampshire Court Records*, 40: 115.

47. Ibid.

48. Ibid., 242.

49. July 4, 1671. *Province and Court Records of Maine*, I: 224 (#53).

50. Alice Morse Earle, *The Sabbath in Puritan New England* (New York: Charles Scribner's Sons, 1891), 247.

51. A "Goodwife Bouley" is mentioned; probably Elizabeth's sister-in-law. See Edgar Yates, "Early Vital Records of Saco and Biddeford, Me," *New England Historical and Genealogical Register* (Boston: New England Historical and Genealogical Society, 1917), 71: 124.

52. *The Diary of Mary Cooper*, excerpts, 1768-1773. The National Humanities Center. Accessed 7/22/15 at: http://nationalhumanitiescenter.org/pds/becoming amer/peoples/text5/marycooper.pdf.

CHAPTER 8. ETHNIC WARS

1. In "Finding the Almouchiquois: Native American Families, Territories, and Land Sales in Southern Maine," *Ethnohistory*, vol. 1, no. 1, Emerson Baker writes that "Champlain used the term Almouchiquois to describe the people living on the coast of New England, south of the Kennebec, and all the way to Massachusetts Bay." See page 79. He also asserts that the natives of coastal Maine south of the Kennebec were distinct from native communities to the north and east, and that they "should all be considered to be Almouchiquois, the peoples who ranged as far south as the north shore of Massachusetts" (p. 94). The communities of natives living in Maine during the seventeenth century are not easily distinguished or categorized. Many individuals moved widely across Maine and southern New England, and marriages and political alliances brought natives together into complex communities that were sometimes difficult for European settlers to sort out. Throughout, I've followed the current convention of using the term "Wabanaki" to refer broadly to the natives of northern New England and Canada's maritime provinces. Where possible, I've tried to be more specific, referring to natives' des-

ignations in seventeenth-century (English) documents, which often associate them with rivers or other place names: Penobscots, Kennebecs, Ammoscoggins (or Androscoggins), Sacos, Ossipees, Pequackets.

2. Christopher Levett explored the Maine coast in 1623-1624.

3. Henry Sweetser Burrage, *The Beginnings of Colonial Maine, 1602-1658* (Portland: Marks Printing House, 1914), 169.

4. Alfred Crosby coined the term "virgin soil epidemics" to describe these occurrences. See "Virgin Soil Epidemics as a Factor in the Aboriginal Depopulation of America," *William & Mary Quarterly,* third series, vol. 33, no. 2 (April 1976), 289-99. See also, Bruce J. Bourque, *Twelve Thousand Years, American Indians in Maine* (Lincoln: University of Nebraska Press, 2001), 118 ff.

5. William Bradford, *Of Plymouth Plantation, 1620-1647,* ed. Samuel Eliot Morison (New York: Alfred A. Knopf, 2011), 271.

6. Josselyn, *John Josselyn, Colonial Traveler,* 138.

7. Parker, *Global Crisis,* 445-46.

8. Hubbard, *The History of the Indian Wars in New-England,* 2: 189.

9. Ibid., 156.

10. Letter of Thomas Gardner to Governor Leverett, September 22, 1675, in James Phinney Baxter, ed., *Documentary History of the State of Maine Containing the Baxter Manuscripts* (Portland: Maine Historical Society, 1900), 6: 92-93.

11. See Lisa Brooks, *Our Beloved Kin: A New History of King Philip's War* (New Haven: Yale University Press, 2018), 122 ff.

12. William D. Williamson, *The History of the State of Maine: from Its First Discovery, A.D. 1602, to the Separation A.D. 1820 Inclusive* (Hallowell, ME: Glazier, Masters & Co., 1832), 1: 517.

13. Brooks, *Our Beloved Kin,* 213.

14. George M. Bodge, *Soldiers in King Philip's War Containing Lists of the Soldiers of Massachusetts Colony Who Served in the Indian War of 1675-1677* (Boston, 1891), 249.

15. Michael Dekker, *French & Indian Wars in Maine* (Charleston, SC: History Press, 2015), 24.

16. George Folsom, *The History of Saco and Biddeford with Notices of Other Early Settlements* (Saco: Alex C. Putnam, 1830), 152-53.

17. At current-day Biddeford.

18. Jill Lepore, *The Name of War: King Philip's War and the Origins of American Identity* (New York: Vintage, 1999), 91.

19. Folsom, *The History of Saco and Biddeford,* 155.

20. Folsom, *The History of Saco and Biddeford,* 154-56, and Letter of Major Richard Walderne, September 25, 1675, reprinted in Bodge, *Soldiers in King Philip's War,* 247–48.

21. Hubbard, *The History of the Indian Wars,* 2: 110.

22. George Wadleigh, *Notable Events in the History of Dover, New Hampshire, from the First Settlement in 1623 to 1865* (Dover, NH, 1913), 54.

23. William Sewell, *The History of the Rise, Increase and Progress of the Christian People Called Quakers: Intermixed with Several Remarkable Occurrences* (Philadelphia, 1728), 324.

24. Letter of September 25, 1675, in Bodge, *Soldiers in King Philip's War*, 248.
25. Sayword, however, appears to have been heavily indebted and mortgaged the property to Bostonians Robert Gibb and Simon Lynde. See Daniel Remich, *The History of Kennebunk from Its Earliest Settlement to 1890, Including Biographical Sketches* (1911), 35-36. Scotchmen's Brook, which enters the Mousam near the present-day village of Kennebunk, is likely named after Brown and Oare. See Remich, n. p. 38.
26. James Phinney Baxter, ed., *Documentary History of the State of Maine Containing the Baxter Manuscripts* (Portland: Maine Historical Society, 1900), 6: 195–96.
27. Hubbard, *The History of the Indian Wars*, 2: 116.
28. Ibid., 2: 118.
29. Ibid., 2: 51.
30. Ibid., 119-20.
31. Ibid., 117.
32. Ibid., 170-71.
33. See James Axtell, "The Vengeful Women of Marblehead: Robert Roules's Deposition of 1677," *William & Mary Quarterly*, vol. 1, no. 4, 652.
34. Bodge, *Soldiers in King Philip's War*, 253.
35. Ibid., 248.
36. Williamson, *The History of the State of Maine*, 1: 530 n.
37. Hubbard, *The History of the Indian Wars,* 2: 130.
38. Ibid., 2: 130.
39. In relating this incident, I have relied heavily on Lisa Brooks' and Margaret Ellen Newell's analyses, which point out many inaccuracies in Hubbard's and other early versions. See Brooks, *Beloved Kin*, 332, and Newell, *Brethren by Nature*, 185-86.
40. Hubbard, *History of the Indian Wars*, II: 132.
41. Letters of Moxes and Indians W. H. and G. recorded by Mrs. Hamond, July 1, 1677, in *Documentary History of the State of Maine*, 6: 179.
42. Brooks, *Our Beloved Kin*, 22.
43. Williamson, *The History of the State of Maine*, 1: 57.
44. Emerson W. Baker and John G. Reid, "Amerindian Power in the Early Modern Northeast: A Reappraisal," *WMQ* LXI, no. 1, 84.
45. Hubbard, *The History of the Indian Wars*, 2: 53–54.
46. Letter of Thomas Gardner to Governor Leverett, Pemaquid, September 22, 1675, in *Documentary History of the State of Maine*, 6: 91-92.
47. *Documentary History of the State of Maine*, 6: 178.
48. Lawsuit of April 2, 1678, against Henry Sayword suggests that Doughty is no longer partnering with James Oare or Henry Brown in Wells. See *Province and Court Records of Maine*, 3: 522.
49. See *Province and Court Records of Maine*, 3: 162-63, for proceedings of April 12, 1682. It is highly likely that Doughty was leasing and running the Phillips's mill at Saco Falls at the time.
50. Doughty vs. Sayword, April 2, 1678, in *Province and Court Records of Maine*, 2: 522. Palmer vs. Doughty, March 31, 1685, in *Province and Court Records of*

Maine, 3: 210. Davis vs. Doughty, March 30, 1686, in *Province and Court Records of Maine*, 3: 227-28.

51. Court record of August 19, 1681 at Wells. *Province and Court Records of Maine*, 3: 20-22. The record doesn't indicate which magistrates presided over that session.

52. Court session of August 21, 1685. *Province and Court Records of Maine*, 3: 215-16.

53. William Willis, *The History of Portland from 1632 to 1864 with a Notice of Previous Settlements, Colonial Grants, and Changes of Government in Maine* (Portland: Bailey & Noyes, 1865), 273.

54. Williamson, *History of the State of Maine*, 1: 609.

55. Court records place Oare and Brown together in Maine at least until 1688. See *Province and Court Records of Maine*, 3:251.

56. Williamson, *History of the State of Maine*, 1: 611.

57. Thomas Church, *The History of Philips's War* (Exeter, NH: J. & B. Williams, 1829), 163 n.

58. Williamson, *History of the State of Maine*, 1: 612.

CHAPTER 9. REFUGEES

1. Samuel Gardner Drake, *The Book of the Indians of North America* (Boston: Josiah Drake, 1833), 109.

2. Everett S. Stackpole, *Scotch Exiles in New England*. 1922. Maine Historical Society, 100.

3. See Thomas Church, *The History of Philip's War*, ed. Samuel G. Drake (Exeter, NH: J. & B. Williams, 1829), 176 n.

4. See Mary Beth Norton, *In the Devil's Snare: The Salem Witchcraft Crisis of 1692* (New York: Vintage, 2002), 104-5; also, letters of April 30, May 1 and May 18, in *Documentary History of the State of Maine*, 4: 91-93, 99-100, 102.

5. Both *The Genealogical Dictionary of Maine and New Hampshire* and Stackpole's *Scotch Prisoners* suggest Malden, though the author has been unable to find reference to any land holdings, taxes paid, or legal proceedings to indicate Doughty's residence there. An August 1690 civil suit against a merchant named Henry Smith places Thomas Doughty in Suffolk County. See *Abstract and Index of the Records of the Inferior Court of Pleas (Suffolk County Court) Held at Boston, 1680-1698* (Boston: Historical Records Survey, 1940), 65.

6. Emerson W. Baker, *A Storm of Witchcraft: The Salem Trials and the American Experience* (New York: Oxford University Press, 2015), 203.

7. Samuel A. Green, "Unpublished Narratives of the Expedition of Sir William Phipps against Canada, in 1690." *Proceedings of the Massachusetts Historical Society*, second series, 15 (1901-1902): 317.

8. Letter from Governor Sloughter to Lord Nottingham, Fort William Henry, March 26, 1691. E.B. O'Callaghan and John Brodhead, Eds., *Documents Relative to the Colonial History of the State of New York* (Albany: Weed, Parsons and Co., 1853), 3: 96.

9. *Publick Occurrences, both Forreign and Domestick*, number 1, September 25, 1690. Accessed 9/28/16 at: http://nationalhumanitiescenter.org/pds/amerbegin/power/text5/PublickOccurrences.pdf.

10. See Cotton Mather, *Magnalia Christi Americana: or, the Ecclesiastical History of New-England* (Hartford: Silas Andrus, 1820), 2: 537-40.

11. The 1680s and 1690s were the worst decades of the Little Ice Age in New England. See Karen Ordahl Kupperman "Climate and Mastery of the Wilderness in Seventeenth-Century New England," in David Hall, D.G. Allen, and P.C.F. Smith, Eds., *Seventeenth-Century New England*, vol. 63 (1984), 26; and Brian Fagan, *The Little Ice Age: How Climate Made History, 1300-1850* (New York: Basic Books, 2002), 113.

12. See Samuel Sewall's diary entries of July 20, July 27, August 25, and September 21, 1692, where he mentions praying and fasting in response to drought. *Diary of Samuel Sewall, 1674-1729* (Boston: Massachusetts Historical Society, 1878), vol. 1. See also Karen Ordahl Kupperman, "Climate and Mastery of the Wilderness in Seventeenth-Century New England," 31.

13. Among other historians, Mary Beth Norton has argued that the trauma of warfare on the eastern frontier and the influx of refugees from those conflicts into Salem and surrounding towns helped to precipitate the crisis. Emerson W. Baker argues that a "perfect storm" of events, including war, local land and political disputes, and larger power struggles, lay behind the witch trials.

14. For a discussion of how land speculation on New England's frontier influenced the witchcraft crisis, see Emerson W. Baker and James Kences, "Maine, Indian Land Speculation, and the Essex County Witchcraft Outbreak of 1692," *Maine History* 40 (3) (Fall 2001): 159-89.

15. Julian Goodare, Lauren Martin, Joyce Miller and Louise Yeoman, "The Survey of Scottish Witchcraft," Introduction, University of Edinburgh. Accessed 10/17/16 at: http://www.shca.ed.ac.uk/Research/witches/introduction.html.

16. Examination of Tituba, *Salem Witchcraft Papers*, eds. Paul Boyer and Stephen Nissenbaum (New York: Da Capo Press, 1977), digital edition, revised, corrected and augmented by Benjamin C. Ray and Tara S. Wood (University of Virginia Scholars Lab, 2010), item no. 125.4.

17. Norton, *In the Devil's Snare*, 105.

18. Ibid., 143, 321.

19. *Documentary History of the State of Maine*, 6: 194–95.

20. Baker and Kences, "Maine Indian Land Speculation," 168–69.

21. *York Deeds* 8: 151. September 8, 1692.

22. Entry of August 19, 1692, *Diary of Samuel Sewall, 1674-1729*, 1: 363.

23. "Letter of Thomas Brattle, F.R.S. 1692," *In Narratives of the Witchcraft Cases*, ed. George L. Burr (New York: Charles Scribner's Sons, 1914), 184.

24. Increase Mather, "Cases of Conscience Concerning Evil Spirits Personating Men, Witchcrafts, Infallible Proofs of Guilt in Such as Are Accused with that Crime (Boston: Benjamin Harris, 1693). See pp. 34, 66.

25. Norton, *In the Devil's Snare*, 279, and Frances Hill, *The Salem Witch Trials Reader* (Cambridge, MA: Da Capo Press, 2000), xxi.

26. George Lincoln Burr, ed., *Narratives of the Witchcraft Cases* (New York: Charles Scribner's Sons, 1914), 369 n.

27. A Goodwife Rule appears on the seating list for the Saco meetinghouse in 1674. Undoubtedly, the Rules were also known to the Doughtys.

28. *Town Records of Salem, Massachusetts* (Salem: Essex Institute, 1934), 3(1680-1691): 9.

29. Paul Boyer and Stephen Nissenbaum, *Salem Possessed: the Social Origins of Witchcraft* (Cambridge: Harvard University Press, 1974), 89–90.

30. Baker, *A Storm of Witchcraft*, 240.

31. See transaction 26:204 in Essex Deeds (Southern District) of October 4, 1700. This deed, however, was not recorded until March 18, 1713, and is found under the grantor name of "Flood." "Flood" was Captain John Floyd, who served, along with Stephen Williams, as attorney for James Menzies, the landowner, who was not present at the transaction. The acreage isn't clear from the deed itself, which is old and difficult to read. But circumstantial evidence indicates it was at least two hundred acres. According to Sidney Perley, "The Cedar Pond Region, Salem, in 1700," *Essex Institute Historical Collections* 51 (1915): 23–40, Menzies' land was part (roughly half) of the original Humphrey Farm (some five hundred acres), which had been divided between two heirs.

32. Brooks, *Our Beloved Kin*, 22–23; 41.

33. Lion Gardner, "Relation of the Pequot Warres," (1660) in *Massachusetts Historical Society Collections*, 3rd series, 3(1833): 154.

34. See entry for 1695, *The Constitution and Bylaws of the Scots Charitable Society of Boston* (Boston: Scots Charitable Society, 1896), 85.

35. See *Essex County Deeds* 14:145 dated March 18, 1700-1701. While the index records the date as 1700, the deed records the date as "March the 18th 1700/1701 (probably Old Style calendar), confirming the more logical notion that the sale took place in 1701.

36. Boyer and Nissenbaum, *Salem Possessed*, 200.

37. See Paul Boyer and Stephen Nissenbaum, Eds., *Salem-Village Witchcraft: A Documentary Record of Local Conflict in Colonial New England* (Boston: Northeastern University Press, 1972), 152-154.

38. See entry for November 11, 1675 in *Salem Town Records*, 3 (1680-1691): 205.

39. Sybil Noyes, Charles Thornton Libby, Walter Goodwin Davis, *Geneaological Dictionary of Maine and New Hampshire* (Baltimore: Genealogical Publishing Co., Inc., 1988) says that Abigail Bully (b. 1655) was the daughter of Nicholas Bully, Jr. George Folsom, *History of Saco and Biddeford*, 180, suggests that Ellen Bully was Nicholas Bully Sr.'s daughter, when she was more likely his daughter-in-law, widowed in 1664 by Nicholas Bully, Jr.'s death. Ellen married John Henderson that year.

40. See *Essex County Deeds* 16:30. Transaction of April 7, 1702.

41. Deloraine Pendre Corey, *History of Malden, Massachusetts, 1633-1785* (Malden, 1899), 684.

42. Ibid., 684-85.

43. Among Plymouth settlers, John Demos noted "a pervasive tendency to expand and scatter—a tendency that leaders of the Colony sought unsuccessfully to restrain." See *A Little Commonwealth: Family Life in Plymouth Colony* (New York: Oxford University Press, 2000), 88.

44. *Records of the Congregational Church in Windham, Conn., 1700-1851* (Hartford: Connecticut Historical Society, 1943), 5.

45. William Willis, *The History of Portland, from 1632 to 1864: with a Notice of Previous Settlements, Colonial Grants, and Changes of Government in Maine* (Portland: Bailey & Noyes, 1865), 321-22, 326-27.

46. Ulster Scots immigrants to America weren't confined to Maine. During the eighteenth century, more than two hundred thousand immigrated to the American colonies, with large numbers settling in Pennsylvania, Virginia, the Carolinas, and into Appalachia and farther west.

47. *Acts and Resolves Public and Private of the Province of Massachusetts Bay* (Boston: Wright & Potter, 1902), IX, chapter 119 (December 3, 1719), 636.

CHAPTER 10. & FURTHER SAYTH NOT

1. Wheelwright was the founder of Exeter, New Hampshire, and had come north with a number of followers exiled by Massachusetts Bay for their Antinomian beliefs. Antinomians believed that faith alone—not a body of established morals—was essential to salvation.

2. See, "A Discourse between John Reeve and Richard Leader, Merchant; recited by Lodowick Muggleton, One of the Two Last Witnesses and Prophets of the Most High God, the Man Christ Jesus in Glory," in *The Works of John Reeve and Lodowick Muggleton, the Two Last Prophets of the Only True God, Our Lord Jesus Christ* (London, 1832), III: 38–47.

3. See Emerson W. Baker and James Kences, "Maine, Indian Land Speculation," p. 172; also, Louise A. Breen, "Judgment at Salem: War, Witchcraft, and Empire," *In* Louise A. Breen, ed., *Converging Worlds: Communities and Cultures in Colonial America* (New York: Routledge, 2012), 298.

4. Long before William Phillips died in 1683, Bridget Phillips was presented at court for "not frequenting of the publique meeting on the Lords day." See *Maine Province & Court Records*, I: 236, court session of November 7, 1665.

5. Roger Williams, "The Bloudy Tenant of Persecution, for Cause of Conscience," 1644.

6. Cotton Mather, "The Negro Christianized" (Boston: B. Green, 1706), 21.

7. Thomas Doutee, probate record, March 12, 1706. Case no. 8196 in *Essex County, MA: Probate File Papers, 1638-1881*. Online database from records supplied by the Massachusetts Supreme Judicial Court Archives. *AmericanAncestors. org*. New England Historic Genealogical Society, 2014. https://www.americanancestors.org/DB515/t/13765/8196-co7/30152058.

8. In *Lost Lives, New Voices*, Gerrard et al. compared twelve of the Scottish prisoners' estates. Doughty's estate (not included in the survey) fell into the third category, £100–249, where "conditions improve markedly." See p. 237.

9. *Documentary History of the State of Maine*, VI: 353. In the seventeenth-century context, "desart" refers simply to an unsettled or uncultivated piece of land.

10. Ibid., 343.

11. Everett Stackpole, "Notes on Scotch-Irish Who Settled in Maine." Maine Historical Society manuscript collection no. 1569. Stackpole cites a file number for New Hampshire court records (volume 5, p. 35), but the author and the archivists at the New Hampshire State Archives were unable to find the record under his ci-

tation. Nevertheless, the text that Stackpole cites is credible, not only because it is carefully quoted in seventeenth-century orthography, but it also concerns one of several known land deals in Greenland, New Hampshire, between Valentine Hill and Captain Francis Champernown, whose farm was located in Greenland.

12. *New Hampshire Court Files*, No. 1090, November 2, 1700. New Hampshire State Archives. Transcribed by the author, 5/20/2016.

Bibliography

Aberdeen City Council. "Green Heritage Trail," 2012. Accessed February 23, 2015, at: www.aberdeencity.gov.uk/web/files/LocalHistory/green_trail_leaflet.pdf.

Abstract and Index of the Records of the Inferior Court of Pleas (Suffolk County Court) Held at Boston, 1680-1698. Boston: Historical Records Survey, 1940.

Acts and Resolves Public and Private of the Province of Massachusetts Bay. Boston: Wright & Potter, 1902.

Acts of the Privy Council of England, 1619-1621. London, 1930.

Archer, Richard. *Fissure in the Rock*. Hanover, NH: University Press of New England, 2001.

Atkin, Malcolm. *Cromwell's Crowning Mercy: The Battle of Worcester 1651*. Thrupp, Stroud, Gloucestershire: Sutton, 1998.

Axtell, James. "The Vengeful Women of Marblehead: Robert Roules's Deposition of 1677." *William & Mary Quarterly*, 31 no. 4 (1974): 647-52.

Bailyn, Bernard. *The New England Merchants in the Seventeenth Century*. Cambridge, MA: Harvard University Press, 1955.

—. *The Peopling of British North America: An Introduction*. New York: Alfred A. Knopf, 1986.

Baker, Emerson W. *The Devil of Great Island: Witchcraft and Conflict in Early New England*. New York: St. Martin's, 2007.

—. "Finding the Almouchiquois: Native American Families, Territories, and Land Sales in Southern Maine." *Ethnohistory*, 51, no. 1 (winter 2004): 73-100.

—. *A Storm of Witchcraft: The Salem Trials and the American Experience*. New York: Oxford University Press, 2015.

——, Edwin A. Churchill, Richard S. D'Abate, Kristine L. Jones, Victor A. Konrad, and Harald E. L. Prins, editors. *American Beginnings: Exploration, Culture, and Cartography in the Land of Norumbega.* Lincoln: University of Nebraska Press, 1994.

—— and James Kences, "Maine, Indian Land Speculation, and the Essex County Witchcraft Outbreak of 1692." *Maine History,* 40, no. 3 (Fall 2001): 159-89.

—— and John G. Reid. *The New England Knight: Sir William Phipps, 1651-1695.* Toronto: University of Toronto Press, 1998.

—— and John G. Reid. "Amerindian Power in the Early Modern Northeast: A Reappraisal." *William & Mary Quarterly,* third series, 61, no. 1 (January 2004): 77-106.

Balfour, James. "Annales of Scotland." In *The Historical Works of Sir James Balfour.* Volume 3. Edinburgh, 1824.

Banks, Charles Edward. "Scotch Prisoners Deported to New England by Cromwell, 1651-1652." *Proceedings of the Massachusetts Historical Society,* 61 (1927-1928): 4-29.

Baxter, James Phinney, ed. *Documentary History of the State of Maine Containing the Baxter Manuscripts.* Vols. 4, 6. Portland: Maine Historical Society, 1900.

Beatty, John D. *Vital Records of Biddeford, Maine prior to 1856.* Camden, ME: Picton Press, 1998.

Beckles, Hilary McD. *White Servitude and Black Slavery in Barbados, 1627-1715.* Knoxville: University of Tennessee Press, 1989.

Bender, Thomas. *Community and Social Change in America.* Baltimore: Johns Hopkins University Press, 1982.

Berry, Stephen R. *A Path in the Mighty Waters: Shipboard Life & Atlantic Crossings to the New World.* New Haven: Yale University Press, 2015.

Black, George Fraser. *The Surnames of Scotland, Their Origins Meaning and History.* New York: New York Public Library, 1946.

Blake, John W. "Irish Transportation to America, 1653–1660." *Irish Historical Studies,* 3, no. 11 (March 1943): 267-81.

Bodge, George M. *Soldiers in King Philip's War. Containing Lists of the Soldiers of Massachusetts Colony Who Served in the Indian War of 1675-1677.* Boston, 1891.

The Book of Bon Accord: or a Guide to the City of Aberdeen. Aberdeen, 1839.

Bourque, Bruce J. *Twelve Thousand Years, American Indians in Maine.* Lincoln: University of Nebraska Press, 2001.

Boyer, Paul and Stephen Nissenbaum. *Salem Possessed: the Social Origins of Witchcraft.* Cambridge, MA: Harvard University Press, 1974.

—, eds. *Salem-Village Witchcraft: A Documentary Record of Local Conflict in Colonial New England.* Boston: Northeastern University Press, 1972.

—, eds. *Salem Witchcraft Papers.* New York: Da Capo Press, 1977.

Bradford, William. *Of Plymouth Plantation, 1620-1647.* Edited by Samuel Eliot Morison. New York: Alfred A. Knopf, 2011.

Breen, Louise A. "Judgment at Salem: War, Witchcraft, and Empire." In Louise A. Breen, ed., *Converging Worlds: Communities and Cultures in Colonial America.* New York: Routledge, 2012.

Brooks, Lisa. *Our Beloved Kin: a New History of King Philip's War.* New Haven: Yale University Press, 2018.

Brown, P. Hume, ed. *Register of the Privy Council of Scotland.* Third series, 2. Edinburgh: H.M. General Register House, 1909.

Burr, George L., ed. *Narratives of the Witchcraft Cases.* New York: Charles Scribner's Sons, 1914.

Burrage, Henry Sweetser. *The Beginnings of Colonial Maine, 1602-1658.* State of Maine, 1914.

Butler, J.D. "British Convicts Shipped to American Colonies." *American Historical Review,* 2, no. 1 (October 1896): 12-33.

Caffell, Anwen. "Palace Green Library Excavations 2013 (PGL13), Human Remains." Department of Archeology, Durham University, July 2014. Accessed May 30, 2017, at: www.dur.ac.uk/resources/archaeology/pdfs/PGL13_Human_Bone_Report.pdf.

Candee, Richard M. "Merchant and Millwright: The Water Powered Sawmills of the Piscataqua." *Old-Time New England,* 60 (Spring 1970): 131-49.

Carlson, Stephen P. *The Scots at Hammersmith.* Eastern National Park & Monument Association and the National Park Service, 1976.

Carlyle, Thomas. *Oliver Cromwell's Letters and Speeches: with Elucidations.* Vol. 2. London, 1846.

Carroll, Charles F. *The Timber Economy of Puritan New England.* Providence: Brown University Press, 1973.

Chadborne, Ava. *Maine Place Names and the Peopling of its Towns: York and Oxford Counties.* Bond-Wheelwright, 1957.

Chambers, Robert. *Domestic Annals of Scotland, from the Reformation to the Revolution.* Vol. 2. Edinburgh, 1859.

Chandler, Abby. *At the Magistrate's Discretion: Sexual Crime and New England Law, 1636-1718.* Dissertation, University of Maine, 2008. www.digitalcommons.library.umaine.edu/etd/114/.

—-. *Law and Sexual Misconduct in New England, 1650-1750: Steering Towards England.* New York: Routledge, 2015.

Chaney, Michael. *White Pine on the Saco River: An Oral History of River Driving in Southern Maine.* Northeast Folklore Series, vol. 29. Orono: Maine Folklife Center, 1993.

Church, Thomas. *History of Philip's War.* Exeter, NH, 1829.

Cobbett, William. *Cobbett's Tour in Scotland; and in the Four Northern Counties of England in the Year 1832.* London, 1833.

Cohn, George C., ed. *Encyclopedia of Plague and Pestilence from Ancient Times to the Present.* New York: Facts on File, 1988.

Coldham, Peter Wilson. *The Complete Book of Emigrants in Bondage, 1617-1775.* Baltimore: Genealogical Publishing Company, 1988.

—-. *Emigrants in Chains.* Baltimore: Genealogical Publishing Company, 1992.

—-. *English Adventurers and Emigrants, 1609-1660.* Baltimore: Genealogical Publishing Company, 1984.

Company of Undertakers of the Iron Works in New England. Records of the iron works at Lynn, Massachusetts, 1650-1685 inclusive. Baker Library, Harvard University Business School.

Connecticut Historical Society. *Records of the Congregational Church in Windham, Conn., 1700-1851.* Hartford, 1943.

Cooper, Mary. *The Diary of Mary Cooper,* excerpts, 1768-1773. National Humanities Center. Accessed July 22, 2015, at www.nationalhumanitiescenter.org/pds/becomingamer/peoples/text5/marycooper.pdf.

Corey, Deloraine Pendre. *History of Malden, Massachusetts, 1633-1785.* Malden, 1899.

Corliss, Adrienne. "A Hoard of 16th and 17th Century Children's Toys." *Irish Archaeology,* 16 February 2013. Accessed January 22, 2015, at: www.irisharchaeology.ie/2013/02/a-hoard-of-16th-and-17th-century-childrens-toys/.

Cotton, John. "God's Promise to His Plantation" (1630). Edited by Reiner Smolinski. Digital Commons at University of Nebraska-

Lincoln, Electronic Texts in American Studies, 22. www.digital-commons.unl.edu/etas/22.

Coughlin, Michelle Marchetti. *One Colonial Woman's World: The Life and Writings of Mehetabel Chandler Coit.* Amherst: University of Massachusetts Press, 2012.

Cronon, William. *Changes in the Land, Indians: Colonists, and the Ecology of New England.* New York: Hill and Wang, 2003.

Crosby, Alfred. "Virgin Soil Epidemics as a Factor in the Aboriginal Depopulation of America." *William & Mary Quarterly,* third series, 33, no. 2 (April 1976): 289-99.

Deane, Charles, ed. *Records of the Council for New England, Reprinted from the Proceedings of the American Antiquarian Society for April 1867.* Cambridge, 1867.

Defenbaugh, James Elliot. *History of the Lumber Industry of America.* Vol. 2. Chicago: American Lumberman, 1907.

Dekker, Michael. *French & Indian Wars in Maine.* Charleston, SC: History Press, 2015.

D'Emelio, John and Estelle B. Freedman. *Intimate Matters: A History of Sexuality in America.* 3rd edition. Chicago: University of Chicago Press, 2012.

Demos, John. *A Little Commonwealth: Family Life in Plymouth Colony.* New York: Oxford University Press, 2000.

Dictionary of the Scottish Language. Accessed May 5, 2018, at www.dsl.ac.uk/about-scots/history-of-scots/origins/.

A Diurnal of Remarkable Occurrents that Have Passed within the Country of Scotland since the Death of King James the Fourth Till the Year MDLXXV. Edinburgh, 1833.

Dobson, David. *Scottish Emigration to Colonial America, 1607-1785.* Athens: University of Georgia Press, 1994.

Donoghue, John. "'Out of the Land of Bondage': The English Revolution and the Atlantic Origins of Abolition." *American Historical Review,* 115, no. 4 (1 October 2010): 943-74.

Dorward, David. *Scottish Surnames.* Edinburgh: Mercat, 2003.

Douglas, William Scott. *Cromwell's Scotch Campaigns 1650-51.* London, 1898.

Doutee, Thomas. Probate case no. 8196, March 12, 1706. In *Essex County, Mass: Probate File Papers, 1638-1881.* Online database from records supplied by the Massachusetts Supreme Judicial

Court Archives, New England Historic Genealogical Society, 2014. www.americanancestors.org/DB515/t/13765/8196-co7/3015 2058.

Douty, Thomas. Deposition. New Hampshire Court Files. No. 1090. November 2, 1700. New Hampshire State Archives.

Dow, George Francis. *Everyday Life in the Massachusetts Bay Colony.* Boston: Society for Preservation of New England Antiquities, 1935.

——, ed. *Records and Files of the Quarterly Courts of Essex County, Massachusetts.* 9 volumes. Salem: Essex Institute, 1911-1975.

Drake, Samuel Gardner. *The Book of the Indians of North America.* Boston, 1833.

Drew, Charles A., ed. *Suffolk Deeds.* Vol. 9. Boston, 1897.

Durham University, Department of Archeology. "The Identification." Accessed September 3, 2015, at: www.dur.ac.uk/archaeology/research/projects/europe/pg-skeletons/find.

Earle, Alice Morse. *The Sabbath in Puritan New England.* New York, 1891.

Fagan, Brian. *The Little Ice Age: How Climate Made History, 1300-1850.* New York: Basic Books, 2002.

Firth, C.H. "The Battle of Dunbar." *Transactions of the Royal Historical Society,* New Series, 14 (1900): 19-52.

—— and R.S. Rait, *Acts and Ordinances of the Interregnum, 1642-1660.* Vol. 1. London: Wyman and Sons, 1911.

Fisher, Linford N. "'Dangerous Designes': The 1676 Barbados Act to Prohibit New England Slave Importation." *William & Mary Quarterly,* third series, 71, no. 1 (2014): 99-124.

Fitch, Audrey-Beth. "Marian Devotion in Scotland and the Shrine of Loretto." In *A History of Everyday Life in Medieval Scotland, 1000 to 1600.* Edited by Edward J. Cowan and Lizanne Henderson. Edinburgh: Edinburgh University Press, 2011, 274-88.

Folsom, George. *The History of Saco and Biddeford with Notices of Other Early Settlements.* Saco, 1830.

Forman, Benno M. "Mill Sawing in Seventeenth-Century Massachusetts." *Old Time New England,* 60, no. 220 (spring 1970): 110-30.

Foyster, Elizabeth and Christopher A. Whatley, eds. *A History of Everyday Life in Scotland, 1600 to 1800.* Edinburgh: Edinburgh University Press, 2010.

Frost, John E. *Maine Probate Abstracts.* Camden, ME: Picton Press, 1991.

Gardener, Lion. "Relation of the Pequot Warres" (1660). *Massachusetts Historical Society Collections,* 3rd series, 3 (1833): 131-60.

Gardiner, Samuel. *History of the Commonwealth and Protectorate, 1649-1656.* Vol. 1. London: Longmans, Green & Co., 1903.

Gerrard, Christopher. "Prisoners of War: Durham and the Fate of the Scots in 1650." Talk delivered at Berwick Academy, South Berwick, Maine, November 2, 2016.

—, Pam Graves, Andrew Millard, Richard Annis, and Anwan Caffell. *Lost Lives, New Voices: Unlocking the Stories of the Scottish Soldiers from the Battle of Dunbar 1650.* Oxford: Oxbow Books, 2018.

Godbeer, Richard. *Sexual Revolution in Early America.* Baltimore: Johns Hopkins University Press, 2002.

Goodare, Julian, Lauren Martin, Joyce Miller, and Louise Yeoman. "The Survey of Scottish Witchcraft." Introduction. University of Edinburgh. Accessed October 17, 2016, at: www.shca.ed.ac.uk/Research/witches/introduction.html.

Gragg, Larry D. "A Puritan in the West Indies: The Career of Samuel Winthrop." *William & Mary Quarterly,* 50, no. 4 (1993): 768-86.

Grainger, John D. *Cromwell Against the Scots, the Last Anglo-Scottish War 1650-1652.* East Linton, East Lothian, Scotland: Tuckwell, 1997.

Green, Mary Anne Everett, ed. *Calendar of State Papers, Domestic Series, 1650.* London, 1876.

Green, Samuel A. "Unpublished Narratives of the Expedition of Sir William Phipps against Canada, in 1690." *Proceedings of the Massachusetts Historical Society,* second series, 15 (1901-1902): 281-320.

Hambleton, Else L. *Daughters of Eve: Pregnant Brides and Unwed Mothers in Seventeenth-Century Essex County, Massachusetts.* New York: Routledge, 2004.

Hamilton, David. *The Healers: A History of Medicine in Scotland.* Gretna, LA: Pelican, 1981.

Hamilton, Marsha L. *Social and Economic Networks in Early Massachusetts: Atlantic Connections.* University Park: Pennsylvania State University Press, 2009.

Hammond, Otis G., ed. *New Hampshire Court Records, 1643-1692.* State Papers Series vol. 40. State of New Hampshire, 1943.

Harrower, John. "Diary of John Harrower, 1773-1776." *American Historical Review*, 6, no. 1 (October 1900): 65-107.

Hartley, E.N. *Ironworks on the Saugus*. Norman: University of Oklahoma Press, 1957.

Hesilrige, Arthur. "To the honorable committee of the Councel of State for Irish and Scotish affairs at White-Hall, concerning the Scots prisoners." London, October 31, 1650. National Library of Scotland, digital.nls.uk/scotlandspages/timeline/1650.html.

Historic American Buildings Survey. "McIntire Garrison House at Scotland, York County, Maine." (HABS-ME-9), District of Maine, June 23, 1937. Accessed November 28, 2015, at Library of Congress: www.lcweb2.loc.gov/master/pnp/habshaer/me/me0000/me0083/data/me0083data.pdf.

Hodgson, John. "A Large Relation of the Fight at Leith Neere Edenburgh." In Henry Slingsby and John Hodgson, *Original Memoirs Written during the Civil War: Being the Life of Sir Henry Slingsby and Memoirs of Captain Hodgson*. Edinburgh, 1807.

Houston, R.A. and I.D. Whyte, eds. *Scottish Society, 1500-1800*. Cambridge: Cambridge University Press, 2005.

Hubbard, William. *The History of the Indian Wars in New England from the First Settlement to the Termination of the War with King Philip in 1677*. Edited by Samuel G. Drake. 2 vols. Roxbury, MA: Elliot Woodward, 1865.

Hutchinson, Thomas. *A Collection of Original Papers Relative to the History of the Colony of Massachusetts-Bay*. Boston, 1769.

Johnson, Claudia Durst. *Daily Life in Colonial New England*. Westport, CT: Greenwood Press, 2002.

Johnson, Edward. *Wonder Working Providence of Sions Savior in New England (1654)*. New York: Charles Scribner's Sons, 1910.

Jordan, Don and Michael Walsh, *White Cargo: The Forgotten History of Britain's White Slaves in America*. New York: New York University Press, 2007.

Josselyn, John. *John Josselyn, Colonial Traveler: A Critical Edition of Two Voyages to New England*. Edited by Paul J. Lindholdt. Hanover, NH: University Press of New England, 1988.

Keys, David. "Skeletons of Scottish prisoners provide evidence of child soldiers in Britain's civil wars." *Independent*. Accessed September 3, 2015, at: www.independent.co.uk/news/science/archaeology/skeletons-of-scottish-prisoners-provide-evidence-of-child-soldiers-in-english-civil-war-10482793.html.

"KING CHARLS HIS SPEECH Made upon the SCAFFOLD At *Whitehall*-Gate, Immediately before his Execution, On Tuesday the 30 of *Ian*. 1648 With a Relation of the maner of his going to Execution. *Published by Special Authority*." London, 1649. Accessed May 24, 2018, at: www.anglicanhistory.org/charles/charles1.html.

Koegel, Otto Erwin. *Common Law Marriage and Its Development in the United States*. Washington, DC: John Byrne & Company, 1922.

Koo, Kathryn S. "Strangers in the House of God: Cotton Mather, Onesimus, and an Experiment in Christian Slaveholding." *Proceedings of the American Antiquarian Society*, 117: 143-75.

Kupperman, Karen Ordahl. "Climate and Mastery of the Wilderness in Seventeenth-Century New England." In David Hall, D.G. Allen, and P.C.F. Smith, eds. *Seventeenth-Century New England*, 63 (1984): 3-37.

Langhorne, W.H. *Reminiscences Connected Chiefly with Inveresk and Musselburgh and Sketches of Family Histories*. Edinburgh, 1893.

Laramie, Michael G. *King William's War: The First Contest for North America, 1689–1697*. Yardley, PA: Westholme Publishing, 2017.

Lepore, Jill. *The Name of War: King Philip's War and the Origins of American Identity*. New York: Vintage Books, 1999.

Lindsay, David. "A Dialogue of the Miserable Estate of the World, Between Experience and the Courtier." Book II. In *The Works of the Famous and Worthy Knight Sir David Lindsay of the Mount*. Edinburgh, 1776.

Lockridge, Kenneth A. *Literacy in Colonial New England: An Enquiry into the Social Context of Literacy in the Early Modern West*. New York: W.W. Norton, 1974.

Macaulay, Thomas B. *The History of England from the Accession of James II*. Volume I. London, 1849.

MacCleery, Douglas W. *American Forests, A History of Resiliency and Recovery*. Durham, NC: Forest History Society, 2011.

MacKenzie, Alexander. *The History of the Munros of Fowlis with Genealogies of Principal Families of the Name: to Which Are Added Those of Lexington and New England*. Inverness, Scotland, 1898.

Marshall, Rosalind K. *Childhood in Seventeenth Century Scotland*. Trustees of the National Galleries of Scotland, 1976.

Martin, John Frederick. *Profits in the Wilderness: Entrepreneurship and the Founding of New England Towns in the Seventeenth Century.* Chapel Hill: University of North Carolina Press, 1991.

Massachusetts Body of Liberties (1641).

Massachusetts Historical Society. *Papers of the Winthrop Family.* Vol. 4. Winthrop Papers Digital Edition, www.masshist.org/publications/winthrop/index.php/view/PWF04d089. Accessed May 29, 2018.

Masson, David, ed. *The Register of the Privy Council of Scotland.* Vol. 10 (1613-1616). Edinburgh, 1891.

Mather, Cotton. *A good master well served. A brief discourse on the necessary properties & practices of a good servant in every-kind of servitude: and of the methods that should be taken by the heads of a family, to obtain such a servant.* Boston, 1696.

——. *Magnalia Christi Americana: or, the Ecclesiastical History of New-England.* Volume 2. Hartford, 1820.

——. "The Negro Christianized." Boston, 1706.

—— & others. *The declaration of the gentlemen, merchants, and inhabitants of Boston, and the countrey adjacent, April 18th, 1689.* Boston, 1689.

Mather, Increase. "Cases of Conscience Concerning Evil Spirits Personating Men, Witchcrafts, Infallible Proofs of Guilt in Such as Are Accused with that Crime." Boston, 1693.

Mays, Dorothy A. *Women in Early America: Struggle, Survival and Freedom in a New World.* Santa Barbara, CA: ABC-Clio, 2004.

McLean, David. "Lost Edinburgh: The Great Plague of 1645." *Scotsman,* March 24, 2014.

McNicoll, Diane D. *The Surnames of East Lothian Based on the Old Parish Registers of Births & Baptisms for Haddingtonshire.* East Linton, Scotland: Scottish Families Researched, 1999.

Mercurius Politicus (London). September 12-19, 1650.

Mittelberger, Gottlieb. *Gottlieb Mittelberger's Journey to Pennsylvania in the Year 1750 and Return to Germany in the year 1754.* Translated by Carl Theo. Eben. Philadelphia, 1898.

Morrison, Alvin. *Tricentennial Too: King Philip's War Northern Front (Maine 1675-1678).* 1977. Maine Historical Society pamphlet 1122.

Muhlenberg, Henry Melchior. *The Journals of Henry Melchior Muhlenberg.* Vol. 1, translated by Theodore G. Tappert and John W.

Doberstein. Philadelphia: Evangelical Lutheran ministerium of Pennsylvania and adjacent states and the Muhlenberg Press, 1942.

National Records of Scotland. Old Parish Registers, 1553-1854. ScotlandsPeople website, www.scotlandspeople.gov.uk.

Newell, Margaret Ellen. *Brethren by Nature: New England Indians, Colonists, and the Origins of American Slavery.* Ithaca: Cornell University Press, 2015.

——. "Indian Slavery in Colonial New England," In *Indian Slavery in Colonial New England,* edited by Alan Gallay, 33-66. Lincoln: University of Nebraska Press, 2009.

Newhall, James R. *Lin: Or Jewels of the Third Plantation.* Lynn, MA, 1862.

Newman, Simon P. *A New World of Labor: The Development of Plantation Slavery in the British Atlantic.* Philadelphia: University of Pennsylvania Press, 2013.

Newton, Hannah. "The Dying Child in 17th-Century England." *Pediatrics,* 136 (August 2015). Accessed October 12, 2017, at www.pediatrics.aappublications.org.

Nicoll, John. *A Diary of Public Transactions and Other Occurrences, Chiefly in Scotland, From January 1650 to June 1667.* Edinburgh, 1836.

Nolan, J. Bennet. "Peter Williamson in America, A Colonial Odyssey." *Pennsylvania History: A Journal of Mid-Atlantic Studies,* 31, no. 1 (1964): 23-29.

Norton, Mary Beth. *In the Devil's Snare: The Salem Witchcraft Crisis of 1692.* New York: Vintage Books, 2002.

Noyes, Sybil, Charles Thornton Libby, and Walter Goodwin Davis. *Genealogical Dictionary of Maine and New Hampshire.* Baltimore: Genealogical Publishing Company, 1988.

O'Callaghan, E.B. and John Brodhead, eds. *Documents Relative to the Colonial History of the State of New York.* Albany, NY, 1853.

Palmer, Colin. *The First Passage: Blacks in the Americas 1502-1617.* New York: Oxford University Press, 1995.

Parker, Geoffrey. *Global Crisis: War, Climate Change & Catastrophe in the Seventeenth Century.* New Haven: Yale University Press, 2013.

Pastorius, Daniel Francis. "Compare the ship that bore them hither with Noah's Ark: Francis Daniel Pastorius describes his impressions of Pennsylvania, 1683." Accessed July 27, 2015, at: www.history-matters.gmu.edu/d/7439.

Paterson, James. *History of the Regality of Musselburgh: With Numerous Extracts from the Town Records*. Musselburgh, Scotland, 1857.

Paterson, Kirsteen. "Child soldiers' remains found in mass grave of troops captured at Battle of Dunbar." *National*, September 2, 2015. www.thenational.scot/news/child-soldiers-remains-found-in-mass-grave-of-troops-captured-at-battle-of-dunbar.7130.

Payne, Linda. "Health in England (16th-18th c.)." *Children and Youth in History*, Item #166, www.chnm.gmu.edu/cyh/items/show/166. Accessed October 12, 2017.

Pendleton, Everett Hall. *Brian Pendleton and his Massachusetts, 1634-1681*. New Jersey, 1950.

Perley, Sidney. "The Cedar Pond Region, Salem, in 1700," *Essex Institute Historical Collections*, 51 (1915): 23-40.

Pestana, Carla Gardina. *The English Atlantic in the Age of Revolution, 1640-1661*. Cambridge, MA: Harvard University Press, 2004.

"Peter Williamson, Aberdeen Slave Child Part 5." *Aberdeen Voice*, June 18, 2011. www.aberdeenvoice.com/tag/peter-williamson/.

Philbrick, Nathaniel. *Mayflower, A Story of Courage, Community, and War*. New York: Penguin Books, 2006.

Plimouth Plantation and the New England Historic Genealogical Society. "Raising Children in the Early 17th Century: Demographics." Accessed December 18, 2013, at: www.plimoth.org/media/pdf/edmaterials_demographics.pdf.

Powers, Edwin. *Crime and Punishment in Early Massachusetts, 1620-1692: A Documentary History*. Boston: Beacon Press, 1966.

Proceedings and Debates of the British Parliaments Respecting North America. Vol. I, edited by Leo Francis Stock. Washington, DC: Carnegie Institution of Washington, 1924.

Province and Court Records of Maine. Vols. 1-3. Portland: Maine Historical Society, 1928-1931.

Publick Occurrences, both Forreign and Domestick. No. 1, September 25, 1690. Accessed September 28, 2016, at: www.nationalhumanitiescenter.org/pds/amerbegin/power/text5/PublickOccurrences.pdf.

Ranlet, Philip, "Another Look at the Causes of King Philip's War," *NEQ*, 61 (1988): 79-100.

Rapaport, Diane. "Scots for Sale, The Fate of the Scottish Prisoners in Seventeenth-Century Massachusetts." *New England Ancestors*, winter, 2003: 30-32.

——. "Scots for Sale, Part II: Scottish Prisoners in Seventeenth-Century Maine and New Hampshire," *New England Ancestors*, Holiday 2004, 26-28.

——. "Scottish Slavery in 17th-Century New England." *History Scotland*, 5, no. 1 (January-February 2005): 44-52.

Records of the Suffolk County Court, 1671-1680. Vol. 29. Boston: Colonial Society of Massachusetts, 1933.

Reese, Peter. *Cromwell's Masterstroke: Dunbar 1650.* Barnsley, UK: Pen & Sword Books, 2006.

Reeve, John and Lodowick Muggleton. *The Works of John Reeve and Lodowick Muggleton, the Two Last Prophets of the Only True God, Our Lord Jesus Christ.* Vol. 3. London, 1832.

Reid, Stuart. *Dunbar 1650: Cromwell's Most Famous Battle.* Oxford: Osprey Publishing, 2004.

Remich, Daniel. *The History of Kennebunk from Its Earliest Settlement to 1890, Including Biographical Sketches.* Kennebunk, ME, 1911.

Report on the Records of the City of Exeter. London: H.M. Stationery Office and *Hereford Times*, 1916.

Robertson, D.H. "Notes of the 'Visitation of The Pestilence,' From the Parish Records of South Leith, A.D. 1645, In Connexion with the Excavations of Large Masses of Human Remains During the Drainage Operations at Wellington Place, Leith Links, A.D. 1861-2." *Proceedings of the Society of Antiquaries of Scotland,* 4: 392-95.

Sansbury, W. Noel, ed. *Calendar of State Papers.* Vol. 1 (1574-1660). London, 1860.

Sargent, Jean A. *Valentine Hill: Sparkplug of Early New England.* Laurel, MD, 1981.

Sargent, William M., ed. *Maine Wills, 1640-1760.* Portland, 1887.

——., ed. *York Deeds.* 18 vols. Portland, ME, 1888.

Scales, John, ed. *Historical Memoranda Concerning Persons and Places in Old Dover, N.H.* Vol.1. Dover, NH, 1900.

Scots Charitable Society. *The Constitution and Bylaws of the Scots Charitable Society of Boston.* Boston, 1896.

Scots Charitable Society, www.scots-charitable.org.

"Scots History." Scots Language Centre. Accessed May 5, 2018, at www.scotslanguage.com/Scots_History.

Scottish Prisoners of War Society. www.scottishprisonersofwar.com.

Sewell, Samuel. *The Diary of Samuel Sewell, 1674-1729.* Vol. 1. *Collections of the Massachusetts Historical Society,* 5 (fifth series). Boston, 1878.

Sewell, William. *The History of the Rise, Increase and Progress of the Christian People Called Quakers: Intermixed with Several Remarkable Occurrences.* Philadelphia, 1728.

Shannon, Timothy J. "King of the Indians: The Hard Fate and Curious Career of Peter Williamson." *William & Mary Quarterly,* third series, 66, no. 1 (January 2009): 3-44.

Shurtleff, Nathaniel B., ed. *Records of the Governor and Company of the Massachusetts Bay in New England.* Vol. 3 (1644-1657). Boston, 1854.

Skelton, Douglas. *Indian Peter: The Extraordinary Life and Adventures of Peter Williamson.* Edinburgh: Mainstream Publishing, 2005.

Smith, Abbot Emerson. *Colonists in Bondage: White Servitude and Convict Labor in America, 1607-1776.* Chapel Hill: University of North Carolina Press and Omohundro Institute, 2012.

Smith, John. *The Adventures and Discourses of Captain John Smith Sometime President of Virginia and Admiral of New England.* London, 1883.

Spaulding Club. *History of Scots Affairs from MDCXXXVII to MDCXLI.* Vol. 1. Aberdeen, 1841.

Stackpole, Everett S. *The History of New Hampshire.* Vol. 1. New York: American Historical Society, 1916.

——. "Notes on Scotch-Irish Who Settled in Maine." Maine Historical Society Manuscript Collection, no. 1569.

——. *Scotch Exiles in New England.* 1922. Archival Material. Maine Historical Society Special Collection.

—— and Lucien Thompson. *History of the Town of Durham, New Hampshire (Oyster River Plantation) with Genealogical Notes.* 2 vols. Durham, NH, 1913.

Steele, Ian K. *The English Atlantic, 1675-1740: An Exploration of Communication and Community.* New York: Oxford University Press, 1986.

Stevenson, Robert Louis. *The Silverado Squatters.* Boston, 1884.

Stewart. George S. Letter to Elizabeth French, January 18, 1911. New England Historic Genealogical Society.

St. George, Robert. "'Heated' Speech and Literacy in Seventeenth-Century New England." In David D. Hall and David Grayson

Allen, eds., *Seventeenth-Century New England*. Boston: Colonial Society of Massachusetts: 1984.

Stinson, Craig B. "Oyster River Scots." August 23, 2016. Scottish Prisoners of War Society, www.scottishprisonersofwar.com.

Suffolk County, Massachusetts Probate. Volume 11. New England Historic Genealogical Society microfilm.

Sylvester, Herbert Milton. *Indian Wars of New England*. 3 vols. Boston: W.B. Clark, 1910.

Tepper, Michael. *New World Immigrants: A Consolidation of Ship Passenger Lists and Associated Data from Periodical Literature*. Vol. 1. Baltimore: Genealogical Publishing Company, 1988.

Torrey, Clarence Almon. *New England Marriages Prior to 1700*. Baltimore: Genealogical Publishing Company, 1985.

Towner, Lawrence W. *A Good Master Well Served: Masters and Servants in Colonial Massachusetts, 1620-1750.* New York: Garland Publishing, 1998.

Town Records of Salem, Massachusetts. Vol. 3 (1680-1691). Salem, MA: Essex Institute, 1934.

Trask, William Blake, ed. *Suffolk Deeds*. Vols. 1-2. Boston, 1880.

Wadleigh, George. *Notable Events in the History of Dover, New Hampshire, from the First Settlement in 1623 to 1865*. Dover, 1913.

Warren, Wendy. *New England Bound: Slavery and Colonization in Early America*. New York: Liveright, 2016.

Whitmore, William Henry. *The Andros Tracts: Being a Collection of Pamphlets and Official Papers Issued during the Period between the Overthrow of the Andros Government and the Establishment of the Second Charter of Massachusetts,* vol. 3. Boston: 1874.

Whyte, Donald. *Scottish Surnames*. Edinburgh: Birlinn, 2000.

Willard, Samuel. *A Compleat Body of Divinity*. Boston, 1726.

Williams, Roger. "The Bloudy Tenant of Persecution, for Cause of Conscience." 1644.

——. *A Key into the Language of America*. London, 1643.

Williamson, Peter. *French and Indian Cruelty: Exemplified in the Life, and Various Vicissitudes of Fortune of Peter Williamson, A Disbanded Soldier*. York, England, 1757.

Williamson, William D. *The History of the State of Maine from Its Discovery A.D. 1602, to the Separation A.D. 1820 Inclusive*. 2 vols. Hallowell, ME, 1832.

Willis, William. *The History of Portland from 1632 to 1864 with a Notice of Previous Settlements, Colonial Grants, and Changes of Government in Maine*. Portland, ME, 1865.

Wingate, Charles E.L. *History of the Wingate Family in England and America*. Exeter, NH, 1886.

Winthrop, John. *The Journal of John Winthrop, 1630-1649*. Edited by Richard S. Dunn, James Savage, and Laetitia Yeandle. Cambridge, MA: Harvard University Press, 1996.

—-. *A journal of the transactions and occurrences in the settlement of Massachusetts and the other New England colonies, from the year 1630 to 1644*. Hartford, CT, 1790.

Winthrop Papers, vol. 5 (1645-49). Edited by Allyn B. Forbes. Boston: Massachusetts Historical Society, 1947.

Wood, William. *New England's Prospect* (1634). Edited by Alden T. Vaughan. Amherst: University of Massachusetts Press, 1977.

Wyman, Thomas Bellows. *The Genealogies and Estates of Charlestown: in the County of Middlesex and Commonwealth of Massachusetts, 1629-1818*. Vol. 2. Boston, 1879.

Yates, Edgar. "Early Vital Records of Saco and Biddeford, Me." *New England Historical and Genealogical Register*, 71 (1917): 123-226.

Acknowledgments

I WISH TO ACKNOWLEDGE the staffs of the Maine Historical Society and Brown Library, Maine State Library and Archives, New Hampshire Historical Society, New Hampshire State Archives, Peabody Essex Museum Library, New England Historic and Genealogical Society, and the Scottish National Library and Archives. Numerous individuals at those institutions provided valuable assistance in researching this book. Charles Butler, historian of Biddeford, Maine, was helpful in deciphering that town's earliest vital records.

I'm grateful to the Scottish Soldiers Project archeology team at Durham University, Durham, England, whose work helped us all to better appreciate the lives of those imprisoned at Durham. That team, led by Professor Chris Gerrard, traveled to New England to share their findings with the Dunbar prisoners' descendants and researchers, and they generously extended invitations to engage in their work and participate in commemorating the Dunbar prisoners at Durham. Chris was also kind enough to review parts of this work.

I'm also grateful to the Scottish Prisoners of War Society—especially founder and executive director, Teresa Rust—for the many helpful leads provided through the website, www.scottishprisonersofwar.com. The Society serves as a vibrant online community for descendants and researchers of the Scottish Prisoners of War.

Alex Comas provided perceptive comments on early and late drafts of this work. Andreu Comas provided insights on the narrative and suggestions for the title. He also designed most of the maps, which have helped enormously in providing clarity and a sense of place.

A book's first reader is often the most important. Xavier Comas supported this idea from its inception, traveled with me to Scotland; Durham, England; and to towns, libraries, historical societies, mill sites, and graveyards throughout New England. He patiently read and commented on endless drafts. His honesty, insightfulness, and encouragement have had an enormous impact on this book.

Many thanks also to publisher Bruce H. Franklin and Westholme Publishing for finding value in this work and for being so accommodating and helpful throughout the production process.

Index